"White is back with another timely topic, complete with his characteristic attention to rich and relevant context, and to engaging, communicative, and inclusive writing. Inclusive though it is, *The AI Music Problem* does not pull punches– expect to be challenged with a strong argument not only for why AI music *currently* falls short but (much more interestingly) why he thinks it always will."
—**Mark Gotham**, *King's College London*

"Chris White provides the definitive guide to one of 21st-century music's most pressing questions. Approaching the topic from a wide variety of angles, *The AI Music Problem* is both clear and thorough in its exploration of what we should expect as technologies continue to advance, and, perhaps more importantly, what we shouldn't."
—**Cory Arnold**, *12tone YouTube channel*

THE AI MUSIC PROBLEM

Music poses unique and complex challenges for artificial intelligence, even as 21st-century AI grows ever more adept at generating compelling content. *The AI Music Problem: Why Machine Learning Conflicts With Musical Creativity* probes the challenges behind AI-generated music, with an investigation that straddles the technical, the musical, and the aesthetic. Bringing together the perspectives of the humanities and computer science, the author shows how the difficulties that music poses for AI connect to larger questions about music, artistic expression, and the increasing ubiquity of artificial intelligence.

Taking a wide view of the current landscape of machine learning and Large Language Models, *The AI Music Problem* offers a resource for students, researchers, and the public to understand the broader issues surrounding musical AI on both technical and artistic levels. The author breaks down music theory and computer science concepts with clear and accessible explanations, synthesizing the technical with more holistic and human-centric analyses. Enabling readers of all backgrounds to understand how contemporary AI models work, and why music is often a mismatch for those processes, this book is relevant to all those engaging with the intersection between AI and musical creativity today.

Christopher W. White is Associate Professor of Music Theory at the University of Massachusetts Amherst.

THE AI MUSIC PROBLEM

Why Machine Learning Conflicts With Musical Creativity

Christopher W. White

NEW YORK AND LONDON

Designed cover image: Getty Images

First published 2025
by Routledge
605 Third Avenue, New York, NY 10158

and by Routledge
4 Park Square, Milton Park, Abingdon, Oxon, OX14 4RN

Routledge is an imprint of the Taylor & Francis Group, an informa business

ISBN: 978-1-032-95976-4 (hbk)
ISBN: 978-1-032-95975-7 (pbk)
ISBN: 978-1-003-58741-5 (ebk)

DOI: 10.4324/9781003587415

Typeset in Sabon
by Deanta Global Publishing Services, Chennai, India

To my parents.

CONTENTS

ACKNOWLEDGMENTS

Many thanks to Jesse Caputo, Sarah Connors, Ian Quinn, Heather Peterson, Nicole Cosme-Clifford, Kavi Kapoor, James Symons, Leo von Mutius, Elizabeth Medina-Gray, Megan Long, Chris Brody, Scott White, Andrew Goldman, Catrina Kim, Mariusz Kozak, Alex Rehding, Justin London, Mark Gotham, Dan Harrison, and my terrifyingly brilliant husband Robert Powell for their insights and input into this project.

1

THE PROBLEMS FACING MUSICAL ARTIFICIAL INTELLIGENCE

"Of course... music is a great difficulty. You see, if one plays good music, people don't listen, and if one plays bad music people don't talk."

The Importance of Being Earnest, Oscar Wilde

"Rabbit's clever," said Pooh thoughtfully.
"Yes," said Piglet, "Rabbit's clever."
"And he has Brain."
"Yes," said Piglet, "Rabbit has Brain."
There was a long silence.
"I suppose," said Pooh, "that that's why he never understands anything."

The House at Pooh Corner, A. A. Milne

It's late at night, and a computer engineer is scribbling in her notebook. An academic journal has asked her to write about some recent innovations in Artificial Intelligence that she's been developing with her collaborator— what's being dubbed the *Analytical Engine*. Her draft outlines how the technology works, its capabilities, limitations, and potential applications. These notes touch on a huge range of topics, including how to program this new technology, how the machine retains information, and what tasks it's best suited for.

The journal expects a short commentary. Her notes are nearing a sprawling 20,000 words.

DOI: 10.4324/9781003587415-1

She starts writing about the machine's potential. She absentmindedly sips her tea, subconsciously searching for a caffeine jolt, and considers how someone might program the machine to generate new creative content. Her thoughts specifically drift toward whether this technology could write new music. She's played piano since she was young and is well acquainted with basic music theory. Her AI is good at processing well-defined mathematical problems, and if it reduced music composition to a series of formulas, it could certainly generate new music following those blueprints.

She starts writing. If compositional procedures were converted into some series of algorithms, then the computer:

> *might compose elaborate and scientific pieces of music of any degree of complexity or extent.*

She grimaces and puts down her tea. She worries her readers will get the impression that her machine might actually mimic a creative human musician. In her estimation, machines can only follow the pathways that engineers have programmed into them, and can only reshuffle the information they've been fed. Again, she starts writing:

> *The Analytical Engine has no pretentions to...*

She stops, searching for the right words. This AI could, in principle, produce an enormous amount of new music by following the formulas laid out its programming. She looks at her bookshelves full of poetry and novels, and at the paintings covering the walls above her desk. Given the right formulas, her programs will be able to generate enough words and images to overflow all of humanity's walls and bookshelves.

She shudders. This firehose of words and images wouldn't be the same as human-made creativity. She thinks back to music, and to the songs she loves to play and sing. This music isn't made by formulas. It sparks from human ingenuity, playfulness, and imagination. She loves performing and singing with other musicians, and she loves knowing that she's playing music made by other living, breathing humans. Even if her AI creates new and interesting melodies and harmonies, these computer-generated tunes won't really be *music*. They won't be *original*. They won't be *human*.

She finishes her sentence. This AI will never actually:

> *originate anything.*

* * *

Ada King, the Countess of Lovelace, would publish her notes in *Taylor's Scientific Memoirs* in 1843. Her work described the steam-powered invention of one of her close collaborators, Charles Babbage, an invention that served as a crucial predecessor to the digital computer.

Yet, Lovelace's sentiments feel like they could have been written today. As innovations in 21st century generative AI increasingly elbow their way into our daily lives, we find ourselves grappling with the same issues that furrowed her brow nearly two centuries ago. Can machines create new artistic, expressive, and creative content? If they can, how do they do it? And when do they do, is their resulting content actually *creative*?

It's no coincidence that Lovelace singles out *music* when she writes about computers' capacities and their limitations. In a lot of ways, music should be easy for AI to create. After all, most music follows sets of norms, structures, and formulas that can be easily adapted to a computer's algorithmic mind. But on the other hand, music can also be complex and unexpected. Music can be a social experience. Music can be felt in our bodies, and it can connect two people emotionally. These are all roles that are difficult—if not impossible—for a computer to step into.

This book is about musical AI, and how there's often a mismatch between what AI is good at and what makes music *music*. It's about the history of this field and how musical AI works. It's also about why it is so difficult for AIs to produce music that is compelling and well-made. It's about what we enjoy about music and why it's so hard for an AI to tap into that enjoyment. It's about why a technology that works so well for written language, voice replication, and even self-driving cars often stumbles when learning music's melodies, rhythms, phrases, and forms.

The AI Music Problem tells the story of musical AI by identifying five forces behind generative computer models: 1) the motivations and potential payoffs for creating a musical AI, 2) the availability of reliable musical examples to create data for these AIs, 3) the ways this data is represented to a computer, 4) the kinds of musical structures these machines can detect, and 5) how humans interpret music created by a computer. Throughout, I will provide a tour of contemporary AI's inner workings, comparing its engineering to the ways that humans make and listen to music, and will show how each of these five forces poses particularly difficult challenges for AIs that generate music. The book will also touch on some larger issues that increasingly powerful and intelligent machines pose—like how we define "creativity" and whether an AI can ever really "feel"—and does so through a musical lens.

The book isn't a technical manual. A little familiarity with music will be helpful, but no ability to read complex orchestral scores or fluently play an instrument is required, nor is writing code a prerequisite. But, I also won't shy away from diving into the nitty gritty of what makes AI tick, or into the specific musical complexities that can prove so difficult for computers to grasp. In short, this book is your window into the music we love and AI's attempt to write it.

Five hurdles for musical AI

Figure 1.1 charts a course through five challenges for musical AI. The gambit begins with *Motivation*. Like any venture, AI's foray into music needs some reason to exist. It needs some obvious payoff, be it academic innovation or the lure of commercial success. It's this initial motivation that fuels the allocation of crucial resources like time, talent, and money. Next up, we hit the problem of *Examples*. AI machines are voracious learners that devour data. For a musical AI to learn to write music that actually sounds like *music*, we need a library of tunes so extensive that it satisfies this computational appetite. Compiling such a library is no small feat.

Once we have chosen and compiled our library of examples, we encounter the craggy landscape of musical *Representation*. Here, the issues become a bit more technical. Before AI can begin to understand musical examples, human engineers need to translate them into a language that computers speak—some format that a computer can read. Essentially, music needs to be cut up and parceled into packets that the computer can process. This is a process of translation, and it is fraught with choices. Will we teach the AI how audio waves work? Or will we ask it to learn the structure of written scores? How do we slice up melodies, describe the length of individual tones, or represent each momentary harmony? Each decision shapes the AI's understanding of music, carving out its abilities and limitations.

Just as written language builds sounds into words, words into sentences, and sentences into ideas and stories, music is organized according to its own levels of *Structure*. Each note and harmony don't behave as simple solitary sounds. Individual notes are like single threads in an expansive Persian rug. The sonic threads gather into themes and harmonies, which in turn weave into larger phrases. Phrases then fall into patterns that warp and weft into larger designs of repetition and contrast, like

Motivation	**E**xamples	**R**epresentation	**S**tructure	**I**nterpretation
Why are people making models of musical AI?	What datasets are people using to train and test their AI models?	How are programmers representing musical events in their AI?	What aspects of musical organization are being learned by the AI?	What value are listeners drawing from music generated by AI?

FIGURE 1.1 Five factors behind musical AI's development.

verses, choruses, and refrains. Each of music's larger structures is made of smaller, interacting components that themselves are made of tinier atoms. For an AI to truly produce convincing music, it must somehow learn the logic of each of these multifaceted, interwoven levels.

Finally, any successful musical AI needs to produce music that people actually *like*. Music is a communal activity in which we hear and *Interpret* emotion and the human experience. The music we value most has some sort of shared social component. We like music because it's beautiful, but also because we hear something of our own lived experience within it. Far from simply assembling notes, a successful musical AI needs to learn to compose something *human*. This is a steep—if impossible—hill for a machine to climb.

Each of these hurdles does not stand alone. The series works like a row of dominos, with each item pushing forward into the next. Should the motivation behind AI research and development ignite with a roar of resources, we'd be met with the challenge of gathering enough musical examples for AI to learn from. Once we amassed a suitable library, we would need to master the translation of music into formats that AI can effectively digest. Supposing AI were to leap over this hurdle, it would then face that intricate, multi-layered puzzle of musical structure.

But let's imagine for a moment that AI sails over all these hurdles and starts producing music as well-constructed as any human could compose. We're then left with that final—and perhaps tallest—hurdle. Would we, as listeners, ever emotionally connect with AI-generated music? In my estimation, this series of challenges presents an enormous, compounding problem for successful musical AIs. In what follows, I explore each of these categories in a bit more depth and suggest ways that music provides a particularly thorny problem for AI at each juncture.

Motivation

I'll dive deeper into the programming and engineering behind musical AI in subsequent chapters, but to give a quick overview of a few important concepts, we can start with one the hottest buzzwords in contemporary AI research—the *Large Language Model*, or LLM. LLMs are digital engines that study vast arrays of text, images, or music to learn how to produce new content. These programs repeatedly pore over their training datasets, learning a bit more with each iteration, shaping their predictions, and refining their understanding of how words, images, or sounds are organized and arranged in their library of data. In this manner, LLMs build up expectations about what kinds of events follow other events, and what sorts of larger sequences occur before or after other sequences. This web of expectations, norms, and statistics forms the basis of the model. Here, the word *model* means the combination of the computer program and its trained expectations, and it's in that sense I'll use the word "model" throughout this book. The data from which these models learn is often called *training data*, and it's from this training data that the model captures and internalizes norms, rules, and tendencies. Any model that learns from training data undertakes *machine learning*. In machine learning, the computer learns information directly from a dataset rather than being explicitly taught or preprogrammed by a human. Such a model can then create new content using the norms and tendencies learned from its training data. When commentators or engineers discuss *generative AI*, they are generally referring to some computer model that can create new content in this manner.

Deep learning is another buzzword of 21st-century AI. When we say that some model uses deep learning, we mean that its artificial mind employs several layers in its learning process. It's like learning the steps, hip action, rhythm, and upper-body movement of a dance all at once. Each individual gesture occupies one layer, and all the layers are united into one seamless dance move. To provide a textual example: it's not enough for a deep learning system to know that the word "cherry" often comes before the word "pie." To be effective, the system needs to understand the layers of possible meanings that govern how and where these words are used—categories like "fruit" and "dessert" and "edible items."

You might think of this process as the AI learning the dance steps of a dataset. Within written language, for instance, an AI identifies the linguistic choreography we perform unconsciously when writing words and sentences. Just as certain steps and turns characterize the subtle routines of a tango or salsa, the AI notices what words tend to occur together and the typical ordering of phrases. It then learns how these sequences can be varied and expanded—what words can substitute for others and the ways that words congeal into phrases that express larger ideas. Just as accomplished dancers learn to improvise and elaborate on basic dance steps, the AI eventually learns to write more expansive and varied sentences, and to draw from related topics. A musical AI works in much the same way, internalizing the kinds of melodies that synch with particular harmonies, and how complexes of sounds group together into phrases, forms, and fully composed songs.

In recent years, generative AI models have become increasingly good at creating new and useful content using deep-learning systems. Media headlines practically scream the praises of various types of deep learning every day, reporting how some new "transformer" or "convolutional neural network"—all types of deep learning systems—are creating alarmingly accurate images, texts, or voice replications.

Throughout this book, I'll be discussing models that learn tendencies, norms, and statistics from training data, internalize the data's statistical tendencies, and use them to create new musical content. My goal is to discuss how these models work and how they interact with music in general instead of focusing on the particulars of any specific engineering or implementation. I'll therefore tend towards referring to these models in their general forms like "machine learning" or "deep learning," as opposed to in their more specific incarnations like "LLMs," "transformers," "convolutional neural networks," and the like. In Chapter 2, I'll outline some of the basic programing and mathematics behind these models, focusing on the overall approaches that unite 21st-century computational AI. The chapter will then turn its attention to *why* companies and researchers pour time and resources into these types of models.

From one perspective, the *motivation* behind creating these sorts of models seems self-evident: to satisfy users' desires to create and consume new and interesting content. In 2024, for instance, the well-known chatbot ChatGPT had over 77 million monthly users in the United States relying on its technology to generate and hone text. In other words, roughly 1 in 5 people in the US were using this technology to produce new content every month. However, reading deeper into these headlines can also show how costly these models can be. The newest AI models often come with a hefty price tag, demanding millions, even billions, of dollars in computing power, data wrangling, and sheer electrical muscle to accomplish their tasks. The 2024 version of ChatGPT, for instance, was reported to have cost over $100 million to develop and train. The motivational calculus of generative AI, therefore, hinges not just on what it can possibly create, but how much it costs to develop and create this content.

From my vantage point, the financial allure of studying musical AI is far from evident. Put simply: music plays a less pervasive role in the capitalist marketplace than other forms of media. It therefore offers lesser incentive for the development of AI-driven applications.

Compare the user base and revenue streams of industry-leading companies like Microsoft Office, Adobe, and Ableton Live. Microsoft Office is a colossus in the realm of text and numerical documents, boasting billions in revenue and a user base stretching into the hundreds of millions. Adobe, a titan of the image-based documents sector, also draws revenues in the billions, with tens of millions of active users.

However, Ableton Live, perhaps the most popular digital music-writing program, plays to a much smaller audience. Its revenues are counted in the mere tens of millions of dollars, and it has a community of around a million users. By either metric, it is less than 10% the size of analogous companies in other media.

This imbalance naturally extends beyond money and into the allocation of human capital. Fewer engineers and researchers work on music AI, and large tech companies spend less time developing musical tools than projects in other media. Chapter 2 will explore this industry imbalance and the motivations shaping musical AI's funding, research, and development.

Examples

In the digital era, AI researchers find themselves in the middle of a veritable ocean of data. With every click of a mouse, they can open vast expanses of content neatly translated into the binary language of computers. This digital transformation ensures an almost endless supply of material for AI's learning and development.

Music is no exception to this digital bounty. At least in terms of sheer content, the online world is awash with music. It would take hundreds and hundreds of years to listen to the complete catalogue of a streaming service like Spotify, and websites like IMSLP.org and CPDL.org host musical scores that number in the hundreds of thousands. Yet, the way music is rendered into digital formats poses significant challenges for deep learning models. Digital music is hard for a computer to read, and hard to collate into *examples* for an AI's training data. While our eyes can easily recognize notes on a page and our ears effortlessly pluck notes and chords out of sound waves, these tasks are quite difficult for computers. In Chapter 3, I'll outline some reasons why musical scores pose such a challenge.

The problem of music notation

Consider the gulf between the relative simplicity of navigating a pdf of text and the complexity of interpreting a sheet of Western music. Reading a page of text requires knowledge of the alphabet and punctuation, and the ability to identify the beginning and end of letters, words, and lines. You'll need to be ready for intermittent paragraph indentations, and now and again you'll encounter an image, graph, or picture that you'll need to realize is *not* part of the written language.

Musical scores, by contrast, present a labyrinthine challenge. Working through any selection of music notation (Figures 1.3 and 1.6 in this chapter, for instance) gives an immediate sense of this warren. In Western notation, the five lines of a musical staff serve as the core. Time signatures can indicate how many beats are in a measure and where downbeats occur. The curved forms at the beginning of each staff are called "clefs," and are added to the staff as a key for deciphering exactly which notes correspond to which lines and spaces. A five-line staff can appear alone, or it can be connected to other staves to indicate multiple musical lines being played concurrently. All the vertically aligned notes across all the connected staves will be played or sung at the same time.

Ovoid noteheads are placed onto the staff's five lines or in the spaces between. The closer notes are to the top of the staff, the higher they sound. To show how long each note lasts, noteheads can be filled in or hollow, and they can have stems—the vertical lines attached to the noteheads—or no stems. Stems can point upward or downward, and they may have flags or bars attached to them. Open noteheads indicate longer notes, while the notes with flags or bars are faster.

I'll stop here, even though there are many other notations connected to phrasing, loudness, instrumentation, and so on. There are many, *many* more aspects of music notation that any music reader must be ready to identify and interpret.

A page of music and a page of written text have many things in common. They are visual representations of suites of information, and we can extract this information by decoding the symbols of the page. But there are simply many more moving parts in musical notation than in text. This heightened complexity significantly amplifies the challenges for a computer attempting to recognize symbols on a score, multiplying the chances for errors during the information extraction process.

The problem of audio

Given the challenges that score-reading presents for computer recognition, why not turn to audio files instead? After all, digital music is readily available online in vast quantities. Unfortunately for musical AI, the task of plucking out individual notes, instruments, and other musical elements from sound waves, while easy for the human brain, proves to be a formidable challenge for computers.

The crux of the problem lies in what acousticians call the *overtone series*, or what musicians sometimes refer to as *partials*. If you sing a tone, the note gains its identity based on how fast your vocal cords make the air vibrate. When we sing a higher note, the sound waves vibrate faster. When we sing lower, the waves are slower. The same principles apply to piano strings, trumpets, drumheads, or any other instrument. Our ears hear different pitches according to how fast the instrument makes the air around it vibrate. The rate of vibration that makes a note sound like a particular pitch is its *fundamental frequency*.

But not all notes with the same fundamental frequency sound the same. Imagine the difference between singing a note with a warm, resonant "aaaa" vowel and the same note sounded through a nasal, piercing "eeee." Any note with the same fundamental frequency sounds different on a piano, a violin, or a harp for the same reasons. These different tone qualities are rooted in the spectrum of *overtones*. Overtones are softer and higher pitches that color the sound of the fundamental pitch. The more nasal and sharp the sound, the more overtones are active in the tone. Warmer sounds like the theremin and violin have fewer overtones acting above the fundamental frequency, and harsher sounds like the oboe and harmonica have more.

From the computer's perspective, the problem is that overtones and fundamentals are both sound waves, and it's often hard to tell whether a particular sound wave is a fundamental or an overtone. Figure 1.2 illustrates this problem using *spectrograms*, visual representations of sound waves. The horizontal dimension on a spectrogram indicates time passing. The sound starts on the lefthand side of the image and continues as you move right. The vertical axis shows the speed at which sounds vibrate. Higher sounds will be on the top, and lower sounds will be on the bottom of the spectrogram. The lefthand pane in Figure 1.2 shows a single computer-generated version of a low C. Here, the computer is generating a pure pitch with no overtones (what an acoustician would call a sine waveform). Since there are no overtones present, one bright white band streaks horizontally across the bottom of the pane. The middle pane shows a piano playing that same low C. Now the spectrogram shows several overtones stacked on top of the fundamental. The white bands that parallel the low C are like floors of a skyscraper, each representing an individual overtone. In combination, the fundamental pitch and its overtones give the piano its distinctive sound. I've flagged one such overtone in the figure

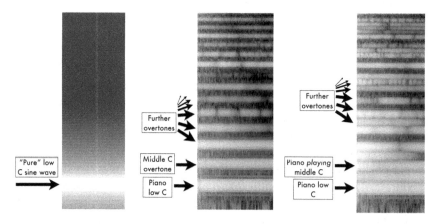

FIGURE 1.2   A spectrogram of the sine wave of low C, a piano playing a single low C, and a piano playing a chord with low C in it.

as the sound wave associated with middle C. When you play a low C on a piano, the overtones for middle C activate along with the fundamental, producing sound waves at the frequency of middle C which are folded into the overall sound. While our ears and brain perceive one single piano note, the envelope of sound waves that build the complex texture of the piano's low C includes this middle C overtone.

The pane at the right in the figure shows another spectrogram, but now of a chord with multiple notes. The lowest note of this chord is low C. You can see that fundamental pitch extending all the way through the graph. Middle C is also played in the chord, and the spectrogram shows a soundwave band at the same frequency we saw for middle C in the previous pane. However, this band now represents a second fundamental frequency, actually played above the low C, rather than an overtone arising from sympathetic vibrations activated by a singular low C. While our ears can easily hear the difference between these two musical situations, computers have a difficult time teasing out whether the middle C is an overtone or the result of an instrument actually playing middle C.

Certainly, the complexities of deciphering sound waves aren't insurmountable. There are tools that extract musical information from audio files. These programs have better success rates when they are primed to know the characteristics of the instruments involved, as this allows the program to anticipate specific overtone patterns. Moreover, some developers simply circumvent the challenge of isolating individual notes from a sound signal. Instead, they train their AI to identify patterns in how sounds are ordered and constructed. In these cases, the AIs learn the expected shapes and contours of a spectrogram rather than any direct information about musical specifics like pitches and rhythms. These strategies and their implications will be explored in Chapter 3.

The relative size of datasets

There's a barrier to entry into musical composition. You can't just pick up a guitar and start playing, and you can't download a digital audio workstation and become a proficient music producer in a single afternoon. Musical fluency typically demands extensive study and practice, and even those who achieve proficiency in playing an instrument may not necessarily excel at composing new music. This high barrier limits the pool of individuals creating music, resulting in musical datasets that tend to be more limited in size compared to other forms of media. For instance, while public domain music repositories like the International Music Score Library Project (IMSLP.org) or the Choral Public Domain Library (CPDL.org) boast impressive collections, the amount of music they have catalogued is dwarfed by the mountains of publicly accessible text offered by sites like

Google Books. Chapter 3 also dives deeper into this challenge, along with various other hurdles that musical AI encounters in its quest for data.

Representation

As an AI sifts through its data, it must parcel it into digestible bites. When engineers build models of visual art, they need to decide whether their AI will dissect the imagery into discrete objects or interpret the pictures pixel by pixel. Similarly, text-based AIs might process their data letter by letter, word by word, or phrase by phrase. A musical AI needs to know whether it's dividing its data into notes, chords, full measures, and so on.

This decision shapes the architecture of an AI's artificial "mind." An AI designed to interpret images pixel by pixel learns the norms and statistics of how those pixels are strung together. Its learning, memory, and generative processes—its *intelligence*—are all anchored in this pixelated perception of images. In contrast, a model that is trained to divide images into recognizable objects populates its intelligence with these entities and the web of relationships between them. These sorts of choices not only dictate how an AI processes information but also how it *represents* the medium in its computational memory.

When the popular chatbot ChatGPT processes text, it does not represent its data as a series of individual letters. Rather, it divides text in words and word components. Figure 1.3 uses vertical lines to show how ChatGPT would parse the sentence, "Generative Pretrained Transformers are super cool."[1] (A GPT, or a "Generative Pretrained Transformers" is the specific kind of deep learning underpinning the chatbot.) Notice how the last four words stand on their own. When ChatGPT learns or produces these words, it considers them individual items and remembers where and when they appear in sentences. The words "Generative" and "Pretrained," however, are split into component parts. The algorithm does not learn where and when to use the word "Pretrained." Instead, it learns how often and in what contexts "Pret" precedes "rained." A model like ChatGPT hones these choices through experimentation, with various tests determining that these *representations* lead the model toward efficient, coherent, and useful outputs.

Music grapples with these same issues. However, due to the many layers of information embedded in any musical moment, there are a multitude

Generative| Pretrained| Transformers| are| super| cool.|

FIGURE 1.3   A sentence divided into the chunks learned by ChatGPT and used in its text generation.

of options for how to divide a musical surface. Consider, for instance, the chord in Figure 1.4 and the veritable avalanche of ways to describe this simple passage. Here, I use two linked staves, indicating that all the notes aligning vertically occur at the same time. Notes that are horizontally displaced are read—and played or sounded—left to right through time. Notes on the upper staff sound higher than the notes in the lower staff. Here, there are four discrete notes in the music corresponding to the four separate parts in a typical choir. From the top of the higher "treble" clef staff to the bottom of the lower "bass" clef staff, the sopranos, altos, tenors, and basses all sing their own notes, with the soprano singing the top note with the upward-pointing stem, the alto singing the note with the downward-pointing stem directly underneath, and so on. The tenor line features a rhythm that is twice as quick as the other voices, as indicated by the bar joining its two notes. The moment begins with the pitches B, G, and D, with the tenor voice changing to an F while the other voices hold their pitches. The notes also occur in specific ranges. Working again from top to bottom, the highest note is a G above middle C in the soprano (top) voice, the alto has the D above middle C, and so on. I've also labeled the *intervals* between the lowest note and the other pitches in the chord. In musical parlance, the distance between B and G is a "6th," because those two letters span the distance of six notes. Western musical practice uses the first seven letters of the alphabet to name its pitches, and moving from B to G, traverses six letters: B→C→D→E→F→G. From this perspective, the chord involves a 6th, a 10th, and a 13th above the lowest note.

But there are yet more ways we can represent this chord. Musicians also often talk about the chord's notes as positions in a scale or key. This chord uses the notes of a C-major scale, which encompasses all the white notes of the piano. These correspond to the seven notes of the musical alphabet,

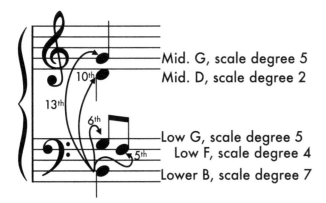

FIGURE 1.4   A chord labeled with several different ways of representing its constituent notes.

i.e., A, B, C, D, E, F, and G. We can also image this chord occurring in the *key* of C major, which means that the pitch C will serve as beginning and end of the scale. The seven letters of the scale are therefore ordered C, D, E, F, G, A, B, and back to C. And, since C serves as the point of origin for the scale, we call it "scale degree 1." At the second position in the scale, D will be scale degree 2. Thinking about the notes in our chords, F occupies the fourth position in the C-major scale, so it is scale degree 4. Similarly, G is scale degree 5, and B—as the last note of the scale—is scale degree 7. The example, therefore, consists of scale degrees 7, 5, 2, and 4.[2]

If all this information feels overwhelming, that's because it is. And there are so many more musical aspects of this moment, including the notes' distance from the previous or next chord, the harmony's relationship to the overarching key, not to mention the notes' rhythms. The problem, then, becomes choosing between this multitude of characteristics when making a concrete, computational representation of some musical chunk. Even with the handful of descriptions I've outlined, which would be the ideal method to represent the events of Figure 1.4 to a computer? Table 1.1 shows several options. Should an AI learn from the information within the "Pitch with height" representation or from the "Lowest pitch with intervals" information? From scale degrees or from note names? And, adding to the already compounding options, I've enclosed in parentheses the data that correspond to the second note sung by the quicker tenor voice. Should this note be integrated into the overall harmony, much like ChatGPT wraps the entire word "Transformer" into one event? Or should the harmony be divided into two separate moments, as the chatbot divides the word "Generative" into two separate components?

There are so many choices that an engineer must make when representing music, and in Chapter 4, I explore these issues in more depth. On the computational end, this large number of options sets up a difficult choice between more general information that is easier for an AI to learn and

TABLE 1.1 Various ways of representing the chord in Figure 1.4.

Characterization	*Representation*
Just note names:	G, B, D, (F)
Just scale degrees:	5, 7, 2, (4)
Names with repeats, ordered from bottom to top:	B, G, (F), D, G
SDs with repeats, ordered from bottom to top:	7, 5, (4), 2, 5
Pitch with height:	Low B, low G, (low F), middle D, middle G
Lowest pitch with intervals:	Low B, 6, (5), 10, 13

more specific, detailed data that is harder to learn but is easier to reassemble into new compositions. For instance, because it erases all information about specific pitches and note names, a scale degree representation is quite general and easy for a computer to learn.

The tradeoff, however, is that a general method of representation like this lacks specificity. Relying on scale degree information alone, for instance, strips away much information about key and exact note placement. If you only told a pianist to play scale degrees 5, 7, and 2, they wouldn't know what key to play in, let alone how many notes to play or how the notes should be arranged. Likewise, a model that trained only on scale degree information would not know how to translate its sophisticated musical knowledge into actual notes in a composition.

Conversely, descriptions like those in the "Pitch with height" or "Lowest pitch with intervals" categories are very specific. As we saw before, armed with this information, a pianist would know exactly which piano keys to push down, and a model equipped with representations of this sort would easily be able to generate notes. However, because these representations are so specific, they often get in the way of a model learning large-scale or general patterns. Engineers, then, need to balance the many options available to them while negotiating between general representations that help an AI learn the music's underlying grammar, rules, and effects with relative ease, and the specific information an AI needs to generate notes, melodies, and chords.

Structure

In April of 2022, OpenAI's Instagram account posted an image generated by Dall-E, the company's visual art LLM. The picture was the result of the prompt, "a teddy bear on a skateboard in Times Square." Dall-E did its job well, with the image realistically depicting a stuffed bear riding a skateboard in front of an out-of-focus midtown tableau. I've recreated the image using my own OpenAI account in Figure 1.5.

Deep-learning models are good at this sort of task, stitching together objects in a logical sequence with simple relationships. After observing many stuffed animals, the algorithm understands how to arrange pixels to represent plush fabric, and it understands how to generate these pixel patterns in the shape of a teddy bear. After similarly creating a skateboard, the algorithm knows how to arrange the two objects because it's seen plenty of things "standing on" other things, some of them skateboards. Additionally, it's seen enough photos backdropped by New York streets and foot traffic to know how to place those objects in Times Square.

Models that learn connections, trends, norms, and statistics within some training data—and this includes deep learning LLMs—tend to be

FIGURE 1.5 DALL-E's image generated from the prompt, "A teddy bear on a skateboard in Times Square."

excellent at identifying what I call *nested determined proximities*. Once the machine knows it's drawing a teddy bear, there are very few options for the kinds of pixels and patterns that occur next to one another. The sorts of pixels that appear *proximate* to one another are highly *determined*. There is a certain predictable regularity in how teddy bear fabric looks. Further decisions about both the fabric, the bear's shape, and its position are *nested*—they all grow out of the larger decision to make a "teddy bear" that is "standing." Similarly, shadows are added based on the position of the primary object relative to some off-screen light source. Throughout, the smallest components combine together to create larger and larger objects, with the global and local details all having clear relationships with one another.

The engineering of these sorts of models allows them to learn nested determined proximities easily. These programs repeatedly move through datasets to notice sequences and connections that happen often, identifying statistically frequent sequential patterns: what items follow what other items, what chunks of items occur adjacent to other chunks. It's simply easier for a program—or, for that matter, a human!—to notice things when they are near to each other than when they are far apart. Additionally, because their learning process is designed to compile the norms and statistics of some dataset, these models and programs are predisposed to those things that happen a lot: things that are determined. After all, strongly practiced norms are easier to notice than seldom-followed preferences. Finally, these statistical models will favor situations in which they can nest several decisions together into one category. It is easier for their learning processes to chunk together several rules and norms under one umbrella than to remember each individual dictum. Pictures of teddy bears and New York backdrops exhibit all these characteristics. To be sure, many machine-learning models have procedures to deal with events that are far apart, infrequent occurrences, and hard-to-predict contingencies. But, nested, determined, proximities are still the easiest sorts of *structures* that a mathematical and statistical machine can learn.

Music is not like pictures of teddy bears. Figure 1.6 shows the melody of "Amazing Grace," annotated to highlight how the music is organized. The piece is written in the key/scale of C major. The entire hymn is divisible into four smaller phrases, as indicated by the grey boxes. The first three sections end on the note G, while the final section comes to rest on a C, scale degree 1 of the key. The second small phrase (labeled A^2) is a slight variation of the first (A^1). The fourth phrase begins as an exact repetition of the first, but it is cut short on the seventh note. Each "A" phrase contains the same melodic core, with the same notes and rhythms. I show these similarities in the solid black rectangles above the music. If you hum the tune, you'll immediately hear how similar each of these sections sounds.

More granularly, the A-section melody is saturated with rhythms that follow long notes with shorter notes. Every measure begins with a note that lasts two beats, as represented by the open noteheads with stems. These relatively long notes are followed in the third and final beat of each measure with a note lasting one beat (the filled-in noteheads with stems), or with two notes crammed into the one beat (the pairs of filled-in noteheads beamed together). While the end of A^2 departs from the melodic prototype of A^1, it also seems to be responding to the first phrase. As I show with the arrows above the staff, A^1 ends by descending to the low G on which the melody began. And, while A^2 also ends on a G, it does so by ascending to the higher G. This ascent ramps up the overall energy while remaining connected to the initial musical idea.

The B phrase uses new musical material, but material that still feels deeply connected with the preceding A phrases. For instance, the high and low Gs that ended A^1 and A^2 now seem to function as the melody's musical floor and ceiling, with the B phrase using these notes but never venturing past them. The rhythmic palette also expands with more variety while still retaining the long–short feel of the A sections. The first note of

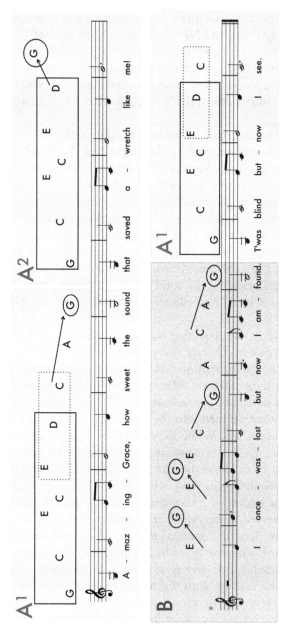

FIGURE 1.6 "Amazing Grace," by John Newton (composed 1772), annotated to show the melody's structure.

each measure remains the longest, though more rhythmic values dot the musical landscape.

The final A^1 section capitalizes on a short melodic idea that was almost hidden in the first phrase, namely, the E–D–C figure enclosed in a dotted box. In the first phrase, those notes were incidental pitches on the pathway to the section's end on low G. However, the last phrase reinterprets this melodic fragment and exploits the fact that it ends on C—scale degree 1 of the key and the first note of the melody's scale—to bring the entire melody to a close.

"Amazing Grace" is not a particularly complicated tune. And yet, very few of its characteristic structural and organizational elements involve immediately *proximate* events. The two uses of E–D–C, for instance, are separated by twelve measures. The low and high Gs that function as the tune's floor and ceiling occur sparsely throughout the hymn and tend to be separated by multiple measures. The return of A in the final measures references the tune's first moments, twelve measures earlier. Furthermore, these connections are not *determined*: just because one musical choice is made doesn't mean the next musical choice *must* be made. The use of a long–short rhythmic pattern in the opening meas-ure didn't mandate its recurrence throughout the phrase, much less the entire tune. In fact, very few melodies replicate the same rhythm with the frequency of this hymn! Also, while many melodies organize their materials in an AABA pattern, there also are many other options for melodic organization. Additionally, most aspects of this musical organi-zation are not *nested*. Unlike the rigid laws of physics that determine how an image's light source casts shadows across a picture, musical deci-sions are flexible and variable. For instance, some performers start the B section of "Amazing Grace" on a high A, careening through the high-G ceiling. Performing that high A doesn't break any laws or make the music sound incoherent, because the initial range of a melody doesn't dictate that subsequent sections must absolutely conform to the same range.

In other words, even a tune as simple as "Amazing Grace" is built on components that are neither adjacent in time, the result of one common cause, nor invariably present in other hymns. Any learning process favor-ing *nested determined proximities* would have a very difficult time notic-ing the structure and organization of this tune alone, let alone within the complexities of a large musical dataset.

In Chapter 5, I will address such issues of music's structural organiza-tion using a combination of music analysis, computational programming, and even research from music cognition to argue that musical structure poses special difficulties for AI. Overall, I'll suggest that any AI system that relies on statistically frequent sequences will stumble when faced with music's variation, complexity, and unpredictability.

Interpretation

Music undisputedly makes people feel things. As a teenager, I was angsty, depressed, and closeted. I would frequently punctuate the end of a school day by squireling myself in my room with my headphones over my ears and blasting a mixture of 90s grunge-pop, Romantic piano concertos, and Andrew Lloyd Weber musicals as a sort of musical therapy. This music helped me process my maturation, sexuality, and interpersonal relationships, and would eventually help me get a handle on my depression.

As far as I can tell, I am far from alone in my relationship with music. People feel emotional connections with music, and music feels like it resonates with and supports the human experience. These are the connections that Ada Lovelace wrestled with when theorizing computational technology in the 19th century, and these relationships contribute to the deepseated role music has in human society the world over.

For centuries, if not millennia, thinkers have grappled with the unique way that music conveys ideas, and their grapplings could—and do—fill volumes of books on their own. Some approaches, for instance, note that music can remind us of real-world sounds. Think of a descending melody that sounds like a human sadly sighing. These thinkers go on to argue that combinations of these references create webs of associations that result in a meaningful musical experience. Others will focus on bodily associations. Consider how descending melodies make us imagine moving physically downward.[3] But, regardless of the specific theories we use to explain this phenomenon—when we find meaning in music, it's about the human experience. We see ourselves, our bodies, our emotions, and our experiences reflected in the music's notes, melodies, and chords.

Of course, this is not to say that other media *never* rely on information about the human experience. A poem about lost love gains its meaning when the reader identifies with the poet's broken heart. A painting of a scream resonates with a viewer's own experience of screaming and its underlying emotions.

But music is an extreme case. In Chapter 6, we rejoin Ada Lovelace in her study, and use her and other historical figures' ideas to outline a distinction between what I call *associational* and *experiential* knowledge. Someone gains associational knowledge by connecting ideas together. If you read extensively about heartbreak, you will learn all the adjectives and turns of phrase that are most often used to describe that state of desolation, and you will form associations between those linguistic elements and the idea of the experience. You will have associational knowledge.

On the other hand, if you get your heart broken, you will search for the adjectives and turns of phrase that capture your feelings. In the process, you will gain experiential knowledge. In both situations, you can write a poem about heartbreak, but only the latter will express a lived human experience.

Deep learning models learn by association. By churning through their enormous datasets, chatbots know the adjectives and phrases associated with the concept of heartbreak. By viewing datasets of labeled pictures, image-generating LLMs know the kinds of facial contortions that go into a gut-wrenching scream. But all this is associational knowledge. A chatbot's heart has never been broken, and no image-generating computer model has reacted to a situation by contorting its face into a scream.

In Chapter 6, I show that audiences deeply care about whether the art, literature, and music they consume is made from experiential knowledge. I outline historical sources and psychological experiments that point to the value humans place on content that reflects lived human experience. Because of this, even if AI produces content that looks exactly like something that a human could construct, we will still value it less if we know it wasn't made by a human. Just like the hypothetical poem penned by a person untouched by heartbreak, we will be skeptical of content that doesn't bubble out of experiential knowledge.

I argue that music exhibits an extreme version of this dynamic. Because musical meaning arises from gestures and metaphors connected to human experience, it is fundamentally disconcerting to have that meaning untethered from an actual life. If we love music for its reflection of our humanity, AI will never be able to provide music that we love simply by virtue of the fact that it is not human. Indeed, it's hard to imagine a teenager ever retreating to their room to process their sexuality through music made by an AI, regardless of the technical qualities of that music.

This book's approach

This book is for anyone interested in AI and its creative ability. Musicians worried about AI's capacity to generate content, college students acquainting themselves with the landscape of generative AI, computer programmers wanting to know more about music. It will also speak to anyone interested in the dramatic rise of AI in the last several years. All of these groups (and more!) comprise this book's intended audience. To maintain a clear focus on the arguments and concepts within the text, I consciously limit direct scholarly citations in the meat of the text, but I provide extensive references at the end of each chapter. I also periodically use the endnotes to dialogue with readers from specialized backgrounds. For instance, if some piece of engineering will be of interest only to readers with coding knowledge, or if part of my music analysis references some important topic in musicology, I will relegate those technical asides to my endnotes.

Additionally, there will be several topics central to 21st-century AI that this book will not immediately address. Legal issues surrounding copyright and plagiarism are outside the bounds of these chapters. I also veer away from the nitty-gritty details of computer programming. While I outline the overall contours of various computational approaches, this book is not designed to teach the mathematics behind machine learning or how to code deep learning networks, nor is it even designed to engage specific types of AI models and their computational implementation. Rather, I aim to discuss broader and general trends in these approaches, and how the logic of statistics and mathematics might misfire when applied to musical composition and expression.

Some larger questions, and music's unique role in AI

Recent commentators have been quick to characterize deep learning LLMs as enigmatic and opaque. As a familiar refrain goes, these models are too complicated for even their programmers to understand. Because of their intricate architectures—the critiques claim—it's difficult to understand *why* these models work. And we're left only to marvel that they *do* work. To boot, media outlets and consumers alike have often been disproportionately focused on evaluating these modes' outputs. They stand agog at what the models are achieving instead of spending their time scrutinizing and understanding the operational mechanisms. Similarly, researchers have been so enamored with the power and potential of deep learning AI that they have spent their time, energy, and resources trying to create better and better results, to the exclusion of studying the models themselves and their roles in art and society.

Several scholars, engineers, and advocates have recognized this oversight and called for a more deliberate approach to AI development. Perhaps most famously, the Future of Life Institute published an open letter in 2023 titled "Pause Giant AI Experiments." It was signed by over 33,000 individuals, including many recognizable names from the tech and computing world. Such critiques advocate for a pivot away from the unyielding pursuit of AI progress towards a slower and deeper investigation into the inner workings of the models and their broader potential consequences for society. Yet, despite calls for caution, the rapid advancement of the cutting-edge in AI continues at a breakneck pace, driven by the formidable economic rewards and incentives involved.

The idiosyncrasies of musical AI make it an invaluable case study for the larger field. Precisely because it's *already* slow and plagued by frequent hiccups, musical AI is an exemplary subject for scrutiny. After all, a slow-moving machine that constantly breaks down is easier to observe and analyze than a whirling, precise, and flawless apparatus. In a world searching for ways to study the broader ramifications of AI, music emerges as a compelling option.

Technology's sustained role in music and creativity

In 1935, Walter Benjamin wrote an influential essay titled "The Work of Art in the Age of Mechanical Reproduction." In it, he grappled with the then-new technologies of vinyl records and radio. These innovations marked a historic pivot, allowing musical performances to be captured and infinitely reproduced for the first time in human history. Prior to this technological leap, experiencing music was confined to ephemeral live performances. If you wanted to hear a piece of music, you needed a musician to perform it or you had to perform it yourself. By the time Benjamin wrote this essay, music played in London could not only be broadcast live to Moscow, San Francisco, and Kolkata, it could also be recorded, preserved to be heard decades later.

Despite almost a century having elapsed since the publication of Benjamin's essay and the incredible moves beyond the technological landscape it addresses, his commentary remains surprisingly relevant. Anticipating debates over nearly every subsequent technological innovation in music creation and distribution, Benjamin argued that there's an intrinsic value in the live transmission of music from performer to listener, a moment, he argued, could never be fully replicated by any mechanical means. Engaging with the innovations immediately surrounding him, Benjamin delved into fundamental issues of how music is constructed, how it functions in society, and how technological changes can run headlong into shifts in musical aesthetics. The enduring relevance of Benjamin's arguments in the 21st century shows how many of these topics transcend any specific era or context. The technology of music may have changed, but the issues Benjamin addressed continue to resonate.

I hope, in some small way, to undertake a similar project with this book. Here in the third decade of the 21st-century, AI—musical or otherwise—is dramatically new and current. I can easily imagine that, fifty years from now, the artistic worries, moral catastrophes, and intellectual hand-wringing that mark our current discussions of AI will seem quaint. But just as Benjamin's engagement with emerging technology fostered an enduring analysis of the nature of music in society, so might thoughtful engagement with state-of-the-art AI have the potential to address larger questions about music. Worries about AI have pervaded creative discourse since the advent of the computer, and the effect of technology on music and musicians reaches back even to the invention of the printing press. This book's arguments are situated within the legacy of these conversations, and it aims to use the issues of our time to analyze music, in general, more deeply.

Notes

1 platform.openai.com/tokenizer.
2 I'm spilling a good bit of ink onto the concepts of key and scale degree because they are foundational to Western musical composition. For instance, scale degrees can quickly capture the basic identity of any given melody or harmony. Let's imagine you're singing some tune—let's say "Amazing Grace"— in some range that's comfortable for your voice—perhaps C major. If you ask your friend to sing the same tune but they have a higher voice than yours, they might sing the tune in some higher key—let's say F major. However, regardless of the key you and your friend use for your respective versions of "Amazing Grace," it will still be recognized as the same tune. This is because the relationships between the notes remain stable, and the melody consists of the same scale degrees. When talking about general ways that music behaves, composers and music critics often use scale degree information to describe its actions and emotive effects. Scale degree 1, for instance, acts as a key's most stable pitch and is often described as something of a "home base" for a melody. In contrast, scale degree 7 evokes instability, and it often feels like it is being pulled homeward toward scale degree 1.
3 For some examples, see Cook (2001), Cox (2016), Meyer (1956), Palfy (2022), Langer (1942), Kivy (1980), and Hatten (1994).

References and Further Reading

Allied Market Research. 2023. *Voice Cloning Market Size, Share, Competitive Landscape and Trend Analysis Report by Component, by Deployment Mode, by Application, by Industry Vertical: Global Opportunity Analysis and Industry Forecast, 2023-2032*. Report Code: A05513. July 2023. https://www.alliedmarketresearch.com/voice-cloning-market.
Agawu, V. K. 1991. *Playing with Signs: A Semiotic Interpretation of Classic Music*. Princeton: Princeton University Press.
Alfaro-Contreras, M., J. M. Iñesta, and J. Calvo-Zaragoza. 2023. "Optical Music Recognition for Homophonic Scores with Neural Networks and Synthetic Music Generation." *International Journal of Multimedia Information Retrieval* 12(12). https://doi.org/10.1007/s13735-023-00278-5
Bengio, Y., S. Russell, E. Musk, S. Wozniak, and Y. N. Harari. 2023. "Pause Giant AI Experiments: An Open Letter." Future of Life Institute. https://futureoflife.org/open-letter/pause-giant-ai-experiments/
Benjamin, W. 1968. "The Work of Art in the Age of Mechanical Reproduction." In *Illuminations*, edited by Hannah Arendt, 214–218. New York: Schocken Books. Original work published 1935.

Blair, E. 2023. "Grimes Says She's Created A 'Digital Voice' to Sing Her Songs so She Doesn't Have To." NPR, April 24, 2023. https://www.npr.org/2023/04/24/1171738670/grimes-ai-songs-voice.

Braguinski, N. 2022. *Mathematical Music: From Antiquity to Music AI.* New York: Routledge.

Christian, B. 2020. *The Alignment Problem: Machine Learning and Human Values.* New York: W. W. Norton.

Chu, Y., and P. Liu. 2023. "Public Aversion Against ChatGPT in Creative Fields?" *The Innovation* 4(4): 100449.

Clarke, L. 2023. "ChatGPT Is Pretty Bad at Poetry, According to Poets." *Vice.* https://www.vice.com/en/article/7kx9d9/chatgpt-is-pretty-bad-at-poetry-according-to-poets.

Cohn, R. 1992. "The Autonomy of Motives in Schenkerian Accounts of Tonal Music." *Music Theory Spectrum* 14(2): 150–170.

Coker, W. 1972. *Music and Meaning: A Theoretical Introduction to Musical Aesthetics.* New York: Free Press.

Cook, N. 2001. "Theorizing Musical Meaning." *Music Theory Spectrum* 23(2): 170–195.

Cosme-Clifford, N., J. Symons, K. Kapoor, and C. White. 2023. "Musicological Interpretability in Generative Transformers." *Proceedings of the 4th International Symposium on the Internet of Sounds in Pisa, Italy.* https://ieeexplore.ieee.org/xpl/conhome/10335168/proceeding.

Cox, A. 2016. *Music and Embodied Cognition: Listening, Moving, Feeling, and Thinking.* Bloomington: Indiana University Press. https://doi.org/10.2307/j.ctt200610s.

Drott, E. A. 2021. "Copyright, Compensation, and Commons in the Music AI Industry." *Creative Industries Journal* 14(2): 190–207.

Gertner, J. 2023. "Wikipedia's Moment of Truth." *New York Times.* https://www.nytimes.com/2023/07/18/magazine/wikipedia-ai-chatgpt.html.

Gotham, M. R. H., K. Song, N. Böhlefeld, and A. Elgammal. 2023. "Beethoven X: Es könnte sein! (It could be!)." In *Proceedings of the 3rd Conference on AI Music Creativity, AIMC.* https://aimusiccreativity.org/2022-aimc/.

Grand View Research. *AI Voice Cloning Market Size, Share & Trends Analysis Report By Component (Software, Service), By Deployment (On-premises, Cloud), By Application (Gaming, Advertising), By Vertical, By Region, And Segment Forecasts, 2023–2030.* Report ID: GVR-4-68040-083-1. Electronic (PDF), 100 pages.

Hanslick, E. (1854) 1986. *On the Musically Beautiful: A Contribution Towards the Revision of the Aesthetics of Music (Vom Musikalisch-Schönen).* Translated by Geoffrey Payzant. Indianapolis: Hackett.

Hatten, R. S. 1994. *Musical Meaning in Beethoven: Markedness, Correlation, and Interpretation.* Bloomington: Indiana University Press.

Huang, C. A., C. Hawthorne, A. Roberts, M. Dinculescu, J. Wexler, L. Hong, and J. Howcroft. 2019. "The Bach Doodle: Approachable Music Composition with Machine Learning at Scale." In *Proceedings of the 20th International Society for Music Information Retrieval Conference*, 100–107. Delft, The Netherlands: ISMIR. https://arxiv.org/abs/1907.06637.

Karpathy, A. 2023. "Let's Build GPT: From Scratch, in Code, Spelled Out. [Video]. YouTube. https://www.youtube.com/watch?v=kCc8FmEb1nY.

Kivy, P. 1980. *The Corded Shell: Reflections on Musical Expression.* Princeton: Princeton University Press.

Krumhansl, C. L. 1990. *Cognitive Foundations of Musical Pitch.* New York: Oxford University Press.

Langer, S. 1942. *Philosophy in a New Key*. Cambridge, MA: Harvard University Press.

Long, H., and R. J. So. 2016. "Literary Pattern Recognition: Modernism Between Close Reading and Machine Learning." *Critical Inquiry* 42(2): 235–267.

Metz, R. 2024. "The AI Music Era Is Here. Not Everyone Is a Fan," *Bloomberg*, accessed June 4, 2024. https://www.bloomberg.com/articles/ai-music-era.

Meyer, L. B. 1956. *Emotion and Meaning in Music*. Chicago: University of Chicago Press.

Palfy, C. S. 2022. *Musical Agency and the Social Listener*. New York: Routledge.

Qian, J. 2022. "Research on Artificial Intelligence Technology of Virtual Reality Teaching Method in Digital Media Art Creation." *Journal of Internet Technology* 23(1): 125–132.

Rebelo, A., I. Fujinaga, F. Paszkiewicz, A. R. S. Marcal, C. Guedes, and J. S. Cardoso. 2012. "Optical Music Recognition: State-of-the-Art and Open Issues." *International Journal of Multimedia Information Retrieval* 1, 173–190. https://doi.org/10.1007/s13735-012-0004-6.

Roberts, A., Y. Mann, J. Engel, and C. Radebaugh. 2023. Magenta Studio. https://magenta.tensorflow.org/.

Rohrmeier, M. 2022. "On Creativity, Music's AI Completeness, and Four Challenges for Artificial Musical Creativity." *Transactions of the International Society for Music Information Retrieval* 5(1): 50–66. https://doi.org/10.5334/tismir.104.

Saint-Dizier, P. 2020. "Music and Artificial Intelligence." In *A Guided Tour of Artificial Intelligence Research*, edited by P. Marquis, O. Papini, and H. Prade. Cham: Springer. https://doi.org/10.1007/978-3-030-06170-8_16.

Samual, S. 2023. The Case for Slowing Down AI. *Vox*. https://www.vox.com/the-highlight/23621198/artificial-intelligence-chatgpt-openai-existential-risk-china-ai-safety-technology.

Sharma, G., K. Umapathy, and S. Krishnan. 2020. Trends in Audio Signal Feature Extraction Methods. *Applied Acoustics* 158, 107020. https://doi.org/10.1016/j.apacoust.2019.107020.

Shang, M., and H. Sun. 2020. Study on the New Models of Music Industry in the Era of AI and Blockchain. In *2020 3rd International Conference on Smart BlockChain (SmartBlock)*, 63–68. Zhengzhou, China.

Sörbom, G. 1994. "Aristotle on Music as Representation." *The Journal of Aesthetics and Art Criticism* 52(1): 37–46. https://doi.org/10.2307/431583.

Tegmark, M. 2017. *Life 3.0 Being Human in the Age of Artificial Intelligence*. New York: Knopf.

Tigre Moura, F., and C. Maw. 2021. "Artificial Intelligence Became Beethoven: How Do Listeners and Music Professionals Perceive Artificially Composed Music?" *Journal of Consumer Marketing* 38(2): 137–146.

Thompson, L., and D. Mimno. 2023. Humanities and Human-Centered Machine Learning. Working paper.

Tomlinson, Gary. 2015. *A Million Years of Music: The Emergence of Human Modernity*. New York: Zone Books.

Turing, A. M. 1950. "Computing Machinery and Intelligence." *Mind* 59(236): 433–460. https://doi.org/10.1093/mind/LIX.236.433.

Tymoczko, D. 2011. *A Geometry of Music: Harmony and Counterpoint in the Extended Common Practice*. New York: Oxford University Press.

Webster, P. 2002. "Historical Perspectives on Technology and Music." *Music Educators Journal* 89(1): 38–43. https://doi-org.silk.library.umass.edu/10.2307/3399883.

White, C. 2022. *The Music in the Data: Corpus Analysis, Music Analysis, and Tonal Traditions.* New York: Routledge.

White, C. 2023. Artificial Intelligence Can't Reproduce the Wonders of Original Human Creativity. *Chicago Tribune* [Op-Ed]. https://www.chicagotribune .com/opinion/commentary/ct-opinion-artificial-intelligence-human-creativity -chatgpt-20230112-mmoxqjgqtfaibgr663lsohtq34-story.html.

White, C., and M. Kozak. 2023. We Need AI Labels on Creative Content — But Not for the Reasons You Think. *Chicago Tribune* [Op-Ed]. https://www .chicagotribune.com/opinion/commentary/ct-opinions-artificial-intelligence -ai-creative-content-labels-20230603-ak26god46bhbfb2ookbqprnfce-story .html.

Wolfram, S. 2023. What Is ChatGPT Doing … and Why Does It Work? https:// writings.stephenwolfram.com/2023/02/what-is-chatgpt-doing-and-why-does -it-work/.

2

HISTORY, ENGINEERING, AND MOTIVATIONS BEHIND GENERATIVE MUSICAL AI

"We can only see a short distance ahead, but we can see plenty there that needs to be done."
Alan Turing, "Computing Machinery and Intelligence," 1950

A lot of graduate students working in my little corner of academia—the intersection of music analysis and computer science—eventually land careers in tech companies. After all, they've devoted years to learning how to code, undertaking statistical analysis, and writing compelling interpretations of these statistics, and these are all useful skills in the 21st-century tech industry. Some of these students find themselves at well-known tech giants, while others join smaller startups or boutique tech firms with their own niches. But almost none of these graduates employed by the tech industry end up working on *music*. Compared with other areas, there are simply fewer tech companies doing music research and development. Moreover, the firms that specialize in music tend to be smaller in scale compared to their counterparts in other sectors.

In this chapter, I explore this imbalance in AI research and look at some reasons the disparity exists. After a short review of the history of generative AI and a discussion of the concept of "creativity," I outline some basic principles behind machine learning and generative AI, focusing on how these tools have been used to engage in musical creativity. I then return to the financial incentives of musical generative AI, contrasting these with motivations within other sectors. I conclude the chapter by contextualizing the various reasons that music receives fewer resources and less attention than other initiatives in generative AI.

DOI: 10.4324/9781003587415-2

The advent of generative and creative machines

For as long as people have been making complex machines, they have designed them to make music. While it is possible that the ancient Greeks or Romans created automated musical instruments, the likely candidate for the first such machine is a water-powered astronomical clock built by Ismail al-Jazari in the late 12th century in al-Jazira, Mesopotamia. The clock featured an automated human figure that struck a cymbal and a mechanized bird that chirped. As pendulum and suspension spring clocks became more ubiquitous over the following centuries, these devices would often involve some sort of music-making element, like cuckoos that whistle or chimes that play on the hour. Technological innovation along this line would eventually extend beyond timekeeping instruments to increasingly advanced mechanisms dedicated solely to creating music. For example, "The Musician," made by Henri-Louis Jacquet-Droz in the late 18th century, features a lifelike female figure that plays an organ. She presses the instrument's keys as she appears to breathe and move her eyes to follow her organ-playing fingers. Wolfgang Mozart even composed a piece for an automated instrument. His Adagio and Allegro in F minor, K. 594, of 1790 was commissioned for a self-playing organ designed to deliver a continuous mechanized funeral mass in the mausoleum of a renowned Austrian general.[1]

All these machines were *generative*. They made music. But none of them were *creative*. Musical clocks, music boxes, mechanized instruments, and automata are all preprogrammed with some sequence of events. When a mechanical organ is programmed to play Mozart's Adagio and Allegro in F minor, it will never play anything but that piece. It can't generate anything new.

Musical dice games were popular among 18th-century European elites, and they represent an early way to create novel music through a non-human process. The games relied on precomposed musical snippets, which players would select at random by rolling dice, thus determining the order of the fragments and creating a "new" piece. While the popularity of these games faded by the 1800s, several 20th-century composers followed in their dice-rolling footsteps by leveraging some randomized procedure or mathematical function to compose new music. The composer Iannis Xenakis created the piece *Achorripsis* by following several probability formulas, while John Cage assembled his *Music of Changes* by using the equivalent of coin tosses. However, in each of these instances, *creativity* lies not in the process itself but in the human behind it. The dice rolls and coin flips simply select precomposed material. If the resulting music sounds good, it's due to either chance or the composer's skill in creating compatible preset fragments. Even if these processes generate new combinations, the actual creativity—the design and composition of musical components—is still done by a human.

One of the first machines that reliably produced seemingly new musical content was Raymond Scott's "Electronium." The Electronium was an enormous analog instrument that created content by randomly reorganizing the melodies, rhythms, and harmonies it kept stored in its memory. Scott engineered this instrument in the 1960s with the intention of assisting composers in generating novel musical ideas. His invention caught the attention of Motown Records, who hoped to integrate the technology into the label's songwriting process. Even though they offered Scott a contract for the use of his device, no Motown songs were ever produced using the Electronium, and he never finished the development of the machine. However, the Electronium still stands as an important milestone in automated music.[2]

While it was certainly a generative machine, the Electronium still wasn't creative. Scott's machine was designed to produce new melodic and rhythmic fragments to seed a songwriter's compositional process with fresh ideas. To be sure, by randomly reorganizing its source material, it was creating combinations of melodies and rhythms that had never been written before. But it was never meant to write songs and grooves on its own, bypassing the human composer. Its melodies and rhythms weren't supposed to stand on their own. They weren't supposed to be *good*.

Scholars like Martin Rohrmeier, Geraint Wiggins, and Margaret Boden have long theorized about the exact criteria needed to consider a music-generating machine to be "creative." And while these thinkers present nuanced analyses and taxonomies of computational creativity, they often hit on two general touchstones in their theories. For a musical machine to really be creative, it must 1) generate music that is new, and 2) be understandable and valued by an audience. To this second issue: "creative" music can't claim to be "new" by being entirely random, incoherent, and haphazard—playing random notes on a piano (or shuffling melodic snippets within the Electronium's memory) might create a sequence that's never been heard before, but the music won't sound *creative*. You can't simply haphazardly reorder a pile of notes and rhythms and expect it to sound like a song. Rather, the music needs to work within some logic and adhere to the norms, aesthetics, and structures that govern some musical style and make it legible and accessible to an audience.[3]

After all, this is how human creativity works. When you compose a new song, you don't haphazardly shovel piles of arbitrary notes into a melody and hope it sounds good. Rather, you choose from a menu of options for a number of different factors. Perhaps you choose to write a song in verse-chorus form, in the key C major, using a standard chord progression, and with familiar melodic shapes. Having made a number of choices about your song's organization, you can then exercise expressive, novel, and even beautiful variations within those presets. Even though you're working within well-defined stylistic guidelines, you aren't simply cutting and pasting precomposed material. You are generating something new through your own creativity.

This is what I'll mean by "creativity," at least as a preliminary definition. When we make content that's understandable to an audience, we are working inside the norms and standards of that artform, creatively varying established structures, and participating in a tradition. It is in this sense that, for a machine to be *creative*, it must make things that an audience understands. Creators—humans or machines—must negotiate the frameworks that render their creations comprehensible and engaging to viewers or listeners.

In Figure 2.1, I locate several musical machines in a graph defined by these two facets of creative ability. The horizontal axis represents how the machine handles its source material. At the left end of this axis, machines simply replicate what's fed to them. As one moves to the right, machines become more sophisticated in reorganizing and manipulating their source content. The vertical axis reflects a machine's ability to conform to an audience's expectations. The higher these machines sit on the vertical axis, the more they are capable of conforming to the stylistic expectations of an audience. Capturing the idea that "creativity" involves both producing new material and working within the guidelines of some system of expectations, human creativity resides in the upper-right corner. In contrast, a mechanical organ, which simply reproduces pre-composed music, sits in the upper-left corner. Moving to the right, dice games and

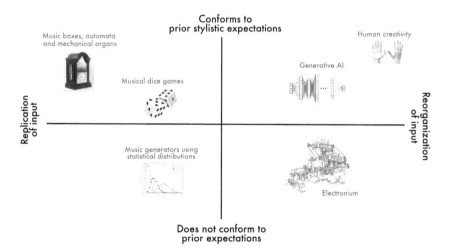

FIGURE 2.1   Generative musical processes graphed according to their abilities to reorganize inputs and conform to stylistic norms.[4]

other random music generators occupy a middle ground. They can shuffle and reorganize precomposed musical snippets, but they can only use this preset material. Because their randomness doesn't necessarily follow stylistic rules, they fall lower on the vertical axis. Finally, the Electronium occupies the lower-right quadrant. It can generate an infinite variety of musical combinations that are not bound by any legibility or constraints, pushing it lower on the vertical axis.

None of the generative machines I've discussed satisfy both criteria for "creativity." This possibility was only offered by the widespread development of the computer in the middle of the 20th century. Machines that utilize some sort of processing unit date back to the work of the 19-century polymath Charles Babbage, but it was the advent of electrical circuits and vacuum tubes, combined with the technological advancements spurred by World War II, that gave birth to the early prototypes of the computers that are ubiquitous in today's world.

These are the types of systems I label as "generative AI" in the upper-right quadrant of my figure. In the sphere of creativity, the power of these computers stems from their capacity to *structure randomness*. Unlike a musical automaton, which cannot deviate from a preset melody, or the Electronium, which generated notes in an often chaotic fashion, computer programs introduced the ability to navigate a middle ground. The digital architecture of these machines enables them to traverse many potential pathways while still allowing for the incorporation of preprogrammed guardrails. A computer program can channel processes along certain preferred paths, offering a structured yet flexible framework that is neither rigidly fixed nor entirely unpredictable. At least in theory, balancing structure and randomness should allow for some level of creativity.

It didn't take long for researchers to suggest that this framework had a lot in common with the human creative process. Alan Turing, the British mathematician, computer engineer, and wartime codebreaker realized the potential for computational processes to imitate human thought in his seminal 1950 article, "Computing Machinery and Intelligence." Turing opens his essay with the provocative question, "Can machines think?" In considering whether computers might one day produce creative content indistinguishable from the work of humans, he posits that achieving such a feat would effectively signify a form of "intelligence" within these machines. Six years later, researchers participating in a summer gathering at Dartmouth College coined the term *Artificial Intelligence* to designate computational programs that, in some way, parallel human thought processes and creativity: making decisions, performing tasks, interpreting information, and generating new content.

Experimentation in musical AI quickly followed. The 1957 piece "Illiac Suite," by Lejaren Hiller and Leonard Isaacson, was one of the earliest instances of AI-created music. In 1960, Rudolf Zaripov published "On algorithmic description of process of music composition," one of the first scholarly investigations of AI music composition. Throughout the next several decades, music theorists like Leonard Meyer, Joseph E. Youngblood, Edgar Coons, and David Kraehenbuehl developed algorithms to analyze and study musical styles, while composers like H.J. Maxwell, Richard Boulanger, Laurie Spiegel, and David Cope used computational systems to generate music. Institutions like *The Center for Music Experiment* at the University of California at San Diego and the *Institut de recherche et coordination acoustique/musique* (IRCAM) in Paris were founded to support the growing number of composers interested in computer-aided music composition.

At this point in our story, many of these musical machines were capable of being "creative." In terms of Figure 2.1, they reorganized digital inputs to create something new while following some set of expectational guidelines. These AIs were not generating random ideas, nor were they regurgitating preprogrammed melodies. And, with a bit of guidance from their composer-curators, the music they produced was engaging to their audiences, even if the engagement involved a fair bit of skepticism. Whether this creativity mirrored the depth and complexity of human ingenuity remains a separate question, one I'll return to in Chapter 6. (Spoiler: I believe it does not.)

But what underpins this machine-driven creativity? How does AI incorporate both the norms its audience expects and the novelty required to invent new music? How does it balance structure and randomness? In the following section, we will rejoin the story of computational composition to explore the mechanisms through which computers generate novel content.

How computers "learn" musical creativity

20th-century computational music used a multitude of approaches that can be grouped into two broad camps. The first camp involves computer programs with rules and preferences built into them. This is what I will call the *expert modeling approach*, so named because the knowledge that an expert might have about musical composition is transferred into a computer. For instance, the "Illiac Suite" was the result of some basic protocols for writing note and rhythmic sequences; H.J. Maxwell programmed his compositional algorithms with rules akin to what one might find in a classical music theory textbook.

Music from the second camp is generated through *machine learning*. Here, computer programs acquire knowledge about composition by computationally observing a dataset of music. For instance, David Cope's "Experiments in Musical Intelligence" (affectionately nicknamed "EMI") processes some musical sequence, observing what chords and melodic notes move between one another. EMI remembers those connections and uses them to generate new music. A key feature here is that Cope's machine "learns" how to compose without supervision from the program's human author— this is "machine learning".

The history of computing is also a history of increasing computing power. In 1951, the UNIVAC-1 became the first computer marketed as a general-purpose instrument to American businesses. It could undertake about 2,000 operations per second. By 1981, the similarly marketed Motorola 6800 chip could do over one million operations per second. And by 1991, the Intel i860 could perform at a rate roughly 50 times that speed. These developments would continue apace, and I'll return to their 21st-century implications below.

The 20th-century surge in computational capacity allowed computer programmers to use increasingly complex architectures in their models. The expert modeling approach relies on structured frameworks and often employs rules and decision trees that determine what the computer will write in certain situations. This method outlines specific compositional directions for the computer to follow under given conditions. An expert modeling approach might include rules such as, "If you are ending a piece, use a stable harmony;" "If you're on a strong beat, follow this set of rules;" or "If you're on a weak beat, follow this other set of rules." The amount of complexity in this paradigm depends on the quantity and intricacy of the rules made by the composer, and more computing power allows for more complex rules.

In the machine learning camp, one straightforward approach is *Markov modeling*, a technique that calculates how often some event follows some other event. While learning, a Markov model maps out how often each different type of event occurs within its dataset and tracks how often those events appear in sequence. It makes these observations into *probabilities*, mathematically capturing how often each event type is followed by each other type of event. When a Markov model creates new music—when it acts as a generative AI—the algorithm turns around and uses the probabilities that it has learned to make new sequences of events. For example, if a particular chord progression appears frequently within its dataset, the Markov model is likely to incorporate that sequence just as often in its compositions. The sequence is *probable*: it occurs a lot in the dataset and will be frequently used in the automated compositional process. Conversely, chord progressions or sequences of notes that rarely occur within the dataset will be *improbable*, and will be seldom replicated by the model in its musical outputs. Here, a model's complexity—how much the model needs to remember in its computational mind—is determined by the gross number of observations the computer is tasked with making and how many kinds of events the computer needs to keep track of. Bigger datasets with more diverse events lead to more computational complexity, and more powerful computers allow for this sort of complexity.

Overall, when you have limited computational capacity, expert modeling approaches make more sense, as they can capture more compositional information with greater efficiency. For instance, H.J. Maxwell's 1992 algorithm for analyzing and generating chord progressions in the style of J.S. Bach was built using only 55 predefined rules. In contrast, David Cope's 1996 machine learning approach for composing in Bach's style used Markov modeling to analyze a dataset of the 33,978 chords from Bach chorales ("chorales" are hymn-like compositions, often for four-part choir). This method required tracking the behavior of each of the 167 unique chord types used by Bach. While Maxwell's approach never had to "learn" anything, Cope's method needed to build up its memory about those 167 chords. The expert approach only contains 55 items in its computational memory, Cope's Markov model had to remember upwards of 27,889 items. This is 167 x 167, or the number of connections between each chord type with every other chord type—or, how probable each chord is to progress to each other chord. If you're working with a computer with limited processing and memory, you're going to prefer the expert model!

But an expert model is limited to the rules programmed into it. If Maxwell wanted to change his algorithm's knowledge, *he* would need to change the code. A machine learning model, however, can expand and refine its knowledge as it processes more data. Cope, for instance, would subsequently add new data from other composers into his model's dataset, thus expanding its stylistic knowledge. He also later enhanced his model by integrating a feedback mechanism, enabling his program to "learn" by recognizing which musical gestures he preferred and which he disliked. None of this is possible with a simpler expert model.

Importantly, both these approaches can be "creative" insomuch as they work within certain guardrails to produce new content that captures the norms of a musical style. Rules-based expert models explicitly show a computer how to follow those norms, while a machine learning Markov model gains some basic knowledge of how to use musical events by tallying the properties of its dataset. However, the creativity of both models is extremely limited, with expert models only being able to use whatever rules and decisions a composer initially coded into it and Markov models essentially replicating the events and sequences in the data.

As computational power and memory continued to expand at the turn of the century, more complex approaches became possible.[5] In particular, these innovations allowed *deep learning* to gain traction in the early years of the 21st century. Where Markov models are predicated on surface-level observations, deep learning relies on generalizations and categorizations made by the computer and the connections it learns to make between them. Deep learning still relies on probabilities and datasets, but it groups its data in more sophisticated ways and applies probabilities to connect these groups. Essentially, deep learning engages in complex connections that categorize events by their similarity, and even groups those categories into increasingly abstract classifications. When a deep learning algorithm learns from a dataset or composes a piece of music, it does not just consider things like how often an individual chord moves to another chord or the probability of a melody note proceeding to another particular note. Instead, it uses its dataset to evaluate how frequently categories of chords and notes move to other categories, emphasizing the relationships between broader groups of musical events. Said more mathematically: deep learning models learn probabilities between categories of events within some dataset. They can then use those probabilities to generate new content by using more probable categories and connections more often and improbable categories and connections less often.

As an analogy, think of the sentence, "The cat sits on my lap." Just as Cope's musical Markov model tracks how often each chord moves to each other chord in Bach's collection of chorales, a linguistic Markov model would analyze this sentence by checking how often each of that sentence's words moves to each other word in a dataset of English-language texts. But, the word "lap" doesn't end the sentence simply because it sometimes follows the word "my" in a dataset of English. Rather, "lap" can end the sentence because it's part of the category of things on which cats sit, a classification nested within the broader category of nouns. In a dataset of English texts, you can imagine finding other items that cats sit on—like "table" or "bed"—occurring in similar contexts. On another level, the broader category of nouns exhibits more generalized contextual resemblances (for instance, as words that occur near verbs). A deep learning model might recognize those linguistic categories. Similarly, a deep learning model of chord progressions will find that there are categories of chords that tend to occur in similar contexts. There are kinds of chords that start phrases, those that end phrases, those that come right before an ending, and so on. In contrast to Cope's Markov model that composes music by referencing which of Bach's chords tend to occur one after another, deep learning models compose music by generating chord progressions and melodies using broader categories.[6]

Naturally, introducing categories and layers significantly increases complexity. Returning to the example of Bach's chorales, a deep learning model will discern various ways to group his 33,978 chords and 167 chord types. The complexity balloons with the addition of multiple categorical layers. What chords go into which category? How many categories are there? In what contexts are certain broader categories appropriate? How do chord types cluster within these categories, and is there any overlap among them? The computational problems (and the required computational power) become intricate indeed.

However complicated, these deep learning models have greater potential to be "creative" when generating new content. Recall that the key for a creative system is to find a middle ground between producing entirely random outputs and simply duplicating pre-existing patterns. The layered categorization within deep learning frameworks provides this equilibrium by organizing events into context-based groups. Such organization enables the models to grasp overarching musical principles, and to learn broader norms about the kinds of events that occur in certain situations. But, when employing these categories, deep learning models also have access to the many options that are appropriate in those situations. In our linguistic analogy, the model might identify all feasible surfaces on which a cat could sit. Musically, it might know every chord that could accompany a particular melody note at the beginning of a phrase. When it comes to generating new material, this capability allows the model to creatively select from the various alternatives and compose something novel yet stylistically coherent, writing something entirely new that still follows the stylistic guidelines of its dataset. Again, whether such artificial creativity can pass for human creativity is a question for Chapter 6. (Spoiler: artificial creativity often fails in this regard.)

But how do these categorizations work from a computational perspective? The next section dives into some specifics of deep learning, particularly the architecture of neural networks.

Machine learning and deep learning

In the last chapter, we did an in-depth analysis of the well-known tune, "Amazing Grace." Figure 2.2 shows the beginning of the melody again, this time using only the note names. This passage uses only five notes from the C-major scale: C, D, E, G, and A. The melody primarily bounces between the notes C, E, and G. The notes D and A occur much less frequently. Outside of being used less often, D and A also behave differently. Based on this observation, we might begin to think of these as two

FIGURE 2.2 The first line of "Amazing Grace" (John Newton, 1772).

categories of notes. While C, E, and G seem to have more melodic free-dom, whenever the melody ventures to a D or A, it immediately moves back to a note in the other category. D and A do not move between one another, and instead move to a C, E, or G. I've shown D and A in gray in Figure 2.2 to highlight this behavior.

Let's imagine we compiled a dataset with many melodies behaving similarly, with the notes D and A moving to the notes C, E, and G, which themselves progress to any note. Figure 2.3a summarizes this melodic behavior with a simple Markov model, represented by notes and arrows between them. The varying thickness of the arrows indicates the fre-quency of note-to-note transitions, with heavier arrows representing more common—more probable—movements and lighter arrows denoting less frequent and more improbable ones. This surface-level information can be learned by observing the melody and simply counting how often each note goes to every other note.

A machine learning algorithm employing a Markov model could "learn" a musical grammar like this by parsing a dataset of similar melodies and tallying how often the notes progress to one another. We can imagine that the pathways between the central notes (C, E, and G) become deeper and more well-worn each time the machine observes them moving to one another. Meanwhile, because D and A never progress to one another, no pathway is hewn between them.

In machine learning, the data used to train a model is called its *training data*. The training data provides the foundation for the model's knowl-edge. It is the source from which the model learns patterns, connections, and trends. This is also the data from which a model calculates the prob-abilities it can use to create new material. Events and sequences that occur more frequently in the training data will be more probable—more expected—by the model, while events and that occur less often will be improbable and less expected.

Indeed, after the machine learning algorithm has processed its training data, the model can use what it's learned to create melodies. To make new music, the computer would follow the pathways shown in Figure 2.3a, with the model producing a new note every time it lands on a pitch. It would move through the space mostly using the well-worn probable path-ways, only occasionally venturing down the narrower improbable side alleys. For example, the machine might begin on C, follow the vertical path to E, move back to C, jump to G, and finally touch on the less-used A before returning to G. In this case, this model would have produced the melody "C-E-C-G-A-G." By using the probabilities, norms, and tenden-cies from training data to produce a new melody, this machine would now become a *generative* model.

Figure 2.3b shows a "deeper" way to imagine this grammar. Following the discussion above, the figure contains two categorical pitch groups, C–E–G and D–A. The thin arrow indicates how the groups can move between one another, while the heavier arrow shows that the first group often moves between its constituent pitches. There is no thicker arrow above the second group, because it cannot return to itself. This level of abstraction represents a more sophisticated description of how the "Amazing Grace" melody works, capturing categorical behaviors rather than mere moment-to-moment note transitions.

Deep learning allows computers to identify these more sophisticated categories and to describe these categorical behaviors with probabilities. The remainder of Figure 2.3 shows one possible way to engineer this learning using multiple computational "layers." In Figure 2.3c, you can see the first step in this process. The *input* or *surface layer* is at the top of the diagram. This layer corresponds to the events or data points the computer encounters in its training data. In a deep learning system focused on text analysis, each node within the input layer might represent a different letter or word. Conversely, in a system designed for image processing, these nodes could correspond to the various colors of pixels within the images being analyzed. In our case, the slots will be filled by the five different notes used in the "Amazing Grace" melody.

Underneath the input are *hidden layers*. These hidden layers add the depth to a deep learning machine.[7] For simplicity, this example uses one hidden layer comprising two nodes, shown in dark and light gray. Before a deep learning system processes its training data, all potential connections remain possible. That is, all hidden nodes have potential connections between them; each hidden node has the potential to connect with every surface node; and potential connections are even present between each hidden node and itself. Before looking at a dataset, all these connections are equally probable—the model does not expect any events or sequences to occur more or less than anything else. These undifferentiated

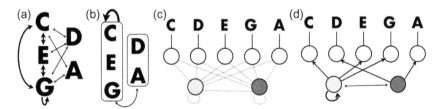

FIGURE 2.3   a) A Markov model of the melodic grammar in "Amazing Grace"; b) A categorized approach to the grammar; c) A deep learning schematic before its learning; and d) after learning the grammar's categories.

connections are shown in Figure 2.3c through the web of light lines. As a deep learning procedure works through its training data, it strengthens those connections that help make sense of sequences and weakens those that don't. Training on a body of melodies that share the salient features of "Amazing Grace," a deep learning machine would make strong connections between the notes C, E, and G and a hidden node that captures their similar behaviors. Because these notes frequently move between one another in the training data, the connections between them will become strong and more probable— the model begins to expect these notes to move between one another. In Figure 2.3d, I show these three notes forming strong connections to the light gray hidden node along with a strong self-pointing arrow below that node, representing a high probability of those notes moving to one another. Then, because D and A have similar behaviors, they'll form strong connections to a second, different hidden node, represented here by the dark gray hidden node. Because we expect notes in these two categories to progress to one another, the connection between the two hidden nodes becomes strong, showing that notes of these two categories can move between one another with a relatively high probability. Because D and A do not progress to one another in the training data, that hidden node's connection to itself atrophies. Moving between D and A is very improbable and unexpected.

In principle, any computational processes that has hidden layers can be considered "deep learning," but *neural networks* are the particular approach to deep learning used in most contemporary AI. (In fact, from now on, I'll treat these two terms as functionally synonymous, given the ubiquity of neural networks in generative AI.) Neural networks get their name because their basic form was initially inspired by the layout of neurons in the human brain, though the metaphor has loosened in recent years. As I show in Figure 2.4a, neural networks involve nodes at an input layer, multiple hidden layers, and an *output layer*. The inputs correspond to the data a network receives, while the outputs are what the network produces. Inputs and outputs are often be the same types of events from the same medium or the same language. A chatbot, for instance, trains on a dataset of text in order to produce new text. Then, after it's been trained, users text the bot questions and the bot responds with text answers. The inputs and output are both sequences of words in the same language. However, a neural network's inputs and outputs can also translate between two different mediums or formats. In an image-producing bot, for instance, the inputs might be a user's description of some object, and the output could be an image created from that description.

Much like my earlier example, as the neural network "listens" to the melodies in its training data, the program strengthens the connections between categories that better describe the data while less useful connections atrophy. However, unlike the deep learning model in Figure 2.3c, a neural network uses its output layer to refine connections. As it moves through its training data, the network isolates short sequences and treats them as inputs. It predicts what will follow each sequence in turn and outputs a proposed continuation. The network then returns to its training data to evaluate its prediction. If its prediction matches the training data, the network will strengthen the connections it used to make that prediction. Said mathematically: if it predicts the sequence of categories correctly, it increases the probability of that sequence. If it does not, the network will assess that sequence as less probable. It repeats this process over and over, chopping up its training data into many different sequences, making predictions, checking itself, remaking sequences, updating its probabilities, and so on.

To illustrate this process, Figure 2.4a shows a hypothetical neural network in mid-training. Capturing the particular way that neural networks train, the diagram should be read from top to bottom, with inputs still appearing at the top but with outputs now added below. Here, the basic inputs are once again the notes of the "Amazing Grace" melody. One difference, however, is that the inputs correspond to a particular melodic fragment—here, the notes sung with the words "…mazing Grace! How sweet the…." Again, this reflects the ways in which neural networks train, processing a sequence of notes in some particular context and predicting the next event. At this point in its learning, the network has derived much the same grammar as that learned by the model in Figure 2.3. The inputs C, E, and G are linked to one series of hidden nodes, and the inputs D and A are connected to another. The C, E, and G output nodes are connected to the hidden nodes associated with those notes' inputs, and these hidden nodes also have connections that run toward the D and A output nodes.

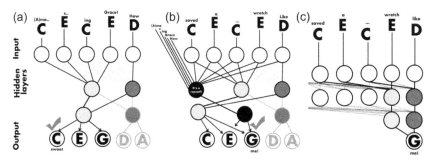

FIGURE 2.4   a) A hypothetical neural network training on a selection from "Amazing Grace"; b) with a hidden layer devoted to repetition; and c) that same training imagined in a more complex transformer-style network.

However, the D and A output nodes are *not* strongly connected to the hidden nodes associated with the C–E–G inputs. This asymmetry captures the imbalance in the melodic grammar. If the network observes C, E, or G occurring as inputs, it will expect any note to follow as an output with a high probability. But, if D or A occur in a melody, the network will only expect C, E, or G to follow.

As we join the model in its training, the note D has occurred on the word "How," at the top right in Figure 2.4a. We can follow the stronger connections downward through the first dark gray hidden node, into the next layer through the light gray hidden node, and finally to the C, E, and G output nodes. This path of strong connections indicates that the network would either predict C, E, or G to be the next likely, most probable notes. When the predicted G occurs with the word "sweet," the network will strengthen the connections that led to its correct prediction, leading the model to make the same prediction in similar contexts in the future.

Just as Markov models can use the probabilities they've learned to generate new musical sequences, once a neural network has undergone its learning process, it can repurpose its output layer to produce new content. These generative models can be engineered in several different ways. But, in one such implementation, a network like Figure 2.4a could follow its connections to produce a series of new notes, and then could repurpose that series as the input to inspire the next series of notes. It could then continue in that manner until it created a full melody. For instance, if the network began a melody with the note C, that note would serve as the input to inspire the next note, perhaps a D. The sequence C–D then becomes the input to generate the next output and so on. Eventually, this neural network—this simple AI—would generate a complete new melody by following its well-worn, more probable connections more frequently and traversing its less probable pathways less often.

The primary benefit of neural networks is that their hidden nodes can capture connections between longer sequences and can notice more distant connections between events. For instance, in "Amazing Grace," the C that appears on "sweet" doesn't only make sense because it follows a D. The note appears as part of a three-note downward cascade ("Grace! How sweet"), and, given that this melodic snippet began on C, that note returns the melody to our point of origin. Surface machine learning approaches like Markov models are not designed to capture larger gestures and organizational patterns of this sort. In contrast, the hidden layers in a neural network can internalize larger and more complex structures.

To capture these broader behaviors, larger sequences that behave similarly can be connected to the same hidden nodes. Perhaps many melodies that start on C tend to frequently return to that note. This tendency/probability might be embedded in some hidden node, with all melodies that emphasize C connected to that node. That node would capture a broader characteristic of these melodies—a "return-to-C-ness"—that wouldn't be available in a simpler, surface model.

We can imagine many similar larger musical contingencies. Perhaps the model might notice that melodic lines act differently at the beginning of a phrase versus the end of a phrase. Here, one series of hidden nodes might embed information about phrase beginnings, while a different group of nodes could be devoted to the probabilities of phrase endings. Perhaps melodies behave differently when they're sung versus played on the violin. Perhaps rising phrases have different tendencies than descending phrases. Perhaps a repeated theme will act differently the first time it's introduced versus in its repetitions.

I've imagined this final option in the hypothetical network of Figure 2.4b. There, I now show the network training on the second time the C–E–C–E–D melodic sequence appears in the hymn, with the words "saved a wretch like." Connections extend to the previous phrase with a hidden layer specifically devoted to the melody's repetition. This hypothetical network predicts that the second repetition would end differently than in its first incarnation. And, given that this is exactly what happens in this hymn, these connections would be strengthened in the network, and the model would learn a larger structural tendency of—and probabilities associated with—repeated themes.

Recent innovations in neural networks have focused on ways to include more and more of these larger connections and contingencies. Figure 2.4c represents one such type of neural network called a "transformer," an approach used often in contemporary generative AI. (Indeed, the "T" in the popular chatbot, ChatGPT, stands for "transformer.") Within the architecture of transformers, longer sequences of connections are fed into a single node, and each node is designed to contain more contextual information about a specific moment. The dark gray nodes in Figure 2.4c are still primarily connected to the notes D and A, while the light gray nodes connect mostly to C, E, and G. And, just like Figure 2.4b, the connections extend to the previous phrase. With its increased connections, a transformer's nodes can include information about repetition, contour, phrase position, and other aspects of larger melodic structure. In other words, when the model predicts the "Amazing Grace" snippet, it's not merely considering the basic category of notes that follow D. Rather, it can use connections that reach back to earlier parts of the phrase.

These diagrams of layered nodes and arrows are metaphors for mathematical relationships within complex computational architectures. But, for the purposes of this book, we don't need to get bogged down in the specific mathematics of these approaches and the specific ways they translate the trends and tendencies drawn from training data into networks of nodes and probabilities. Nor do we need to dive into the engineering differences between the many types of neural networks that dot the landscape of generative AI.[8]

Rather, I want to end this tour of machine learning by highlighting some general summarizing characteristics of these types of models. There are five main components of deep learning neural networks that both summarize these models' underlying processes and underpin the mismatches between music and AI.

First, these deep learning systems learn patterns from datasets by predicting what they believe will happen next, checking their training data to see whether they're correct, and repeating the process to hone their predictions. Second, their hidden layers allow the model to generalize between different events by connecting similar observations and situations to the same series of hidden nodes. Third, the hidden layers allow the network to learn complex, long-term patterns from data by devoting particular hidden nodes to certain situations. Fourth, each connection between nodes is computationally represented as a probability, with more frequent sequences of events being more probable, and less frequent sequences being less probable. Finally, these networks can create content—they become generative—when they use their connections to produce something new. Instead of predicting what they expect to occur next, the networks actually create that next event. These neural networks produce content by learning the norms of some dataset by identifying patterns and generalizing the behaviors it's observing. In terms of my formulations in Figure 2.1, these neural networks create original content by following the larger compositional guidelines they've learned from a dataset. It is in this sense, these generative AIs.

The resources neural networks need

Neural networks have been present in computational engineering since the dawn of the modern computer. In a 1943 paper, neurophysiologist Warren McCulloch and logician Walter Pitts proposed that the human brain's neuronal connections could provide a useful analogy for computational engineering. This idea was amplified in 1948 by Alan Turing, often considered the father of modern computing, in his own publications. The US Navy noted these developments within academia and quickly directed substantial resources into investigating the usefulness of computer programs based explicitly on the neural architecture of the brain.[9]

Through much of the 20th century, neural network models were found lacking. They underperformed relative to computational systems from both the expert modeling and simpler machine learning approaches. In the early 1990s, for instance, the music research community explored the potential of neural networks for modeling how listeners learn musical concepts such as key, scales, and chords. Despite the intriguing theories behind these proposals, the computational models were not practically effective, and the work remained largely speculative.[10] These systems needed far more data and computing power than 20th-century technology could provide, but 21st-century advancements in computer engineering combined with the vast amounts of data available on the internet to usher in a heyday for deep learning and neural networks.

Neural networks' hunger for huge amounts of data and computing power arises from three important facets of their design. The first, and perhaps most obvious, is that the greater complexity of neural networks simply requires more computational memory. As I noted earlier, an expert modeling algorithm needs to keep only the preprogrammed rules in its computational memory, and a surface-level machine learning model need only keep track of connections between adjacent items in its dataset. But neural networks need to have enough memory to process surface events, connections between those events and the many hidden layers, *and* the connections between nodes within the hidden layers. These models have only become more complicated in recent decades. When my students create mockups of the very simplest versions of musical transformers, they tend to use about a thousand input nodes related to four hidden layers. Google's network for writing music in the style of Bach uses the rough equivalent of twelve layers. ChatGPT's architecture uses more than 16,000 surface nodes and has a depth roughly analogous to 90 layers.

The second aspect of neural networks that drives the increasing need for data and computing power is the way these models learn. Simpler algorithms like Markov models can assimilate their entire datasets in one pass. After all, their learning process simply involves cataloging the frequency with which sequential events occur in their training data. Deep learning models, on the other hand, cultivate the connections in their hidden layers gradually over many iterations. That is, they learn by repetition. As we saw in my hypothetical neural network, these models make predictions, strengthen connections when they predict correctly, and weaken connections associated with incorrect predictions. In this manner, they pass over their dataset repeatedly, jigger probabilities, and refine connections with each cycle. Complex and subtle ideas, such as how musical phrases begin and end, are built up slowly over many passes through the training data. Making satisfactory connections often involves thousands, if not millions, of iterations over a dataset. For instance, when my students build the simplest musical transformers, they find that their models need to run through their training data around 100,000 times before they begin to produce recognizable musical outputs. They only start to create larger musical gestures reliably after about a million iterations.

This gives some indication of the formidable computational power, including high-speed processors and substantial memory, that training sophisticated models requires. If 20th-century computing power allowed researchers like David Cope to experiment with basic machine learning, 21st-century innovations have opened the door for enormous neural networks. For instance, ChatGPT-3, OpenAI's third-generation chatbot, was created using computers that can process approximately eight quintillion operations per second. That's eight with 18 zeros after it. To put this in perspective, to undertake the equivalent of one second of this computing power, a computer from the early 1990s would have had to run constantly from the end of the last ice age to the current day!

Finally, these models need *lots* of data. Subtle and complex events are hard to notice. If a particular species of concluding phrase is used rarely by composers, or if it occurs with slight variations, a computer is unlikely to identify it as a salient gesture. A machine-learning algorithm requires a massive pile of examples to identify such patterns within its dataset. Just as students need more classroom time to understand complicated concepts, an AI's need for data escalates proportionally with the level of complexity inherent in its subject, and of the desired quality of its outputs. An algorithm must be fed an astonishing volume of data to even begin identifying nuanced events or large-scale organizing principles.

In the 20th century, computer scientists often had to construct all their data from scratch. Music researchers, for example, would make their own computer-readable versions of the repertoires they were studying. This required the meticulous programming of each note in every piece into their files. The size of a dataset was therefore limited to the amount of time a person could spend creating it.

However, the internet of the 21st century has fundamentally changed that dynamic. With immediate access to an almost unlimited amount of information from all corners of the globe, researchers can now construct datasets from materials they collect online. As I am writing this paragraph, English Wikipedia contains 4.3 billion words, Google Books has scanned 130 million books, and the website DeviantArt has 550 million user-uploaded images. These numbers are constantly rising, both acting as fodder for deep learning systems, and quenching these neural networks' insatiable thirst for data. The effect of this volcano of available data cannot be overstated.

When computer scientists talk about *Large Language Models* (LLM), they're talking about deep learning neural networks that use very complex systems with many hidden layers with vast numbers of nodes, and that usually train on enormous piles of data. LLMs harness huge repositories of data, leveraging state-of-the-art computing power and memory to process, learn from, organize, and retain a mountain of information.

Due to their size and complexity, LLMs can be awfully *expensive*. All of this technology, computing power, electricity, data processing, and research costs money. PaLM, one of Google's language models, cost upwards of $8 million to train. Microsoft's comparable Megatron-Turing NLG cost $11 million to train. And while it cost $5 million to train ChatGPT-3 for its release in early 2023, the cost of training the more recent ChatGPT-4 was $100 million. OpenAI estimates that training their newest model may cost upwards of $2 billion. These costs include electricity, hardware, data collection, research resources, and user feedback, among other things. In other words, it can take time, talent, and a lot of money to make a successful LLM.

These financial considerations throw musical AI its first hurdle. Since it takes so much time and money to create a state-of-the-art LLM, companies have to allocate their resources carefully and in ways that make fiscal sense, and music seems to get only a small piece of the fiscal pie. In what follows, I show some evidence of music's underrepresentation in the AI market, after which I speculate on several reasons why this might be.

Musical AI and resource allocation

It can often be difficult to get a clear picture of exactly how tech companies spend money, especially when it comes to proprietary research and development. We can, however, use a few proxies to peek into this world. For instance, the tech behemoth OpenAI publishes research papers, and they tag these papers by topic on their research website. The volume of papers under each category can serve as an indication of the relative emphasis placed on each area. This provides a tangible measure of the institution's research priorities.

Figure 2.5 presents a pair of pie charts illustrating the distribution of published papers by topic. The chart on the left shows all reported topics, while the chart on the right focuses on topics specifically related to generating media content. In both charts, I've highlighted the segment labeled "Audio generation" with a box, as this is the tag for most of their papers that focus on music generation. The number of papers related to audio generation occupies only a tiny portion of either pie chart. The company's researchers publish overwhelmingly on "Language" (associated with the development of chatbots), "Games," and "Robotics." In terms of media and product research, music-related publication only eclipses work in speech recognition.

We can also get a sense of the allocation of investment in startups by examining the data compiled by ai-startups.org, a website that tracks up-and-coming AI companies in a variety of fields and reports their levels of funding. The website includes a list of startups that are developing AI

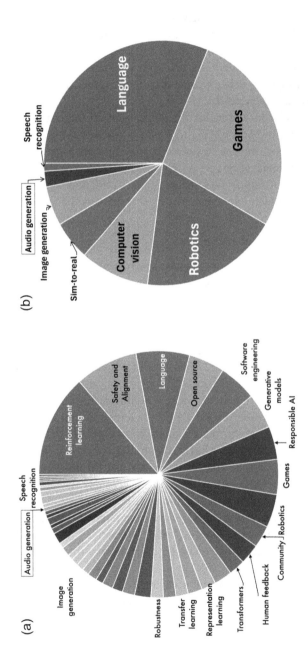

FIGURE 2.5 Pie charts showing the relative number of papers published by OpenAI researchers in a) all reported topics and b) media and other products.

for music-related enterprises. Excluding those that use AI to serve music to users (like TikTok or Spotify) or to recognize or categorize music (like SoundHound and Musiio), their list contains seven companies. As I show in the graph on the left in Figure 2.6, the average funding for these seven companies was about $28 million in 2023, with a median of $7 million. Startups working to generate text or visuals, however, raised an average of $52 and $48 million, respectively, with median investments of $31 and $20 million.

These numbers are further dwarfed by AI funding in other fields, as I show in the graph at right in Figure 2.6. Ai-startups.org indicates that the top 20 biomedical AI startups received an average of $595 million in investment capital, with a median of $457 million. And startups focused on self-driving car technologies averaged a staggering $1.9 billion in funding, with a median of $650 million. Investment in text-based generative AI represented a mere 3% of the funding allocated to self-driving cars, and music garnered even less, coming in at only 1.5% of that amount. Overall, generative media receives only a small fraction of the monetary interest in AI, and music AI occupies one of the smallest areas within that niche.

Academic research in computational music faces similar disparities in resource allocation. For example, the National Science Foundation's Seed Fund suggests topics for prospective applicants. Under AI, these areas include cognitive science, images, language, and conversation, but not music. Of course, this does not mean that music is entirely excluded, as music research could potentially align with several broader categories. Still, music is not offered as a primary focus.

While Figure 2.6 relies on data from 2023, the following year witnessed a surge in AI music generation with the launch of the two highly successful bots, Suno AI and Udio. With these bots, users can create short musical pieces by providing text prompts specifying the genre, instrumentation, and even the affect of their desired piece. From this information, these AI bots generate fragments that users can build upon, extending them into full-length tracks. Debuting in early 2024, these user-friendly platforms garnered significant media attention and a veritable boatload of

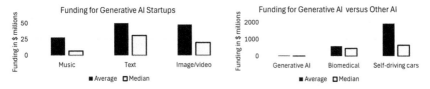

FIGURE 2.6 2023 funding for generative AI startups in media (left) and all generative AI startup funding compared to that for AI research in biomedical and self-driving cars (right).

funding. In the months after launch, Udio raised $10 million from a series of high-profile investors, while Suno announced a staggering $125 million raised. The rise of these bots did not go unnoticed by music creators either. An open letter signed by over 200 musicians, including well-known names like Norah Jones, Jon Bon Jovi, and Camilla Cabello, raised concerns that these tools might pose a threat to human composers and performers.

I'll discuss the strengths and weaknesses of these bots in Chapter 5 and touch on the challenges they may—or may not—pose to human artists in Chapter 6. But while the rise of these bots was meteoric, the bots themselves are awfully small meteors compared to AIs in other sectors. Consider the successes of some other AI startups over the same period that saw Suno and Udio's initial fundraising rounds. Cohere AI, a competitor to ChatGPT, secured a staggering $450 million. Similarly, a self-driving car developer, Wayve, raised a whopping $1 billion. Midjourney, an image-generating AI company, generated $200 million in *revenue*, raising funds from its users rather than outside investment. While music AI's funding is impressive, it is clearly dwarfed by investments in other sectors, even during times of maximal interest.

The media buzz around these different AI sectors mirrors the funding imbalance. By my count, Suno and Udio garnered exactly one story in the *New York Times* in March and April of 2024, the two-month window around their launches. In contrast, during the two-month window around ChatGPT's entry onto the public stage, December 2022 to January 2023, it was the subject of at least 39 articles. Public concern seems to follow the same trend. While the open letter against music AI garnered around 200 signatures, a similar letter regarding the release of ChatGPT-4 received over 30,000. Online search volume points to the same imbalance. Google's Keyword Planner—a technology that determines pricing for keyword-directed advertising—suggests that an add connected to searches for the words "Udio" and "Suno" would reach 10,000 to 100,000 people per month in mid-2024. However, if you purchased ad space for the search term "Gemini," the name of Google's own text-generating AI, you would land between 100,000 and one million views in the same time window. The search term "ChatGPT" tops out at a staggering ten million expected views.

Google itself is a huge player in musical AI. In 2016, the company launched its Magenta project, an open-source initiative designed to explore the potential of deep learning in the creative arts, including music. The project has yielded impressive outcomes, such as the 2019 Bach Google Doodle, which used a neural network to harmonize melodies in the style of J.S. Bach. Google's investment in musical AI extends beyond this. It includes the development of AI tools for adding rhythm to digital compositions; MusicLM, an experimental program that generates music from text prompts; and Lyria, which allows YouTubers to experiment with composing music in the style of contemporary pop artists. In addition, Google and its subsidiary YouTube collaborated with Universal Music Group in 2023 to establish an incubator aimed at supporting research and startups dedicated to AI-generated music.

While Google's contributions to musical AI are notable, it's important to contextualize them within the company's broader spectrum of projects. Alphabet, Google's parent company, reported an expenditure of over $40 billion on research and development in 2023. Pinpointing the exact distribution of these funds across various projects is challenging. But even if Google's music research budget equaled the combined funding of the seven music startups referenced in Figure 2.6, a total of $233 million, this would represent a mere 0.5% of its total R&D budget. Google's investments in musical AI may be significant when compared to other entities in the market, but this likely remains a small portion of its overarching research endeavors.

Music's lack of resources

In a way, the underlying reasons for music's comparative lack of funding and other resources are beside the point. When viewed through the lens of free-market capitalism, capital is typically allocated to opportunities based on their potential to yield substantial returns on investment. The relative lack of investment in musical generative AI would seem to be an indicator of the music sector's diminished ability to offer convincing and reliable returns in general. But we can complement this capitalist logic by pointing to several reasons that music research exerts such a small amount of financial gravity. To my mind, there are at least three reasons that musical AI attracts relatively meager resources.

1. **Limited cross-application synergies.** Music, unlike other forms of expression, doesn't directly extend or enhance other modes of communication or expression. While literary works use the same grammar and vocabulary as everyday communication, and visual arts often depict recognizable objects and scenes from daily life, music operates under a distinct set of rules and structures. Music is, to be sure, an artistically elevated version of everyday sound. However, when humans make music, they aren't exactly using everyday sounds. Rather, they use specially made instruments and vocal techniques to transform sound the into pitches and rhythms that follow grammars and norms entirely unlike the sounds of the non-musical world. "Music" is simply different from other types of sound, and everyday sounds don't often find their way into what we consider "Music."

The sounds of dogs barking don't sound much like musical instruments, a closing door doesn't follow rules of phrasing, the rhythm of passing cars does not exhibit beat patterns, and the patter of a conversation doesn't follow verse-chorus form.

Because artistic expression in most media enjoys significant overlap with everyday experience, AI developed for artistic or commercial use can often be repurposed. An LLM trained to write poetry can be adapted to compose business emails, and an AI designed to create visual art can be used to design sales brochures. This versatility is not as evident in musical AI, and commercial ventures in generative AI across most media benefit from a greater potential for financial returns. Musical AI isn't going to help you in your business endeavors, nor is it going to make any household task easier. The scope of musical AI is more narrowly defined, and its utility is limited to a specific domain. This equates to more restricted opportunities for commercialization and profit. I'll return to this issue in the next chapter, as it will also affect the size and availability of musical datasets.

2. Specialized knowledge and computational hand-me-downs. Most individuals have strong intuitions about their native languages and can easily recognize the visual forms populating the world around them. English speakers have internalized the structure of the English language, allowing them to quickly grasp unfamiliar words or phrases. People with normal vision have some basic understanding of unfamiliar objects they encounter in the surrounding world. Most people can taste specific ingredients and components in the meals they're eating ("there's cheese in this taco!") and can usually identify the origin of the sounds hitting their ears ("that's a dog barking through that window!"). Just by moving through the world, we gain a pretty good fluency with the sights, tastes, sounds, and even language we encounter on a daily basis, and can accurately analyze and describe the components and makeup of these moments.

The same cannot be said for music. Not everyone who enjoys music can describe its technical aspects, such as notes, melodies, harmonies, and phrases. Music performance and composition are specialized artforms and require years of study to gain fluency. Even becoming proficient in reading basic musical notation can take months of practice. Consequently, researchers in the field of musical AI are required to possess dual expertise in music and computation. This requirement significantly narrows the field, reducing the number of individuals equipped to contribute to this niche area of study.

One notable way this constraint manifests is musical AI's tendency toward "algorithmic hand-me-downs." There is a notable inclination among musical AI practitioners to repurpose technologies initially devised for other domains. Instead of developing algorithms tailored specifically for music, they often adapt existing solutions from other areas. The early researchers in the 1950s used algorithms initially designed for telephone technology. Composers in the 1980s borrowed approaches from linguistics. Advancements in the 2000s incorporated methods from image studies.[11] Although these hand-me-downs have often been successfully adapted to music, it raises the question of whether music-specific innovations could provide a more solid foundation for musical AI in the 21st century.[12]

This also means that computational music research has a high barrier to entry. It's harder to find researchers with dual expertise, and it's harder to synergize computational and musical knowledge. This difficulty simply adds to the amount of time and funding that any potential research project in musical AI will require. These barriers further complicate the calculus around a project's return on investment and the challenge of human resources available to complete them.

3. **Limited audience.** It's not obvious that there is a large audience for AI-generated music. True, AI music has a certain novelty and often elicits fascination, but listeners often view music as a reflection of the human experience and appreciate it for its emotional resonance.[13] This issue is the central focus of Chapter 6, but in short, if we want music that reflects our humanity, then music made by a machine will always be found lacking, no matter how technically proficient musical LLMs become. It's very possible that this prescribes a limited market for AI-generated music, or at least one more limited than for other AI-generated media. I return to these issues in Chapter 6.

Summary

It's no surprise that students studying musical AI don't always end up working in the field of music. There's simply more action—more research and financing—in other domains of AI than in music. This imbalance stems from a combination of several significant factors. Most basically, the research, development, and training of *creative* machines demand extensive resources.

After defining "creativity" as a process that produces new and novel content within some guardrails of norms and usability, this chapter outlined the basics behind the neural networks that underpin generative AI. It showed how they use machine learning to formulate the norms and tendencies of a given medium by analyzing vast datasets. As examples of deep learning, neural networks connect the surface events in their training datasets through hidden layers. These layers embed the patterns, nuances, norms, and tendencies present in the dataset into the computational model. The capability to generate new, coherent content hinges on creating networks of interconnections in the hidden layers, something that requires huge datasets and repetitive training cycles. The complexity of these models, combined with the enormity of their datasets, necessitates that they use thousands, if not millions, of iterations over their data to refine these connections. The intensive iterative process requires the use of advanced computers equipped with substantial memory and significant computing power. This prospect becomes very expensive very quickly.

Music doesn't necessarily justify this expense. While artforms like poetry, visual art, and cinema are artistic versions of the practical components of our everyday lives, music is not. Because of this, musical AI is more constrained in its potential commercial applications. While the same chatbot that writes narrative essays could also help edit an email, and a visual AI that produces artistic images could also engage in website design, a musical AI can only produce music. Furthermore, because of music's traditional connections to human expression, it's very possible that consumers will remain skeptical of AI-generated musical content altogether.

The challenge of securing resources for musical AI is reflected in the broader landscape of research funding, where music-related startups routinely receive less financial support than startups in other fields. Additionally, within established companies, the allocation of research and development resources to musical AI projects tends to constitute only a minor fraction of the overall R&D budget. This trend underscores the comparative difficulty of attracting investment in musical AI and raising its status within the priorities of technological innovation and development.

The scarcity of resources allocated to AI music research will have downstream effects on every other topic addressed in this book. The absence of adequate funding and time hampers the process of creating and curating the large, detailed datasets necessary for the effective operation of complex deep learning models that train on large datasets. Moreover, the lack of focused research lengthens the timeline for determining the most effective strategies for representing and modeling musical data for neural networks. It also delays the development of specialized algorithms capable of accommodating the distinctive structural and organizational aspects of music.

Notes

1 See Moussas (2018), Haspels (1994), Savage-Smith (1984), Ord-Hume (1995), and Bruderer (2020).
2 For more on the Electronium, see Chusid (1999).
3 Boden (1990), Wiggins (2006), Rohrmeier (2022). My thinking is also influenced by the concept of "communicative pressure" (Temperley 2007) in which creators balance the pressure to be accessible to their audience with their desire to challenge that audience with unpredictable and novel content.
4 All images are published under a Creative Commons License and can be found at the following URLs:
https://commons.wikimedia.org/wiki/File:Tischfl%C3%B6tenuhr_Matthias _Naeschke_komplettes_Fl%C3%B6tenwerk.JPG. Accessed June 15, 2024.
https://commons.wikimedia.org/wiki/Category:Dice#/media/File:Dadi_per _lo_riichi_mahjong.jpg. Accessed June 15, 2024.
https://commons.wikimedia.org/wiki/Keyboard#/media/File:Qwerty.svg. Accessed June 15, 2024.
https://commons.wikimedia.org/wiki/File:Example_of_a_deep_neural_network.png. Accessed June 15, 2024.
https://commons.wikimedia.org/wiki/Category:Machines#/media/File :Bonsack_machine.png. Accessed June 15, 2024.
https://en.wikipedia.org/wiki/Poisson_distribution#/media/File:Poisson_pmf .svg. Accessed June 15, 2024.
5 Different computational architectures developed to support this increased complexity. For instance, a Central Processing Unit (CPU) has acted as the foundation of most computers since their early development. The CPU functions as a computer's "brain" and performs much of the actual computation that a machine undertakes. "Graphics Processing Units" (GPUs) were developed later in the 20th century specifically to support increasingly sophisticated graphics displays, particularly for gaming. They gained this capacity by processing several tasks in parallel, which cut down the computing time for very complex computations. Over time, GPU engines became more flexible, with their parallel processors being applied to any number of applications, including AI research.
6 For more on deep learning in music, see White and Quinn (2018).
7 This example depicts what computer scientists call a "Hidden Markov Model."
8 For a more sophisticated presentation of neural networks and their mathematics, see Bharucha (1991), Heaton (2013), and Aggarwa (2020), (2023).
9 See Schmidhuber (2015), Macukow (2016), Rochester (1956), Rosenblatt (1958), and Haykin (2009).
10 See Bharucha (1987), (1991), and Large et al. (2016).
11 See Shannon (1948), Gagniuc (2017), and McFee and Kinnaird (2019).
12 A noteworthy exception is the work of Carol Krumhansl and Edward Kessler in the 1990s. They developed a unique machine learning method to determine the key of musical works. Their method stands out as a musically native computational innovation. It remains a foundational element in the field of musical computation and is likely still used by many tech firms and music applications to determine the key of music tracks.
13 See Shank et al. (2023), and Tigre Moura and Maw (2021).

References and Further Reading

Alphabet Inc. 2024. "2023; Q4; Annual Report (PDF)." Alphabet Investor Relations. Accessed March 20, 2024. https://abc.xyz/investor/.

Aggarwal, C. C. 2020. *Linear Algebra and Optimization for Machine Learning: A Textbook.* New York: Springer.

Aggarwal, C. C. 2023. *Neural Networks and Deep Learning: A Textbook.* 2nd ed. New York: Springer.

Ben-Tal, O., M. Harris, and R. Sturm. 2020. "How Music AI Is Useful: Engagements with Composers, Performers and Audiences." *Leonardo* 54: 1–13. https://doi.org/10.1162/leon_a_01959.

Berkowitz, A. L. 2010. *The Improvising Mind: Cognition and Creativity in the Musical Moment.* New York: Oxford University Press.

Bharucha, J. J. 1987. "Music Cognition and Perceptual Facilitation: A Connectionist Frame-Work." *Music Perception 5*: 1–30.

Bharucha, J. J. 1991. "Pitch, Harmony and Neural Nets: A Psychological Perspective." In *Music and Connectionism*, edited by P. M. Todd and D. G. Loy, pp. 84–99. Cambridge, MA: MIT Press.

Bruderer, Herbert. 2020. *Milestones in Analog and Digital Computing.* New York: Springer.

Boden, M. 1990. *The Creative Mind: Myths and Mechanisms.* New York: Routledge.

Buisson, M., B. McFee, S. Essid, and H. C. Crayencour. 2024. "Self-Supervised Learning of Multi-level Audio Representations for Music Segmentation." *IEEE/ACM Transactions on Audio, Speech, and Language Processing*, 1–13. https://doi.org/10.1109/TASLP.2024.3379894.

Chusid, I. 1999. "Beethoven-in-a-box: Raymond Scott's electronium." *Contemporary Music Review* 18(3): 9–14.

Coons, E., and D. Kraehenbuehl. 1958. "Information as a Measure of Structure in Music." *Journal of Music Theory* 2(2): 127–161.

Cope, D. 1987. "Experiments in Music Intelligence." In *Proceedings of the International Computer Music Conference*, 170–173. San Francisco: Computer Music Association.

Cope, D. 1990. "Pattern Matching as an Engine for the Computer Simulation of Musical Style." In *Proceedings of the International Computer Music Conference*, 288–291. San Francisco: Computer Music Association.

Cope, D. 2005. *Computer Models of Musical Creativity.* Cambridge, MA: MIT Press.

Chusid, I. 1999. "Beethoven-in-a-Box: Raymond Scott's Electronium." *Contemporary Music Review* 18(3): 9–14.

Editorial Team. 2022. "AI Music Tech Startup LifeScore Raises €13M Led by Octopus Ventures to 'Soundtrack Life.'" Silicon Canals. Accessed June 12, 2024. https://siliconcanals.com/news/startups/ai-music-tech-lifescore-raises-13m/.

Foscarin, F., Karystinaios, E., Nakamura, E., and Widmer, G. 2024. "Cluster and Separate: A GNN Approach to Voice and Staff Prediction for Score Engraving." In Proceedings of the 25th International Society for Music Information Retrieval Conference, San Francisco, United States.

Gagniuc, P. A. 2017. *Markov Chains: From Theory to Implementation and Experimentation.* Hoboken, NJ: Wiley.

Haspels, J. J. 1994. *Musical Automata: Catalogue of Automatic Musical Instruments in the National Museum, "From Musical Clock to Street Organ."* Utrecht: National Museum.

Haykin, S. 2009. *Neural Networks and Learning Machines.* 3rd ed. New York: Pearson.

Heaton, J. 2013. *Artificial Intelligence for Humans, Vol. 1: Fundamental Algorithms.* St. Louis: Heaton Research.

Hiller, L., and Isaacson, L. M. 1959. *Experimental Music: Composition with an Electronic Computer.* New York: McGraw-Hill.

Huang, C.-Z. A., C. Hawthorne, A. Roberts, M. Dinculescu, J. Wexler, L. Hong, and J. Howcroft. 2019. "The Bach Doodle: Approachable Music Composition with Machine Learning at Scale." In *Proceedings of the 20th International Society for Music Information Retrieval Conference (ISMIR).* https://arxiv.org/abs/1907.06637.

Krumhansl, C. L. 1990. *The Cognitive Foundations of Musical Pitch.* Oxford: Oxford University Press.

Krumhansl, C. L., and E. J. Kessler. 1982. "Tracing the Dynamic Changes in Perceived Tonal Organization in a Spatial Representation of Musical Keys." *Psychological Review* 89: 334–368.

Large, E. W., J. C. Kim, N. Flaig, J. Bharucha, and C. L. Krumhansl. 2016. "A Neurodynamic Account of Musical Tonality." *Music Perception* 33(3): 319–331.

Lupker, J. 2023. "The Origins of AI Music." *Staccato* (blog), March 15. https://blog.staccato.ai/en-US/The-Origins-of-AI-Music.

Macukow, B. 2016. "Neural Networks – State of Art, Brief History, Basic Models and Architecture." In *Computer Information Systems and Industrial Management*, edited by K. Saeed and W. Homenda. New York: Springer.

Maxwell, H. J. 1984. "An Artificial Intelligence Approach to Computer-Implemented Analysis of Harmony in Tonal Music." PhD diss., Indiana University.

Maxwell, H. J. 1992. "An Expert System for Harmonic Analysis of Tonal Music." In *Understanding Music with AI: Perspectives on Music Cognition*, edited by M. Balaban, K. Ebcioglu, and O. Laske, 335–353. Palo Alto: Association for the Advancement of Artificial Intelligence.

McCulloch, W. S., and W. Pitts. 1943. "A Logical Calculus of the Ideas Immanent in Nervous Activity." *Bulletin of Mathematical Biophysics* 5: 115–133. https://doi.org/10.1007/BF02478259.

McFee, B., and K. M. Kinnaird. 2019. "Improving Structure Evaluation Through Automatic Hierarchy Expansion." *Proceedings of the 20th International Society for Music Information Retrieval Conference, October 2019.* PDF available from smith.edu.

Meyer, L. B. 1956. *Emotion and Meaning in Music.* Chicago: University of Chicago Press.

Meyer, L. B. 1957. "Meaning in Music and Information Theory." *Journal of Aesthetics and Art Criticism* 15(4): 412–424.

Moussas, X. 2018. *The Antikythera Mechanism: The First Mechanical Cosmos.* Athens: Canto Mediterraneo.

Ord-Hume, A. W. J. G. 1995. *The Musical Clock: Musical and Automaton Clocks and Watches.* Ashbourne: Mayfield.

Patel, A. D. 2007. *Music, Language, and the Brain.* Oxford: Oxford University Press.

Price, D. S. de. 1984. "A History of Calculating Machines." *IEEE Micro* 4(1): 22–52.

Raz, C. 2018. "Anne Young's Musical Games (1801): Music Theory, Gender, and Game Design." *SMT-V: Videocast Journal of the Society for Music Theory* 4(2). https://doi.org/10.30535/smtv.4.2.

Rochester, N., J. Holland, L. Haibt, and W. Duda. 1956. "Tests on a Cell Assembly Theory of the Action of the Brain, Using a Large Digital Computer." *IRE Transactions on Information Theory* 2(3): 80–93. https://doi.org/10.1109/TIT.1956.1056810.

Rosenblatt, F. 1958. "The Perceptron: A Probabilistic Model for Information Storage and Organization in the Brain." *Psychological Review* 65(6): 386–408.

Savage-Smith, E. 1984. Review of *Arabic Water-Clocks*, by Donald Hill. *Technology and Culture* 25(2): 326–328.

Schmidhuber, J. 2015. "Deep Learning in Neural Networks: An Overview." *Neural Networks* 61: 85–117. arXiv:1404.7828. https://doi.org/10.1016/j .neunet.2014.09.003.

Shank, D. B., C. Stefanik, C. Stuhlsatz, K. Kacirek, and A. M. Belfi. 2023. "AI Composer Bias: Listeners Like Music Less When They Think It Was Composed by an AI." *Journal of Experimental Psychology: Applied* 29(3): 676–692. https://doi.org/10.1037/xap0000447.

Shannon, C. E. 1948. "A Mathematical Theory of Communication." *Bell System Technical Journal* 27: 379–423, 623–656.

Shannon, C. E., and Warren Weaver. 1949. *A Mathematical Model of Communication*. Urbana: University of Illinois Press.

Sturm, R. L., J. Santos, O. Ben-Tal, and I. Korshunova. 2016. "Music Transcription Modelling and Composition Using Deep Learning." Paper presented at the 1st Conference on Computer Simulation of Musical Creativity. https://arxiv.org/ abs/1604.08723.

Sturm, R. L., O. Ben-Tal, U. Monaghan, N. Collins, D. Herremans, E. Chew, G. Hadjeres, E. Deruty, and F. Pachet. 2018. "Machine Learning Research That Matters for Music Creation: A Case Study." *Journal of New Music Research* 48(1): 36–55.

Temperley, D. 2007. *Music and Probability*. Cambridge: MIT Press.

Tigre Moura, F., and C. Maw. 2021. "Artificial Intelligence Became Beethoven: How Do Listeners and Music Professionals Perceive Artificially Composed Music?" *Journal of Consumer Marketing* 38(2): 137–146. https://doi.org/10 .1108/JCM-02-2020-3671.

Tillmann, B., J. J. Bharucha, and E. Bigand. 2000. "Implicit Learning of Tonality: A Self-Organizing Approach." *Psychological Review* 107(4): 885–913.

Tomlinson, G. 2018. *A Million Years of Music: The Emergence of Human Modernity*. Princeton: Princeton University Press.

Turing, A. (1948) 1992. "Intelligence Machinery." In *Collected Works of A.M. Turing, Vol. 1, Mechanical Intelligence*, edited by D. C. Ince, 107–127. Amsterdam: North-Holland.

Turing, A. 1950. "Computing Machinery and Intelligence." *Mind*, Volume LIX, Issue 236, October 1950, pp. 433–460. https://doi.org/10.1093/mind/LIX.236 .433 Epigraph used with permission.

White, C. W., and I. Quinn. 2018. "Chord Context and Harmonic Function in Tonal Music." *Music Theory Spectrum* 40(2): 314–335. https://doi.org/10 .1093/mts/mty021.

Wiggins, G. A. 2006. "A Preliminary Framework for Description, Analysis and Comparison of Creative Systems." *Knowledge-Based Systems* 19(7): 449–458.

Youngblood, J. E. 1958. "Style as Information." *Journal of Music Theory* 2(1): 24–35.

Zaripov, R. 1960. "On Algorithmic Description of Process of Music Composition." *Proceedings of the USSR Academy of Sciences* 132(6): Title translated from Russian.

Zatorre, R. 2023. *From Perception to Pleasure: The Neuroscience of Music and Why We Love It*. Oxford: Oxford University Press.

Zbikowski, L. M. 2002. *Conceptualizing Music: Cognitive Structure, Theory, and Analysis*. New York: Oxford University Press.

3
COLLECTING EXAMPLES FOR MUSICAL DATASETS

"It is a capital mistake to theorize before one has data."
Sherlock Holmes, Arthur Conan Doyle

Deep learning AI models are always hungry for data. In the last chapter, we saw these systems combing through training data to learn patterns and tendencies. We also saw generative AI leverage these patterns to create new content. But this process hinges on a crucial element: available data. Let's start this chapter with a few stories about data and how it becomes available.

In 2005, two recently minted PhDs from MIT, Tristan Jehan and Brian Whitman, founded the Echo Nest to collect and study all the musical data the internet had to offer. Using automated web-scraping bots that pored over the wide expanses of the internet, they compiled about 30 million songs by 2011. In the same year, they made one million of those songs available to researchers. Thierry Bertin-Mahieux and Dan Ellis, two Columbia-affiliated researchers, used these songs to create the Million Song Dataset.[1] In 2014, Spotify acquired the Echo Nest, and the data was added to Spotify's catalog to augment its developer interface. The resulting data represents over 400 million minutes (762 years!) of content.

In 2006, Edward Guo, an undergraduate student at New England Conservatory in Boston, started the International Music Score Library Project (IMSLP). As a repository for musical scores in the public domain, the website initially focused on creating complete collections of works by famous composers. However, by 2011 the site hosted over 100,000 scores, and by 2020 it held half a million. Currently, there are about 750,000

DOI: 10.4324/9781003587415-3

scores on IMSLP by over 27,000 composers. The Choral Public Domain Library (CPDL) is a similar website focused on vocal music. It was founded in 1998 by Rafael Ornes, and ten years on, CPDL contained about 10,000 scores. The number doubled by 2015. CPDL now has around 50,000 scores by about 5,000 composers. If you spent a mere five minutes reading through each piece on IMSLP, it would take you 285 years to get through the entire catalog. CPDL would take about three decades.

When Google co-founders Sergey Brin and Larry Page were in graduate school, they became interested in the prospect of encoding printed books and articles in a digital format that would make them accessible on home computers. In 2002, Page began working with Google's Marissa Mayer on "Project Ocean," the early codename for what would become Google Books. When the project premiered in 2004, they had scanned about 25 million books. Since then, that number has nearly doubled to 40 million. If it took you a mere hour to read every book on the website, it would take you 4,566 years to consume all of them.

The early 2000s also saw the burgeoning of websites that allowed users to upload their own content. In 2002, Werner Schweer, a developer working on Musical Instrument Digital Interface (MIDI) technology, spun off the music notation aspects of his code to create MuseScore, a free and open-source music writing program. In 2008, Schweer launched the MuseScore website, which allowed users to upload their own, homegrown scores. Currently, about 1.5 million scores are hosted on the website. In the world of audio, SoundCloud was founded in 2007 for users to upload their own music compositions, performances, and recordings. By 2012 the website had ten million registered users, and by 2019 it hosted 200 million tracks. Currently, SoundCloud contains 250 million files from 30 million artists. If you spent a mere three minutes on each track, you'd be listening for 1,426 years. If you played through each MuseScore composition for just five minutes, you'd be at it for about 15 years.

Of course, many other websites were founded in the first decade of the 21st century to host user-generated content. YouTube was launched in 2005 by three former employees of PayPal: Steve Chen, Chad Hurley, and Jawed Karim. At its inception, the site counted its content in the tens of thousands of hours. However, with hundreds of hours soon being uploaded to the website every minute, YouTube's content quickly expanded to millions of hours. About a quarter of YouTube's content is music, which means that the website currently hosts 39 million hours (4,452 years) of music and 117 million hours (13,356 years) of non-musical content.[2]

The digital landscape is awash with mind-boggling quantities of user-generated content. Facebook boasts around 250 billion user-generated images of people and scenery, while Pinterest isn't far behind with 240 billion. Artistic images? We could consider pages like DeviantArt (550 million images) or Shutterstock (300 million). Short-form videos? There are roughly ten billion videos on TikTok and 1 billion on Reels. Text? Wikipedia contains 6,802,658 articles consisting of more than 4.5 billion words, while Reddit has around two million subreddits with an estimated 1.8 billion comments.

Figure 3.1 visually represents the amount of content across these different websites by mapping them onto a historical timeline. The figure shows the amount of time required for a hypothetical, immortal human to consume the entirety of each site's content, placed in relationship with some historical milestones. Events earlier in time are on the left. As you move right, events get closer to the present. The timeline compresses as it extends into the past, so a given amount of time takes up less space on the left-hand side of the page than it does on the right.

The figure shows several very large datasets of music. The musical content of YouTube and SoundCloud is graphed comparably to the ancient Egyptian and Roman civilizations, for instance. But the figure's musical datasets do tend to be smaller than their counterparts in other media—more often aligned with the American and Maoist revolutions than with cave paintings and ice ages. What's more, musical datasets that are specifically compiled to be easily accessible to researchers (like the Million Song Dataset) tend to be vastly smaller than similar datasets in other domains (like Google Books).

This chapter addresses the fact that AI researchers and developers have so much less musical data to work with than other media, and why that data is more difficult for computers to analyze. I'll discuss some reasons why musical data is limited in the first place. I'll then turn to why the scores and recordings that humans use to perform and listen to music are often difficult for computers to make sense of. I'll look more specifically at why musical scores are challenging for a computer to parse, especially those in our Western notation of staves, noteheads, and rests. Finally, I'll describe the difficulties of analyzing audio, and why a format that is so simple for our ears and brains to understand has proven such a thorny issue for computational engineers.

The limitations in making and collecting music

We are constantly surrounded by sounds. As I type this sentence, passing traffic rumbles outside my window, my dog's toenails are clicking on the floor, and the monotonical hum of the refrigerator reaches me from the kitchen. Certainly, there can be something beautiful—even musical—in sounds like these. But these sounds won't help train an AI to produce the kinds of music that we might find on the Billboard charts or our local

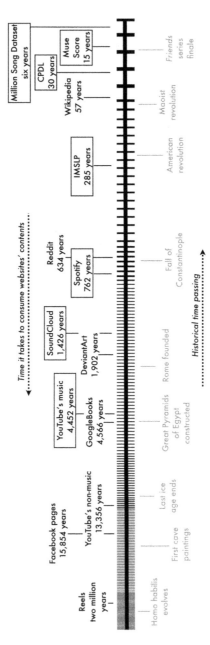

FIGURE 3.1 Size of datasets, framed as the amount of time it would take to read, listen to, or view an entire web repository's contents, with time indexed by historical events.

NPR station. For this, you need sound that's organized in some way, following stylistic norms, sung or played by instruments, and then written down or recorded. You need music.

Music is difficult to make, and it is difficult to collect. And even when you've compiled a collection of music, not all of its data will be usable. To my mind, there are four main reasons datasets of music tend to be relatively small.

1) **Making music requires training, especially when creating scores or recordings.** Training and practice will help you do any artistic task well. Experience and study in literature, painting, photography, or dance tend to result in higher-quality novels, paintings, photos, and choreography. However, it is much easier for someone with no background in poetry to spontaneously decide to try their hand at writing a limerick than for someone with no musical background to impulsively decide to compose and perform a tune for the oboe. Music usually involves specialized tools and instruments that have a significant learning curve. While elementary school students casually and incidentally learn to use a pencil or a computer just through the process of learning to read and write, one doesn't casually or incidentally learn to play the drum or harp. Should you want to write down a musical idea, you need to study music notation or learn to use a Digital Audio Workstation (DAW) computer interface. Even someone's informal singing is lost to posterity unless happen to be using an audio recording device.

This learning curve means that fewer people have even the basic capacity to create musical content than content in other media. If fewer people can create musical scores, there will be fewer musical scores available in the world. If fewer people can play the banjo, there will be less banjo music performed in the world. The specialized nature of music production limits the amount of music that is produced.

2) **Repetition is part of the artform.** When a Spotify user gets their year-end listening summary, the app lists the artists they've listened to most often, which songs they've listened to most frequently, and how many total hours they've listened. In 2023, for instance, I reportedly listened to Miley Cyrus's "Flowers" for about two and three-quarter hours. This means that I listened to her three-minute and 20-second track about 45 times over the course of the year.

In her book, *On Repeat*, Lisa Margulis argues that, as an artform, music is meant to be listened to over and over. Listeners have an "appetite for musical repetition," she writes (p. 90). This repetition helps us enjoy the music more, and it can also support the social components of the musical experience. When I listen to "Flowers" 45 times, I'm becoming more and more familiar with the track. My pleasure increases as I more readily anticipate each turn of phrase and as I slowly memorize the lyrics. This knowledge lets me opt into communal musical experiences, such as singing along in the car with my husband when the song shuffles onto our playlist or moving in pseudo-choreographed motions to Cyrus's melodic gestures when dancing with friends.

Repetition can certainly add to the pleasure we get from engaging with other artforms as well. Many of us watch our favorite movies many times over, re-read novels we enjoy, or come back repeatedly to our favorite piece of art. I rewatch the TV series *30 Rock* every few years, and whenever I go to New York's Museum of Modern Art, I make sure to see Vincent Van Gogh's *Starry Night*. But none of this compares to the 45 or so times I listen to my favorite pop songs in a given year.

This means that Miley Cyrus and her team did not need to write two and three-quarter hours of unique content to fill that duration of my musical enjoyment. Instead, they needed only one track with slightly more than three minutes of music. This dynamic throws the relationship between musical creation and consumption into a particular imbalance. Because we consistently come back to the same musical material, less musical content can satisfy our musical cravings.

Compounding this phenomenon, music typically features a good bit of internal repetition. "Flowers," for instance, is in verse–prechorus–chorus form. This simply means that the song rotates through these three distinct sections, and that this succession is repeated in its entirety. The only change is the addition of new words in each subsequent verse. In "Flowers," the verse–prechorus–chorus combination lasts about a minute, and it repeats nearly wholesale two more times. I invite the skeptical reader to scroll between the track's time points of 1:02, 2:03, and 2:59, where they will hear precisely the same music. This means that I'll have heard each of the three internal musical units three times every time I listen to the song. In other words, after 45 listenings, I'll have heard Cyrus's verse, prechorus, and chorus 135 times.[3]

We also repeat music in our performances. As the theorist and philosopher Nicholas Cook notes, a composer or producer provides a "script" for the performer to enact in performance. Popular tunes like the Irish folk song "Danny Boy," Robert Schumann's often-performed German art song "Ich grolle nicht," or the jazz standard "Take the 'A' Train," by Duke Ellington, have been performed and recorded countless times. Each performance features its own subtle (or not so subtle) variations, with musicians interpreting the musical script differently. Having a multitude of interpretations of the same pieces introduces another level of repetition into the musical landscape. This type of repetition introduces the potential for untold hours of content in musical datasets to be little more than the same few pages of melody and chords repeated over and over. There are over 700 performances of "Danny Boy" on Spotify. That's about 35 hours of "Danny Boy" renditions. The song's notated music, however, takes up only about 32 measures. If you go one step further and account for the fact that the song itself internally repeats, these 35 hours of musical content boil down to a core of about a minute of unique melodic and harmonic material.

These various aspects of musical repetition will affect the amount of unique data in a musical dataset. In Figure 3.1, I tallied YouTube's musical content as lasting an incredible 4,452 years. But let's imagine that each tune in the dataset repeats an average of four times. That's very generous, especially compared to Spotify's 700-to-1 "Danny Boy" ratio! Let's also imagine that each song internally repeats its material twice. Once again, we're being generous: recall the triple repetition of "Flowers." Discounting these repetitions in turn, the dataset shrinks to about 400 years of unique data. From this perspective, only around one-tenth of YouTube's data is unique, non-repeated music.[4]

Because of the way we consume and play music "on loop," there will always be an enormous amount of repetition within a musical dataset, along with a consistent pressure from musical consumers to create less unique musical material. However, as we saw in the previous chapter, machine learning systems—and large deep learning models in particular—crave as much data as they can possibly get. The redundancy in musical datasets therefore puts musical AI at a significant disadvantage by deflating the amount of unique information available for machine learning.

3) Unlike almost every other art form, music doesn't directly elevate some other type of perception or communication. Poetry and storytelling are elevated versions of verbal communication. The letters, words, and sentences that comprise a Reddit post or a friendly text message are, fundamentally, the same building blocks used by authors to write Pulitzer Prize-winning literature. The color palette employed in traffic signage is identical to that of the artworks hanging in your local museum. The design principles of any small-town post office follow the same fundamentals as the work of any famous architect.

As I noted at the end of Chapter 2, music does not work this way. To be sure, many aspects of music are *drawn* from other domains. For example, we raise the pitch of our voice at the end of a sentence to form a question. Similarly, when we increase our walking pace to close the distance with someone ahead of us, faster bodily rhythms propel our movements. More subtly, various styles of music use vocabularies and grammar in much the same way as spoken languages. For instance, when you say a song is in C major, you're referencing the dictionary of pitches and chords available in that key. The way we expect those chords to be ordered has a lot of similarities to the way parts of speech govern sentence structure. Indeed, neuroscientists have even identified several areas of the brain shared between music and spoken language.[5]

But these connections with other domains involve partial borrowings and metaphoric analogies rather than a wholesale overlap. Poetry *is* language. Visual art *is* images. But music is, well, just music. Knowing the lexicon and grammar of a language will help you read both poetry and Reddit posts, but it won't help you understand music. Having an understanding of the nuanced ways we modulate our voices to convey meaning and emotion doesn't directly translate into the ability to compose a melody. Music plays by its own rules. The norms and tendencies that govern how a particular note acts within a scale are purely musical principles—they're not imported from some less artistic form of communication. Understanding the principles of music theory doesn't grant insights into other domains, just as fluency in other areas doesn't equip one with the knowledge of how to treat various notes and scale degrees within a melody.

Music's unique behaviors limit the kinds of data available for training a musical AI. Recall that deep learning systems iterate over a dataset to identify norms and trends in that data. These processes therefore need datasets with some consistency. In other words, there need to be patterns to be found. Because poetry, Reddit posts, novels, movie scripts, and recipes all share similar linguistic structures—they share the same lexicon and grammar—datasets that mix all sorts of English-language content will be useful in learning how the English language works. Training on persuasive essays will help an AI write poetry, training on poetry will help it write persuasive essays, and training on both genres will help the AI edit emails. From the artistic to the mundane, all English-language content shares some consistent linguistic structures. Similarly, the fine art portion of DeviantArt's 500 million diverse images will potentially help an image-generating LLM design website logos, while the dataset's repository of logos can contribute to the AI's capacity to create images recalling more "artistic" traditions. Artistic and non-artistic images rely on the same lexicon of shapes, colors, and objects.

But an audio dataset that casts as wide a net as these language- or image-based AIs would include *all sound*, mixing together everyday sounds with music. Non-musical sounds don't speak the same language as musical sounds. Because non-musical sounds don't exhibit the structures, patterns, organization, and norms of music, a broad dataset containing nonmusical sounds would not help an AI learn how to create music. Musical AI research and modeling is therefore limited to using only artistic versions of sound, further limiting the availability of data for musical AI. This is a constraint unique to music.

4) **Music isn't useful.** I love music. I have devoted my life to studying, performing, and teaching music. In the words of Jane Austen's *Emma*, "I absolutely cannot do without music… without music, life would be a blank to me." However, as any worried parent of a music major will tell you, pursuing music isn't the most practical endeavor.

On the one hand, music's lack of utility is a fallout of the dissociation from other media that I've already discussed. Because poetry and business contracts have similar linguistic properties, the knowledge about how to write a poem has at least some synergy with the world of finance. Because the same AI that can imitate a museum piece can also generate graphics for a retailer's website, that model has some commercial utility. But as we have seen, music doesn't share its organizing principles with any other domain. You'll only be able to make music with a music AI.

On the other hand, music's place in the commercial pantheon is a downstream effect of the forces we discussed in the last chapter. Music simply doesn't have the same financial applications as other media. You don't use rhythm and meter to close a real estate deal. You infrequently see violins on the floor of the New York Stock Exchange. Contracts don't have a melody. By definition, any society oriented toward capitalism will spend more resources producing things that make more money. Music-making does not help a capitalist make money as directly as other media.[6]

These four factors—music's specialized training, its unique rules, its repetition, and its lack of commercial payoff—combine to ensure that there is less data available for computational research in music than for other types of media. Additionally, each of these forces independently compromises advancements in the others. In an alternate reality where making music was a surefire way to make money, AIs would still need to grapple with music's inherent repetition. In a world where music was made of only unique, non-repetitive content, the field of musical AI would still suffer from the fact that musicians need some manner of training to create new content. These issues even reinforce one another. For instance, one of the reasons music needs such specialized training is because music doesn't share a language or lexicon with other forms of art, cognition, or communication.

The psychologist Steven Pinker once described music as "auditory cheesecake" when highlighting music's repurposing of more mundane and utilitarian ingredients into something deeply enjoyable. While his original formulation was connected to a largely debunked theory of music's role in human evolution,[7] the metaphor is surprisingly applicable to the dynamics behind musical datasets. Cheesecake transforms basic culinary components—cheese, sugar, eggs—into something that is uniquely pleasant and desirable, and fundamentally different from its individual ingredients. Cheesecake also represents a more labor-intensive and expensive use of its internal components than other, potentially more nutritious dishes that might be made with the same ingredients.

Just as cheesecake elevates basic proteins, fats, and sugars, music escalates some baseline resources available to human cognition. The natural pitch of our voice is sweetened into song; bodily movements are transformed into musical downbeats; basic human linguistic capacities support musical grammars. But just like cheesecake, this musical repurposing doesn't serve the same practical goals as its source material. Song is less immediately useful than speech, and feeling a downbeat is less immediately useful than walking. And just like cheesecake, you need to go out of your way to make music, using specific tools and undergoing training. It takes more effort, time, and resources to make both cheesecake and music than it does to use their utilitarian components in more immediately productive ways.

We love music. And we love cheesecake. But there's less cheesecake in the world than there is cheese, and there's less music in the world than the other, more practical modes of expression on which it draws.

Music is hard for computers to read

Older millennials like me will recall an age when PDF documents were merely pictures of text, and computers could not recognize letters or words within them. In the dark days of the early 2000s, we could not highlight text within a PDF. We couldn't copy text between PDFs and word processors. The very idea of editing text directly in a PDF seemed hopelessly futuristic.

Now, a couple of decades later, the technological landscape has evolved. Scanned documents can be swiftly transformed into computer-readable text. Even the camera apps on most phones automatically highlight and convert any text within an image. In a sequence that would have flabbergasted me in the early 2000s, I could print this page, snap a photo of the printout, and then open that image as a PDF. From there, I could easily copy and paste the text into a word processor document, seamlessly returning to where I began. This is possible because contemporary image technology can identify the letters, spaces, punctuation marks, and words present in a picture. Such technology undertakes *character recognition* using computer models to process a page of text or other media and extract the text from it.

The challenge, of course, is that the character recognition model needs to be familiar with all the variations in how the letters, spaces, and punctuation marks might appear on a page. Books will present these characters differently than multi-columned newspapers and magazines. Fonts differ from one another in how they render each letter, and font size can change within the same page. Figures, illustrations, and photos can be interspersed throughout a page, and a character recognition model needs to be able to distinguish this non-linguistic content from actual text. To extract text successfully and consistently from an image, the model needs to be prepared for all potential variations.

Text-based deep learning AIs can leverage character recognition technology to build their datasets. The massive number of scans available on Google Books, for example, is only useful to an AI if the words can be extracted from the images in the scans. Character recognition technology allows for the vast trove of words contained in printed and scanned material to be made available to text-based machine learning processes.

For a musical AI to use information from scanned scores, it needs to undertake a similar character recognition of musical notation. You can't just show some deep learning system a picture of score; the data on the page needs to be extracted from the image in some way. Just as a text reader pulls the letters and words from an image of text, a music reader needs to extract notes, measures, and rests from an image. It needs to be able to identify which markings on the page are the five lines of the staff, which are notes, which are phrase markings, and so on. Once these items are isolated, the score becomes "computer readable," and the computer can identify what's on the musical page. The readable items can then be used for a computational process like deep learning.

However, musical character recognition has many more moving parts—and opportunities for failure—than linguistic character recognition. For one, text documents have a limited number of characters. Counting the 26 letters in upper and lower cases and the 14 or so regularly used punctuation marks, there are roughly 66 discrete characters a scanner needs to be familiar with.[8] Additionally, these characters appear in predictable places, as they are grouped into words which are separated by punctuation marks, spaces, and line breaks within paragraphs and pages.

Western musical notation—with its depictions of rhythm, meter, pitch, loudness, instrumentation, phrasing, and articulation—relies on complex combinations of signs. The mixing of these signs becomes exponentially more complicated with the addition of more factors. Furthermore, depending on the musical style and instruments being used, those signs can be distributed on the page in many different ways. Composers put notes on the five lines of the staff to indicate which pitches a performer should sing or play, and individual staves can be linked together to indicate that multiple instruments or voices are moving simultaneously. Each note can have any number of durations, indicated by whether the notehead is filled or open, and whether it has a stem, flag, beam, or dot attached to it. Vertical lines show where measures begin and end. Single letters—often abbreviations for Italian words—show how loud one should perform a note or phrase. Horizontal arcs can show where phrases begin and end. Short abbreviations like "*Ped*" or "*Pizz*" can indicate things like when pianists pump the instrument's pedals or whether a violinist should use their bow or pluck the string. This is only a tiny sample of the characters that make up Western music notation. Additionally, the norms around these indications change with the genre of the music, with jazz, classical, and country music all having distinct notation styles.

The opening eight bars of Ludwig Beethoven's Fifth Symphony appear at the top of Figure 3.2, here arranged for piano by the Hungarian composer Franz Liszt. Readers will recognize this theme as the famous (and ominous) *Da-da-da-dunnnn* theme that appears in so much pop culture (think: Bugs Bunny cartoons. The example begins with a half-beat ("eighth-note") rest, followed by three quick eighth notes. These faster note values are indicated by the single beam connecting the individual notes and constitute the "*Da-da-da*" initiation of the theme. These three notes descend to a longer two-beat note (a "half note") that takes up the entirety of the following measure. The longer rhythmic value is shown by the fact that the body of the note (the "notehead") is an empty circle. This is the "*dunnnn*" conclusion of the theme. The note is made even longer by the symbol above it. This is a "fermata," a half circle with a dot inside that indicates the performer should sustain the sound for some duration longer than the indicated rhythm. The *Da-da-da-dunnnn* is then repeated. This time, the final notes are "tied" into a second measure with curved horizontal lines, indicating that the pitches' duration should last for two whole measures before the fermata extends it even further. The symphony continues by spinning out this musical idea with groups of three short eighth notes appearing above sustained harmonies tied across multiple measures.

Even this short excerpt contains a lot more information than simple pitches and rhythms. The example starts with the indication "Allegro con brio," meaning to perform this passage "briskly, with vigor." A small parenthetical tempo indication states that "a half note equals 108," meaning that the half note is the fundamental beat of the piece, and that the half notes should pass at a rate of 108 per minute. The "*ff*" abbreviates the Italian word *fortissimo*, which tells the performer they should play the

FIGURE 3.2 The original score of the opening to Ludwig van Beethoven's Symphony No. 5, as transcribed for piano by Franz Liszt, and three renderings of that score using music character recognition.

passage loudly, while the following "*p*" markings mean *piano*, an indication to play softly.

In addition to these basic notational symbols, Liszt adds some markings specifically for the performer of his piano transcription. These include indications for when the pianist should push down the instrument's sustain pedal to allow the pitches to ring and resonate. "*Ped*" shows where to push down the pedal, and the subsequent star indicates where to release it. The passage begins with a short parenthetical "*Instruments à cordes et*"

Clarinettes," which reminds the pianist that the original version for full orchestra uses strings and clarinets here. Finally, the numbers above the final notes of the passage suggest which finger a pianist should use to play these notes.

Below the published Liszt score, Figure 3.2 shows outputs generated by the Audiveris software's music character recognition software[9] from three different scans of the score. In much the same way that text-oriented character recognition software converts images of writing into computer-readable letters, spaces, punctuation, and words, this program is designed to convert images of scores into computer-readable music. I have translated the information Audiveris extracts from the scans back into scores to compare the computer-readable data with the original.

The results illustrate three separate types of errors, demonstrating how the process of musical character recognition might go awry. In the first scan, the software misidentifies various characters on the page. The fermatas above measures 2 and 5, for instance, are misidentified as notes, and the fingering numbers in measures 6 and 7 become multiple redundant loudness markings—note the several instances of "*p*" at the end of scan 1. Scan 2, on the other hand, misidentifies many of the markings in measures 2, 4, and 5 as musically extraneous, placing, at most, only one note in each of those measures. Additionally, this version seems to confuse staff lines with beams used to show rhythmic duration. The extra beams added to the "*Da-da-da*" parts of the melody make these notes twice as fast as they should be. The software identifies more of the correct notes and rhythms from scan 3 than it did the other versions, but it drastically misunderstands the page layout. This output links all the staves with a continuous line at the very left side, mashing together all the music on the page by indicating all lines should be performed at the same time. This cacophonous result plays multiple phrases concurrently. In each their own way, these mistakes show how difficult it is for a computer program to extract accurate information from the lines, spaces, words, letters, and shapes on a musical page.

We could, of course, sidestep the thorny issues of music notation by focusing on audio files instead. After all, a comparatively small amount of notated music is available online compared to the internet's trove of recorded music. This was illustrated in Figure 3.1, where smaller musical datasets are typically those containing scores (CPDL, IMSLP) and the audio datasets (SoundCloud, YouTube Music, and Spotify) contain much more content.

However, audio is also extremely difficult for computers to extract reliable information from. This is primarily due to the complexity of sound waves. A sounding note is not made of just one singular sound wave, but rather, it contains many complementary waves that contribute to the quality of its sound. When any instrument plays a middle C, it produces the *fundamental* of middle C. This fundamental provides the sound wave that makes a middle C sound like a middle C. When a harp and a trumpet both play a middle C, both produce the same fundamental sound wave. But these instruments sound different from one another because of the different higher and softer component sound waves that accompany the fundamental. These *overtones* change the quality of the note. They determine how bright, muted, warm, or nasally a pitch sounds. When an instrument or voice sounds more piercing or intense, it's because that instrument or the singer activates more and stronger overtones concurrent with the fundamental pitch. The nasally trumpet's middle C has more overtones than one played by the warm and mellow harp. This is because a harp's strings emit fewer overtones than does the bell of a trumpet.

In Chapter 1, I used *spectrograms* to show these fundamentals and overtones. Spectrograms are detailed maps of a sound, showing how pitch and loudness change over time. With a vertical axis showing pitch and a horizontal axis corresponding to time, spectrograms capture which soundwaves are flowing through the air at each moment. You can see more piercing or nasally sounds within a spectrogram because they activate more and higher sound waves, while warmer sounds will show sound waves closer to the fundamental pitch.

The problem is that it's very difficult for a computer to determine which waves are fundamentals and which are overtones flickering above some other fundamental. A nasally trumpet playing a single note will have many strong overtones above one fundamental, and a harp playing multiple notes at the same time will have waves associated with each of the different notes' fundamentals. Both situations involve multiple layers of sound waves stacked on top of one another, and it's hard for a computer to distinguish between the two.

Figure 3.3 shows some of the pitfalls for programs that extract pitch information from audio files using two short passages from Lizzo's 2017 breakout hit, "Truth Hurts." The lefthand side of the figure shows the piano's introductory material from the first moments of the track. The righthand side shows Lizzo's vocal entry in the first verse. In the top row, I show transcriptions of the notes played and sung by the piano and voice that I made using my own ear. In the middle, I show corresponding spectrogram representations of Lizzo's track. Finally, I used Spotify's audio feature extraction software to convert the audio file of Lizzo's track into digital pitch and duration information.[10] The program outputs this information as a MIDI file, a standard computer readable music notation format. In other words, the program converts the audio file's sound waves into computer readable notes and rests as best it can. In the figure's final

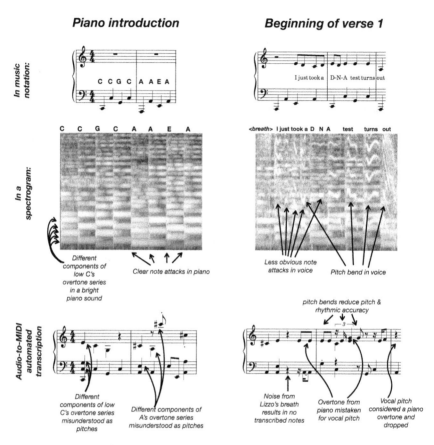

FIGURE 3.3 Comparison of human and automated transcriptions of two short passages from Lizzo's "Truth Hurts" (2017).

row, I show the resulting MIDI file converted to traditional music notation, which we can now compare with my original transcription.

The transcription at the upper left of the figure shows "Truth Hurts" beginning with two zigzagging piano patterns that start on the piano's low C and low A. Lizzo selects a very bright piano for this underscoring, and this brightness can be seen in the well-ordered stacks of overtones in the spectrogram immediately below the transcription. The spectrogram also shows a burst of energy with each attack in the piano, clearly delineating each note's beginning. As the pitches change, the towers of overtones shift. These bursting stacks of fundamentals and overtones follow the zigzag of the piano patterns, first jumping upward and then back downward like lightning bolts.

However, the brightness of the piano throws the transcription software for a loop. As the piano slams into the track's initial low C, the program believes that the stack of bright overtones indicates four different pitches, as seen in the bottom example on the left side of the figure. The sound waves that our ears hear as the sonic trappings of a single intense piano note become confused for multiple pitches. This phenomenon continues into the second measure. The software identifies several C-sharps in that measure—the notes preceded with "#" in the score—though the piano plays nothing of the sort. Rather, the piano's notes contain C-sharp as an overtone. The instrument is so bright and crisp that the software assumes that those overtones must represent fundamentals in their own right.[11]

Lizzo's vocal entry to the first verse, which is shown down the righthand column of Figure 3.3, provides an even messier example. At this moment in the track, she sings, "I just took a DNA test," while the piano continues its zigzag pattern. Lizzo takes an audible breath before beginning her verse, and I highlight this moment in the spectrogram. The spectrogram also shows that Lizzo slightly bends the pitch of her notes up and down, adding expression (and sass!) to her delivery. Also, while some of her notes have obvious beginnings in the spectrogram, she slurs the beginning of many words in the passage, giving these moments less clear starting points. Looking at the text placed above the spectrogram, notice how there are rather clear delineations of pitch onsets at "D," "test," and "turns," and how these are much less pronounced at "just," "took," and "N."

Each of these factors poses different problems for Spotify's software. The breath, for instance, creates a lot of noise—a lot of unstructured sound—so the software assumes that *no pitches* appear at that moment. Also, the combination of her pitch bends and slurred note attacks hampers the software from recognizing several of her sung notes. Because the slurred note attacks make it ambiguous as to where notes begin and end, the transcription uses very unusual, incorrect, rhythms at these points. The brightness of the underlying piano seems to throw a further wrench into the works at several moments. Notably, the program deletes the last note she sings in the excerpt ("out"), believing that her vocalization is part of the piano's overtones.

Of course, I'm picking illustrative mistakes, and these open-source free programs do not represent the state-of-the-art, highest-quality software available. However, they do show the kinds of things that can easily go wrong when converting music into computer-readable formats. Overall, using either score images or raw musical audio can produce messy and unreliable data. Any dataset based on such information would be riddled with errors, and a deep learning system training on this data would not be using anything like the actual music. Rather, it would be training on distorted and often unrecognizable information. The AI would not learn how to create music. It could only learn to replicate the mistakes and gibberish in the faulty data.

This is not to say that there is no hope for this technology, that the problems facing musical character recognition and audio processing are unsolvable, or that better programs won't be able to minimize these problems. To be sure: these technologies have improved by leaps and bounds over the past handful of years, and this progress will surely continue. Every time I try music scanning technology, the results are noticeably better, and recent research into audio analysis has seen some very impressive improvements.[12] However, as my examples demonstrate, music is simply a tough nut to crack when it comes to extracting reliable, computer readable information from scores and audio files, and its fidelity seems to lag behind similar technologies in other media.

Computer readable musical data

A significant portion of music research relies on data that was originally made in a digital format, rather than on data extracted from scores or audio. This digitally native data is generally made by and for people using computers to make or study music. MIDI—the file type that Spotify's audio parser used as its output—is the most widely used format. Effectively, a MIDI file functions like an old-fashioned piano roll. On a piano roll, different pitches occupy unique horizontal rows on the paper. Higher rows are assigned to increasingly higher pitches, and notes are produced by cutting a small hole in the appropriate place on desired row. Longer rhythmic durations are made simply by making longer holes in the roll. In MIDI, the rows on the paper roll are replaced by assigned numbers, and durations are controlled by an electronic on/off switch. For instance, a MIDI representation of the first piano note in "Truth Hurts" would consist of a computational signal to "turn on" pitch number 36 (low C) at the beginning of the track and another signal to turn it off one beat later.

Such a representation is eminently usable by researchers and AI developers. A computer can simply move through these signals and identify when notes turn on and off, thereby reconstructing the full score. There are other types of computer readable music files using similar approaches, but with modifications to add particular features or solve for specific problems. For instance, the MusicXML format is designed to include more aspects of Western notation, including phrasing and articulation, while the Music21 and kern formats are designed to embed information specifically useful for music research.[13]

Developed to be computer friendly, all these file formats are perfectly suited for training deep learning systems. In fact, the research conducted in my own lab predominantly uses datasets comprised of MIDI files.

However, there's an enormous problem with these types of files. Because people only make them for unique circumstances, only a relatively tiny number are available. Digitally notated music files are created only when composers, performers, or researchers deliberately invest the effort to encode their music into these formats. A composer writing a piece for computer or a researcher interested in analyzing a particular music genre might opt to create music files in one of these specialized formats, but these cases represent a miniscule amount of the music-making in the world around us.

I'll give a few statistics to illustrate the paucity in computer-native music data files. IMSLP contains 16,000 MIDI versions of its scores. ClassicalArchives.com contains a bit more than 10,000 MIDI files. The music library associated with the Music21 research software contains 1,006 XML and kern files. The Electronic Locator of Vertical Interval Slices (ELVIS) research project at McGill University has compiled 3,358 XML files, mostly of European Medieval and Renaissance music. The Lieder Encoding Project has created XML files of 300 European art songs. The Turkish Makam Music Symbolic Data Collection contains 2,200 XML and MIDI files from that tradition. PolishScores.com contains about 7,000 kern scores of music from a variety of traditions.[14] While the list goes on, each repository numbers their content in the hundreds or in the thousands. Taken together—and with the caveat that counting anything on the internet will be riddled with imprecision—I believe there are no more than 200,000 digitally native scores on the internet.

This sum is miniscule compared to the size other datasets. It is one quarter of the PDFs available on IMSLP, and one fifth of one percent (0.2%) of Spotify's audio library. The number is even more miniscule when you compare it to datasets in other media. It's 2% *of 1%* of the number of videos on YouTube (.025%), and it's a third of *1% of 1%* of the number of images on DeviantArt (.003%). The entirety of all digitally native music files available on the planet would register a mere one or two decades on the timeline of Figure 3.1. Even if I've underestimated the amount of available digitally native files by some order of magnitude, this type of music data is still some microscopic fraction of the data available in other domains.

The availability of musical data, then, faces something of a bottleneck. The fact that the data extracted from scores and sound files is unreliable and messy combines with the extra effort and specialized contexts required for creating computer readable formats to limit the number of files readily available online. The result is that musical deep learning models are confined to train on only a tiny fraction of the data available in other media.

Summary

This chapter outlined several reasons that musical datasets are small, especially when compared to those available in other media. Music requires specialized knowledge, and this restricts the number of people making it. This is especially true for recorded or notated forms that are easily accessible on the internet and compilable into training datasets for AIs. Also, music's inner grammar, materials, and rules are not shared by other media, which further limits the availability of data for deep learning systems. Art forms like poetry and photography use elements that are much the same as those we encounter in everyday life. A poetry-generating AI can therefore be supplemented by the immense amounts of text available on the internet, and an image-generating AI can use pictures of everyday objects. Music, however, is an independent medium. Because no other medium plays by similar rules, any music-making AI needs to train on music alone. You cannot supplement a dataset of music with other types of sound.

Further deflating the size of available data, music involves an enormous amount of repetition. Music tends to involve much internal repetition, like the consistent return of a refrain or rotations through multiple verses employing the same melody and harmony. And as performers, we repeat old content, putting our own spin on classic tunes that have been performed and recorded countless times before. This all combines to limit the amount of unique data produced and consumed in the broader musical environment.

On top of the relatively small amount of raw data in the musical landscape, computing software has difficulty converting audio recordings and notated scores into computer readable data. Compared to written language, with its constrained number of letters and punctuation marks that consistently appear in horizontal lines that group into words separated by spaces, scores are complicated and unpredictable. In Western notation, the notes that appear on the staff's five lines may or may not be arranged to occur concurrently in simultaneous chords, and the staves may or may not be linked together to indicate various instruments or lines moving together. Further, the beams, lines, flags, articulation marks, repeat signs, holds, words, tempos, lyrics, and phrase markings that may or may not occur add increased variability and complexity. Processing score images is a complex problem with many opportunities for error.

It's also difficult to extract reliable pitch and duration information from audio music files. When an instrument plays a note, the sound involves both a fundamental sound wave that establishes an identifiable pitch and a series of overtone sound waves that determine how harsh or warm that pitch sounds. While our brains are very good at distinguishing whether a battery of vibrations hitting our ear drums is from one single note or from multiple notes being played at the same time, the complexities of fundamentals interweaving with overtones make for a very difficult computational task. And the infinite possibilities of instrument combinations, performance techniques, and background noise found in recorded music add further difficulty to an already difficult task. Any software attempting to identify notes and durations from sound waves has a huge number of opportunities to make mistakes.

Finally, while several musical file formats exist that are specifically designed to be easily read by a computer, the available datasets of such files are tiny. MIDI files, for instance, consist of computational indications of which notes are played and at what time. However, MIDI files have most often been created for very particular situations, either when composers make music specifically for a computer or when researchers compile musical data to study. Because of this, there are very few digitally native files available online, compared both to the number of scores and audio files available on the internet and to datasets of other media. In a world where AI models are racing to acquire the biggest datasets possible, music is at a disadvantage. Many of the improvements in deep learning AI have arisen from access to increasingly huge pools of data. Not only is the pool of musical data shallower, but our technology to extract the resources from it is limited.

That said, these hurdles are shrinking. Each year sees major improvements in score scanning and automated transcription. A few years ago, the technology was only usable in the most basic and simple cases—scanning a clean and consistent piano score or transcribing a single instrument playing in a quiet room. Every year, we see these technologies succeed in increasingly complex situations. And the rise of music streaming services means that more and more audio data is available online. Perhaps most encouraging, more and more digitally native scores are finding their way online, mostly through user-sourced websites like MuseScore. These trends are slowly increasing the size of the musical datasets of Figure 3.1.

However, even if music transcription dramatically increases its fidelity, and even if musical datasets massively increase their size, these breakthroughs will have been achieved *after* and *behind* similar milestones in other media. From the complexities of its notation to its frequent repetition to the idiosyncrasies of its overtones, this chapter shows how music poses particularly difficult problems when curating large, high-quality, computer-readable datasets.

Many of these issues are the downstream effects of the forces I described in the previous chapter. If there was a huge demand for piles of musical data, or if the possibility of a substantial payoff for music transcription software loomed around the corner, music's datasets would be larger, and the surrounding technology would be more developed. Conversely, the relative size of musical datasets will continue to have effects on other issues in musical AI. Even if we solve the problems surrounding the collection and curation of musical examples, we will still need to solve these downstream issues. In the next chapter, I will address what I view as the next major difficulty for musical AI: how to represent musical data in machine learning.

Notes

1 Bertin-Mahieux and Ellis are one of the most striking examples of the musical brain drain I described in the last chapter. While they were instrumental in creating the largest and most used musical dataset of its time, Ellis now works as a research scientist at Google, and Bertin-Mahieux founded a startup that applies AI to retail.
2 Lindner (2023).
3 This sort of internal repetition appears across musical cultures sufficiently frequently that the ethnomusicologist Bruno Nettl (1983) identified it as a potentially universal characteristic, writing, "All cultures make some use of internal repetition and variation in their musical utterances" (p. 46). Most sonatas written in Western Europe at the turn of the nineteenth century repeat their opening theme four times. West African jembe repertoire often rotates through the same timeline of rhythms over and over again. In jazz, the ensemble generally repeats the main melody (the "head") after various members take improvised solos.
4 While we've been generous in our assumptions, this argument overstates the point in some important ways. For example, a reggae-ska cover of "Danny Boy" would provide its own unique musical information and is not entirely redundant. Similarly, the fact that verses and choruses repeat is crucial information about how pop songs are organized.
5 See Patel (2008).
6 For a fascinating and in-depth analysis of this dynamic, see Ritchey (2019).
7 See Pinker (1997) and Piilonen (2024).
8 While these 66 are the most frequent, successful character recognition apps can identify many more characters. See Mithe *et al.* (2013) and Islam *et al.* (2016).
9 Audiveris is an open-source software that is built into the pdf scanning capacities of the popular notation software MuseScore. It can also be downloaded for free at its github page: github.com/Audiveris/audiveris.
10 The software is publicly available at basicpitch.spotify.com.
11 Many programs that extract pitches from audio files literally treat the spectrogram as a visual object, and parse it in much the same way as a program might analyze visual art. I'll return to this topic in the following chapter, but for more, see Choi *et al.* (2016), Dhariwal *et al.* (2020), Lee *et al.* (2018), Gourisaria *et al.* (2024), and Joung and Lee (2024). For an alternate approach, see Briot and Pachet (2018) and Xu *et al.* (2021).
12 See Burgoyne (2012), Andersen (2017), and Raffel (2016).
13 Huron (1992), Cuthbert and Ariza (2010).
14 Interested readers can peruse the Musical Corpus Register at github.com/dharasim/MCR/wiki.

References and Further Reading

Andersen, J. S. 2017. "How to Think Music with Data: Translating from Audio Content Analysis to Music Analysis." PhD Dissertation. Copenhagen: Faculty of Humanities, University of Copenhagen.

Bertin-Mahieux, T. 2013. "Large-Scale Pattern Discovery in Music." PhD diss., Columbia University. https://academiccommons.columbia.edu/doi/10.7916/D8W66HPM.

Bertin-Mahieux, T., D. P. W. Ellis, B. Whitman, and P. Lamere. 2011. "The Million Song Dataset." In *Proceedings of the 12th International Society for Music Information Retrieval Conference* (ISMIR 2011).

Briot, J.-P., and F. Pachet. 2018. "Deep Learning for Music Generation: Challenges and Directions." *Neural Computing and Applications* 32(4): 981–993.

Burgoyne, J. A. 2012. "Stochastic Processes & Database-Driven Musicology." PhD diss., McGill University.

Burgoyne, J. A., Wild, J., & Fujinaga, I. 2011. An expert ground-truth set for audio chord recognition and music analysis. Proceedings of the International Society for Music Information Retrieval Conference, 633–638.

Burgoyne, J. A., Fujinaga, I., & Downie, J. S. 2015. Music information retrieval. In S. Schreibman, R. Siemens, & J. Unsworth (Eds.), A new companion to digital humanities (Chapter 15). Wiley. https://doi.org/10.1002/9781118680605.ch15

Cook, N. 2001. "Between Process and Product: Music and/as Performance." *Music Theory Online* 7(2). http://societymusictheory.org/mto/issues/mto.01.7.2/toc.7.2.html.

Choi, K., G. Fazekas, and M. Sandler. 2016. "Explaining Deep Convolutional Neural Networks on Music Classification." https://doi.org/10.48550/arXiv.1607.02444.

Cuthbert, M. S., and C. Ariza. 2010. "Music21: A Toolkit for Computer-Aided Musicology and Symbolic Music Data." In *Proceedings of the 11th International Society for Music Information Retrieval Conference*, edited by J. Stephen Downie and Remco C Veltkamp, 637–642. Utrecht, Netherlands: International Society for Information Retrieval.

Dhariwal, P., H. Jun, C. Payne, J. W. Kim, A. Radford, and I. Sutskever. 2020. "Jukebox: A Generative Model for Music." arXiv preprint arXiv:2005.00341.

Gourisaria, M. K., R. Agrawal, M. Sahni, and P. K. Singh. 2024. "Comparative Analysis of Audio Classification with MFCC and STFT Features Using Machine Learning Techniques." *Discover Internet of Things* 4(1): 1.

Huron, D. 1992. "Design Principles in Computer-Based Music Representation." In *Computer Representations and Models in Music*, edited by A. Marsden and A. Pople, 5–59. London: Academic Press.

Islam, N., Z. Islam, and N. Noor. 2016. "A Survey on Optical Character Recognition System." *Journal of Information & Communication Technology-JICT* 10(2): 1–4.

Jehan, T. 2005. "Creating Music by Listening." PhD diss., Massachusetts Institute of Technology. https://web.media.mit.edu/~tristan/phd/dissertation/index.html.

Joung, H., and K. Lee. 2024. "Music Auto-Tagging with Robust Music Representation Learned via Domain Adversarial Training." arXiv preprint arXiv:2401.15323.

Lee, J., J.Park, K. L. Kim, and J. Nam. 2018. "SampleCNN: End-to-End Deep Convolutional Neural Networks Using Very Small Filters for Music Classification." *Applied Sciences* 8(1): 150.

Lindner, J. December 16, 2023. "Must-Know YouTube Music Statistics." Gitnux (website). https://gitnux.org/youtube-music-statistics/.

Mithe, R., S. Indalkar, and N. Divekar. 2013. "Optical Character Recognition." *International Journal of Recent Technology and Engineering (IJRTE)* 2(1). ISSN: 2277-3878.

Nettl, B. 1983. *The Study of Ethnomusicology: Twenty-Nine Issues and Concepts.* Urbana: University of Illinois Press.

Patel, A. D. 2008. *Music, Language, and the Brain.* Oxford: Oxford University Press.

Pinker, S. 1997. *How the Mind Works.* New York: W. W. Norton.

Piilonen, M. 2024. *Theorizing Music Evolution: Darwin, Spencer, and the Limits of the Human.* Oxford: Oxford University Press.

Raffel, C. 2016. "Learning-Based Methods for Comparing Sequences, with Applications to Audio-to-MIDI Alignment and Matching." PhD diss., Columbia University.

Ritchey, M. 2019. *Composing Capital: Classical Music in the Neoliberal Era.* Los Angeles: University of California Press.

Whitman, B. A. 2005. "Learning the Meaning of Music" PhD diss., Massachusetts Institute of Technology. http://dspace.mit.edu/handle/1721.1/32500.

Xu, S., W. Zhao, and J. Guo. 2021. "RefineGAN: Universally Generating Waveform Better Than Ground Truth with Highly Accurate Pitch and Intensity Responses." arXiv preprint arXiv:2111.00962.

4
REPRESENTING MUSIC TO AN ARTIFICIAL INTELLIGENCE

"Once you label me, you negate me."

Either/Or, Søren Kierkegaard

In 1973, the conductor and composer Leonard Bernstein gave a series of lectures at Harvard University in which he outlined some basic components of music. He provocatively described how these concepts fit together in a language-like manner. Bernstein began by describing the overtone series, which—as we saw in the previous chapters—combines some fundamental sound wave with complementary higher sound waves (overtones) to make the actual sound we hear coming from an instrument. He analogized this level of musical production to the basic sounds our mouths can create in spoken language, or linguistic "phonemes." Just as phonemes are the essential building blocks of any spoken language, the sounds our voices and instruments make are the basic construction materials of music. The analogy here is straightforward. These sounds are music's basic building blocks just as phonemes are the most basic components of spoken language.

However, Bernstein's descriptions and analogies soon become far less straightforward. His lectures start jumping between many aspects of musical construction. He mentions how musical phrases move to one another, the ways particular harmonies progress to other harmonies, how a melody's shape creates certain expectations, the characteristic tendencies of certain rhythms, and even how musical themes can develop across an entire symphony.

Bernstein likens this hodgepodge of musical devices to linguistic *syntax*, the ways in which parts of speech—nouns, verbs, prepositions,

DOI: 10.4324/9781003587415-4

etc.—behave in spoken language. Here, his connections with language begin to get thorny. Viewers looking for clear and obvious analogies between music and language might become frustrated with Bernstein's apparent inconsistency and lack of focus. Are individual chords the "words" in this analogy? Or is the analogy to full musical phrases? Where do single notes fit in? And what of rhythm and meter?

But Bernstein's mercurial changeability is a feature of musical grammar rather than a bug in his lectures. In contrast to the way that spoken language uses sounds that group into words that chunk into phrases, music involves a messy interrelation of harmony, melody, meter, rhythm, themes, and phrases whose components often overlap with, and feedback into, one another in a tangled web of consanguinity. It's hard to cleanly analogize what a musical "word" or "part of speech" might be because there are so many aspects of music that work together at multiple timescales to fill this role.

This chapter is about music's messiness and how that messiness poses a problem for musical AI. Because so many different, overlapping components and characteristics contribute to each moment in music, it's hard to choose exactly how to represent music to a computer, and it's hard to know what musical components should be used in machine learning. I'll first outline some of the basic concepts underpinning how media is represented within machine learning algorithms and how those representations undergird the model's "knowledge" about a given medium. I'll then show how these dynamics work in computational representations of music, emphasizing music's particular complexity in this domain. I end by arguing that this issue poses a resource allocation problem for musical AI research. With so many possible ways of representing music to a computer, researchers face the problem of dividing their attention among several different avenues for musical modeling, spreading the field's already limited resources thinly between these different approaches.

Representing tokens to deep learning models

You can't just turn on the radio in front of a machine-learning model and expect it to learn music. You can't wave sheet music in front of a computer screen and expect it to see the notes and chords on the page. Computers can't use computational ears to listen to music any more than they can open their digital eyes to read poetry or view paintings. No: as we saw in the last chapter, computers need to have their data packaged in a way that is computationally readable. The soundwaves in the air or the scribbles on a score need to be changed into some digital format that a computer can process.

But this data also needs to be useful. In machine learning, the model needs to be able to observe the data to identify norms and tendencies in the medium. In generative AI, the model also needs to be able to use those patterns and norms to make new content. For instance, to create a deep learning model capable of composing poetic quatrains, the dataset of poetry must be formatted in a way that the learning model can detect linguistic features such as stress and rhyme. The model must then be able to use this format to generate new, human-readable verses that recognizably emulate the poetic form.

Tokenization is the process by which an AI divides data into manageable chunks that are useful for both learning and generating content. Tokens are essentially the list of ingredients an AI's engineers have decided the program can use when learning and generating media. For example, a chatbot program could tokenize a digital text document in several different ways. If it divides the text into individual characters, then each letter, space, and punctuation mark becomes a separate *token*. Alternatively, if it segments the text by spaces, then each word becomes its own token. As I noted in Chapter 1, when OpenAI trains ChatGPT, it divides the text into recognizable chunks that its prior research has found to act in predictable and useful ways. These chunks are the ingredients the chatbot is ready to recognize within a text and prepared to use when generating new content. These are its tokens.

Figure 4.1 schematizes this process, using a short quatrain by Emily Dickinson—the second half of the poem, "Alter? When the hills do," published in 1890. The figure is divided into five vertical columns, with the steps ChatGPT would take to write a new quatrain outlined at the bottom. The second column shows how OpenAI's tokenizing process divides the Dickinson text into its constituent segments. Smaller words like "dew" and "you" become their own tokens, but larger words like "daffodil" are divided into smaller units.[1] This is how the text would be represented to the chatbot. We can think of these small linguistic units as the specific pieces of information the model learns about, and which appear in its computational mind. The chatbot will have a representation of the word "dew," and it will understand the word "daffodil" as the sequence of *d*, *aff*, *od*, and *il*. The tokens also show the exact limit of the chatbot's knowledge. For instance, it doesn't really understand anything about the word "daffodil" *per se*. If you opened the dictionary within ChatGPT's artificial mind, there would be no entry for the word. You would only find entries for its components. Because "daffodil" is not a token in this system, that word would not be represented.

To get a bit more technical, even though this stage cuts the text into digestible chunks for the computer to process, these words and word fragments still aren't exactly what the computer "sees." When the tokens enter

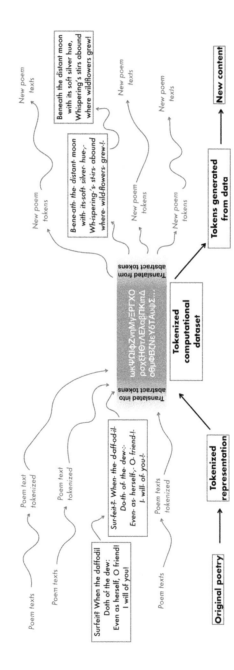

FIGURE 4.1 An outline of the representation, tokenization, learning, and generation processes in a simple hypothetical poetry model.

the computer's "mind," they become abstracted even further. As illustrated in the center of the figure, each token is converted into an abstract reference. I use arbitrary Greek letters to represent these references. At this point in the process, the abstracted references can be thought of as tokens stripped of all ancillary information. This is akin to how a book in a library is reduced to a call number in a reference catalog. Once something becomes a token in machine learning, its original content is set aside, transforming it into a mere reference point. At this stage, the machine learning procedure recognizes a token not by its content, but by its referential similarities relative to other tokens. This is similar to how a library's catalog of call numbers tracks the order of books on shelves without direct reference to the content of the books. The token for the word "dew" is no longer understood as a three-letter word starting with "D." Instead, it is now an abstract reference (marked in the figure as "Γ") indicating only the position of the token in relation to other tokens. Because the "d" of "daffodil" and the word "dew" are represented as different tokens (the token for "d" is φ in the figure), they become associated with a different abstract reference. They are now totally different tokens in the computer's mind, regardless of any spelling similarity a human might notice. But like a library cataloging system, this translation process keeps track of which symbols correspond to which human-readable tokens. After all, if the AI wants to generate new poems, it's going to need to know how to translate its tokens back into letters and words.[2]

These abstract representations form the basis of a machine learning model's training set. As I described in Chapter 2, the nodes within a neural network's surface layer—its inputs and outputs—each correspond to a token. The deeper layers of the neural network are tasked with learning the patterned norms and tendencies within these tokens. During the iterative learning process, the network improves its understanding of the token sequences, making better and better predictions. With each iteration, it refines the connections between the deep layers, enhancing its ability to process and interpret the underlying data effectively. A generative model then uses these abstract tokens when it creates new content. Once the layers of a deep learning model can predict the patterns and norms in a sequence of tokens, it can create a new sequence. If, for instance, we asked the poetry model in Figure 4.1 to create a new quatrain, it would activate its neural network to spit out a new series of tokens that follow the poetic logic the AI has learned.[3]

With Figure 4.1, we can imagine an AI observing regularities in a dataset of poetry and producing new sequences of tokens based on its machine learning process. When prompted to write a new quatrain in the style of Emily Dickinson, it reaches into its computational data, finds connections and norms in that data, and produces some new sequence of tokens. The computer then translates its abstract tokens back into letters, spaces, and punctuation marks. Extending my library metaphor, this would be like using a list of references to pull books off a shelf and using those reference numbers to inform how you create new literature rather than the actual content inside the books. With this translation done, the final poem can be assembled and served to the user.

All deep learning systems and generative AIs undergo a tokenization process. You cannot simply dump data on a neural network's doorstep and expect coherent results without chunking up that data in some way. An image-generating AI divides pictures into tokens that reference lines, shapes, and objects, and its computational mind will be filled with connections between these tokens. A voice recognition AI will tokenize sounds into a dictionary of possible utterances voices make. Tokens used by code-writing AIs consist of the functions, objects, and procedures available in computer languages. And tokens used in musical AIs are... complicated. Before addressing the issues specific to musical tokens, I will outline some of the various decisions involved in the tokenization process.

What makes a good token?

How do engineers decide what to use as the slate of recognizable ingredients in an AI? Why, for instance, does ChaptGPT *not* slice up its texts into individual characters? Alternately, why doesn't it always use full words as tokens? In other words: *What makes a good token? How do you choose what your AI "sees"?*

This decision involves balancing the general with the specific; the need for efficiency with effectiveness. Engineers want a dictionary of tokens to be big enough to cover all the cases a model might encounter in some dataset, and to allow it to be sensitive to highly specific patterns. But they also want the dictionary to be simple enough for the model to learn quickly. Such efficiency requires that the dictionary not be saturated with redundant or useless information.

A kitchen analogy can illustrate this balance. When you open up a recipe for a cake, it will almost certainly list "baking powder" as an ingredient. Baking powder works as a leavening agent because it combines a base with an acid. These are usually baking soda (sodium bicarbonate) and cream of tartar (potassium bitartrate), respectively. Even though many pantries are stocked with baking soda and cream of tartar, it would be inefficient and redundant for the recipe to list both components. Because this chemical mixture is used so consistently and in such reliable ratios, it's sold as its own prepackaged entity, and bakers reliably keep a can of baking powder sitting on their shelves. It would add confusion and potential error to the baking process to list baking powder's individual component ingredients rather than simply listing "baking powder."

In contrast, even though almost every cake involves whipping ("creaming") together butter, sugar, and eggs, recipes tend to not list an ingredient like "creamed sugar." The process isn't standardized: different recipes will vary the process and use the ingredients in different proportions. And besides, no ingredient called "creamed sugar" sits on our shelves or in our refrigerators. Even though it would capture something standard about cake baking, if a recipe were to list "creamed sugar" as an ingredient, it would not convey the specific ways that eggs, sugar, and butter are used in different cakes. This would only confuse and frustrate the baker.

In this analogy, baking powder is a good token, while creamed sugar is not. The former is a recognizable ingredient to a baker, and the latter isn't. Just as the word "dew" is used so reliably and straightforwardly in ChatGPT's dataset that the word is treated as its own linguistic chunk, so too is baking powder treated as a stable and predictable component of cake recipes. It would overcomplicate both the chatbot and the recipe to divide the tokens into their components. The word "daffodil," on the other hand, is *not* used consistently enough to make sense as its own token. Just as cake recipes vary their use of eggs, butter, and sugar in important ways, the word's components (*d*, *aff*, *od*, and *il*) each act in sufficiently independent ways, and the model can learn more about its dataset by treating them as individual tokens.[4]

A good tokenization scheme, therefore, needs to balance the general with the specific. Tracking how often every single letter moves to every other letter would become ungainly for a text-generating model very quickly. In addition to tracking letter-to-letter changes, the model would need to make connections between pairs of letters, trios of letters, and so on until it could form words. Like the annoyed baker looking at a needlessly long ingredients list, such a chatbot would need a staggering amount of information just to make words.

On the other hand, a model could be generalized by treating parts of speech as tokens. Such a model would be much more straightforward, as it wouldn't need to know anything about how letters or words behave. It could focus solely on general grammatical rules. It would, for instance, quickly learn that prepositions tend to come before nouns, and adverbs often appear adjacent to verbs. While this type of model would be a grammatical expert, it would have a difficult time producing actual sentences. Just like a baker would need to guess at how to produce "creamed sugar," a grammar-based model wouldn't know which noun should follow a given preposition and what specific verbs and adverbs to pair together. This model's tokens—like the recipe's ingredients—have been overgeneralized, and so they do a poor job of producing sentences and cakes.

The particular problems of musical tokenization

Engineers face several problems in musical tokenization. As in every other medium, they need to strike a balance between representations that are too general and too specific. Do we consider each individual note as a token? Or perhaps each chord should become a token? Perhaps we should consider a chord *and* the melody note it accompanies as a single event, or perhaps we should treat a chord and a melody as separate entities. If two instruments are playing at the same time, do we represent their notes as separate tokens, or do we combine what both instruments are playing into a single token? And then there's the question of audio features. How do you incorporate loudness or timbre? Do you strive to reduce events to something like notes on a page, or do you use something closer to the spectrograms we encountered in Chapter 3?[5]

The ways that musical features intertwine and interact with one another further muddies these waters. As we began to see in Bernstein's description of musical grammar, harmony and melody influence one another. In turn, both influence—and are influenced by—the music's rhythm and meter. And all of these elements contribute to the formation of themes and phrases. Understanding the beat on which a note occurs informs its rhythm. And, the connection can be flipped, vice versa: a passage's rhythms can indicate the beat pattern. Knowing a note's position within a scale can indicate what harmonies to use, and vice versa. Recognizing the harmony can suggest where this musical moment will fit within a phrase... and vice versa. This intricate Gordian thicket presents an explosion of choices and potential pathways for deciding what should and should not count as a musical ingredient.[6] Before I go into any more detail about how these interconnections complicate the construction of musical tokens in machine learning, I will first provide a brief overview of some musical concepts and terminology that will be useful in navigating this topic.

A tour of some musical concepts

To clarify some technical concepts important in musical tokenization, I'll outline a few basic musical characteristics prevalent in Western European and American music, and I'll use Bernstein's linguistic analogies as a jumping-off point.

Most basically, Bernstein (along with most music theory teachers!) discourages his audience from defining pitches primarily by their note names and instead encourages them to think about how pitches behave within the scale. Here, a *scale* is an ordered arrangement of the notes in the musical universe (A, B, C, D, E, F, and G). A *scale degree* is the position of a note within the scale. For the C major scale, we take the notes of the musical universe and arrange them so that they start and end on C:

C–D–E–F–G–A–B–C. Being that it is the first note in the scale, C is scale degree 1. D is scale degree 2, and so on. As we move up through the scale, we eventually reach scale degree 7, the note B. Being that we recognize only seven discrete notes in the basic major scale, there is no scale degree 8: scale degree 7 moves upward to a higher scale degree 1, and the scale begins again. Music is in "the key of C" when scale degree 1 aligns with the note C.

Describing how scale degrees behave, rather than focusing on the names of individual pitches, can help us find patterns in music across different keys. For instance, many descriptions of classical music point out that scale degree 7 frequently progresses to scale degree 1. This means that, in the key of C major, the note B often feels like it's being drawn toward the note C. Regardless of whether you're in C major, F major, or G-sharp major, the seventh degree of the scale will pull toward scale degree 1. Every scale degree has its own set of probable behaviors, and these can be generalized across all parallel keys.[7]

We can also extend this scale degree logic to chords. By viewing harmonies as groups of scale degrees, we can describe how chords behave across different keys. The *Roman numerals* method is a popular way to do exactly this, naming each chord using the Roman numeral corresponding to the scale degree on which the chord is built. In this world, we can talk about V chords moving to I chords, which are chords built upon the fifth and first degrees of the scale, respectively. It's important to remember that individual scale degrees will always be labeled with Arabic numerals while Roman numerals will always refer to chords.

Bernstein also discussed the distances between notes, or musical *intervals*. Intervals are named according to the number of notes they comprise. If scale degree 1 jumps up to scale degree 5, that interval would be a *fifth*, as the distance encompassing both scale degrees contains five notes: 1–2–3–4–5. The interval from scale degree 1 all the way up to the next highest scale degree 1 is what musicians call an *octave*, the musical term for "eighth," as it passes by all seven notes of the scale up to the next scale degree 1, encompassing eight total notes. ("Octave" is usually abbreviated as "8ve," a shorthand I will adopt in this chapter.)

One example of the grammatical expectations associated with intervals is the leap/reversal paradigm. When a melody features an interval that leaps upward, the melody will want to reverse direction and fall back downward, backfilling some of the distance jumped. For instance, a melody jumping an octave upward from scale degree 1 all the way to the next highest scale degree 1 would tend subsequently to move downward in the opposite direction after the large leap.

Intervals combine with scale degrees to create the chords used in this style, the most frequent and fundamental being the *triad*. Triads are three notes (hence the name!) made from stacking two-thirds—a particularly stable and harmonious interval—on top of one another. A "C triad" would start with the note C and add a third above that note, E. Finally, a third above E is added, completing the triad with a G. The C triad, therefore, is made up of the notes C, E, and G. These three notes may be doubled and repeated in any number of octaves; but, any combination of C, E, and G will still be a C major triad. Triads are so basic to harmony that when composers (especially jazz and popular musicians) want to indicate a "C major triad" in a score, they will often simply write the letter "C" as a shorthand for the full triad. Additionally, Roman numerals also usually indicate triads. Because C is scale degree 1 in C major, the I chord in the key/scale will be a C triad.

The notes of a triad can be reordered, and if a composer wants to reorder a triad such that its initial pitch is no longer the lowest, they'll often add a slash after the triad's letter name with another letter to indicate the new, lowest, bass note. For example, C/E means that the chord is a C major triad but E is the bass note. Notes can also be added to a triad to color the harmony. Superscript numerals following the chord names indicate that a particular interval should be added to the triad. A superscript "7" after G (G^7), for instance, indicates that a note an interval of a seventh above G should be added to the G major triad. A V^7 would similarly add a seventh to a V triad.

Meter, or a pattern of strong and weak beats, also plays a crucial role in musical construction. Usually, these beat patterns are either in *quadruple meter*, in which there are four beats per measure, or the waltz-like *triple meter*, with three beats per measure. The former feels something like "ONE–two–*three*–four–ONE–two–*three*–four," while the latter could be counted as "ONE–two–three–ONE–two–three." These patterns create significant expectations, with listeners expecting strong accents and melodic/harmonic arrivals on the first, strongest beats of the measure.

Rhythm, on the other hand, defines how long notes last. Rhythmic durations will fall within the meter's beat pattern. A half note (a note that lasts two beats) that begins on the beginning of a measure will last the full duration of beats 1 and 2, "filling in" those two beats. Rhythms lend melodies recognizable thematic qualities. Recall from Chapter 3 the *short–short–short–LONG* rhythmic idea that pervaded the famous opening theme of Beethoven's Fifth Symphony. Rhythms also have strong connections with meter, as we usually expect longer notes to appear on stronger beats and weaker beats to host shorter notes.

The sticky web of musical representation

Each of these musical characteristics slip between general and specific musical representations, while all intertwine in foundational and complex ways. Figure 4.2 shows how complicated even a simple musical representation can become. Here, we return to the tune "Amazing Grace," now with a simple harmonization underneath the melody.

Readers should be warned: what follows is going to get deep into musical weeds. My Amazing "Grace" excerpt is about 16 measures of music, containing a simple melody harmonized with some simple chords. But, I will spend about a dozen pages, three illustrated figures, and two tables describing all the complex factors underpinning that short excerpt. Unfortunately for my readers, *the depth and breadth of the weeds are the point.* Music is complex, and its complexity breeds layers on layers of computational problems and questions. Readers who might not have the priorities or patience to trek through this muddy musical terrain with me can be easily forgiven to take my word for some of the musical complexities the next several pages place under the microscope.

I've notated "Amazing Grace" in the key of C major, which means that all the notes and chords align with the C major scale. I've added note names and scale degree numbers above the melody. Below the melody, I show "Chord names" that indicate the letter names of each triad being used, using the slashes and added numbers that I described earlier. "C/G," for instance, indicates a C triad with G as the lowest note. G^7 means a G triad with a seventh added. I also add Roman numerals below the chords. As I noted above, the note "C" is scale degree 1, because it's the first note in the C major scale. Therefore, the C triad becomes I, while a D triad would be II because that note is scale degree 2, and so on.

I've also added the intervals between the melody notes in gray. In the first full measure, the melody's C goes up to E, which is an ascending third, while the melody descends by a second in the next measure from E down to D. Additionally, vertical gray arrows show some of the intervals within each chord, along with the interval between the harmony's lowest note and the melody note. For instance, in the first measure, you can see that the harmony's lowest pitch is connected to the melody's C with a gray arrow and the label "8ve," because the melody note is an octave above it. To keep the figure as uncluttered as possible, I have only used these interval notations in the excerpt's first line.

The example also begins with a 3-over-4 designation. The "3" means that "Amazing Grace" has three beats in each measure; the "4" means that a beat lasts one-quarter note. So, each measure will last for a total duration equivalent to three-quarter notes. The piece is therefore in a triple, waltz-like meter.[8] Between the two staves in each system—staves that are bracketed together to indicate that they should be played or sung concurrently are called a *system*—I show the triple beat pattern of each measure with the Arabic numbers "1, 2, 3" in the middle of the systems.

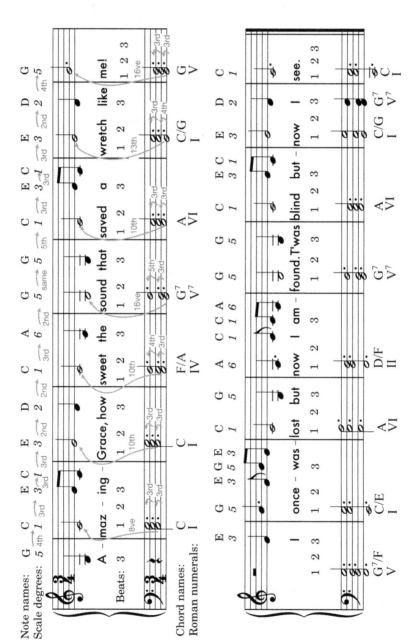

FIGURE 4.2 "Amazing Grace" with chord, melody, and meter/beat annotations.

The piece begins with an incomplete measure that consists of only one beat, and this one beat is fully occupied by one-quarter note.[9] The first syllable of "Amazing" is felt as an "upbeat" on the weak beat 3. It falls into the "downbeat," the strong beat 1 of the first full measure with the second syllable of the word, "maz." That note, the first melody note in the first full measure, is a half note. Half notes last two beats, twice the length of a quarter note.[10] The "maz" of "Amazing" therefore takes up beats 1 and 2 of the first measure, and the following events—the two faster notes on "ing"—occupy beat 3.

The veritable geyser of music theory information flooding this example demonstrates how many musical characteristics are at play in even the simplest of musical passages, and this volcano of details also shows several difficulties in balancing the *general* with the *specific* when representing musical events. For instance, there are five I chords in this piece, and each uses scale degrees 1, 3, and 5, or the notes C, E, and G. Yet each looks a little different. The first measure's I chord has a different note in the melody than the I chord in the second measure, while the I chords in the second line—under "once" and "now"—have different notes in the lowest, bass voice. And, while the I chords used under the words "wretch" and "now" have the same bass and melody notes, a closer look shows that the inner notes are arranged with slightly different intervals. Furthermore, we could distinguish between some of these chords based on their rhythm. For instance, the chord under "now" is shorter than all other I chords in the excerpt. In *general*, these are all I chords, but all have *specific* differences.

Instead of focusing on the harmony as the general event, we could instead focus on the melody. The melody uses scale degree 1 nine times (a *general* event), but there are many *specific* differences in its use. Some instances of scale degree 1 are harmonized by I chords (the "maz" and "ing" of "Amazing," and "see"), but scale degree 1 is also harmonized once by a IV chord ("sweet"), once by a II ("now"), and several times by VI ("saved," "lost," "blind"). Some of these instances share the same bass note, as with the words "sweet and "saved," but even with the same scale degree in the melody and the same bass notes, the harmonies are different. And, as we saw with the I chords under "wretch" and "now," many of these chords are nominally the same, but the internal interval structure is changed ("lost," "blind"). Some of these chords also have different durations, like the final note on "see," which is the only time we see scale degree 1 last three whole beats. One occurrence of a melodic scale degree 1 even happens at a different metric position: the "ing" of "Amazing" is at the very end of its measure, while most other instances of this scale degree occur at measures' beginnings.

This huge amount of information associated with each event makes it difficult to choose exactly how to describe a musical moment. I frame some of this ambiguity in Figure 4.3. The figure highlights how different musical characteristics nest into one another, with more specific features connecting into a more general feature. The general event—the chord or melodic scale degree—sits at the center of a web, with the more specific distinguishing features emanating from that central point. We can distinguish between different types of I chords, for instance, by referencing their different internal intervals or bass notes, and we can distinguish different ways the melody uses scale degree 1 by noting varying metric positions or underlying chords.

But which of these features do we *actually choose* when representing music to a computer? From the standpoint of tokenization, a machine learning method must decide which—if any—of these specific characteristics it should represent with its tokens. As a computer converts music into digital tokens, it needs to choose what musical events it wants to treat as the same, and which events to treat as different. Should all I chords be represented by the same token? For instance, would the first and last measures' I chords be represented as the same token because they both contain C, E, and G? Or should they be distinguished because they involve different intervals, rhythms, and melodies? Should all instances of scale degree 1 be represented identically? Would the C sung in the first full measure be assigned a different token from the C sung in measure 5 because they're harmonized with different chords? If these harmonies and melodic notes are converted into different tokens, should they be connected in some way, or should they be treated as entirely separate? If there are similarities, how will these similarities be compared and measured? For instance, would two chords with the same bass note be more similar than two chords with the same melody note? Is the I chord of measure 1 more similar to that of measure 2 or to the excerpt's final I chord? And, if we are making these sorts of distinctions, how specific should we get? If many subtle differences are built into a model, will it become too complex and ungainly to

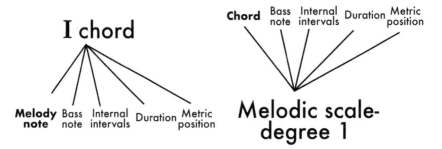

FIGURE 4.3   Two general musical objects connected with their more specific components.

be effective? If instead, we veer toward generalizing, how general should the tokenization become? If we remove all these differences, will the model become too simple to generate effective content?

It's just not clear where to begin when tokenizing this music. And when you do start chunking this music up into digital packages of information, it's not clear where to stop.

I'll return to nitty-gritty of these computational issues below, but there's another abstract issue at play in Figure 4.3. Each domain influences each other domain, and the general and specific collide with one another in feedback loops. As I show with bolded text in the figure, a subservient detail in one situation becomes the most general feature in the other. We distinguish different chords based on the melodic scale degrees above them, and we distinguish different iterations of the same melodic note by their underlying chords. And as the following section shows, these topsy-turvy interrelations are just the tip of the iceberg.

The pianist across the room, and the frustrating redundancies in musical information

When balancing the general with the specific, musical AI engineers must also deal with the interrelations of music's various components. Redundancy is often unavoidable when capturing different pieces of musical information, making it difficult to even discern which components are more general and which are more specific, and complicating an already complex web of possible tokenizations.

Imagine trying to describe exactly what to play at the very beginning of the first full measure of "Amazing Grace" to a pianist sitting across the room. Looking at the music in Figure 4.2's dotted box, you could begin by detailing each note occurring at that moment, telling them something like, "The notes are the C below middle C, the E and G above that, and middle C." Or, if you didn't care which key or scale the piece is in, you might instead say, "Play scale degree 1 as your lowest note, then play a third, fifth, and octave above that scale degree."

With these instructions, however, your pianist doesn't know which of the notes they are playing is the melody, and so they won't know which note to emphasize. You could therefore call out, "The melody uses middle C!"; or "The melody uses the highest scale degree 1!"; or "The melody note is the octave above your lowest note!" As the piece continues, you would need to continue specifying the melody notes. You might say, "Play the E above your first melody note and then return to the first C," or "The next two melody notes are a tenth and an octave higher than your lowest note."[11]

You'd also need to specify the rhythm of these notes. In that first measure, the C triad in the lower staff lasts through the full three beats of the measure.[12] You could therefore add, "The lowest three notes last three beats!"; or "Hold notes that *aren't* the melody for the full measure!" You'd then need to further distinguish the melody's rhythm from the underlying chords, as the melody's first two-beat note is followed by two quicker notes that carve up the measure's last beat. You could invoke the meter's beat pattern by saying, "Start the melody on the downbeat of the first measure, and play E and C sequentially in the beat right before the next measure's strong beat." Alternately, you could treat the rhythm like a timeline and say something like, "Start by playing all the notes, and then two beats later play E and C."

And so on.

Table 4.1 tallies all the characteristics we relied on when dictating "Amazing Grace" to our hypothetical pianist, and Table 4.2 lists the details more specifically. The lefthand column of Table 4.1 shows some basic musical features we used: which notes to select, how long to hold those notes, and where to put them in a measure. We then had several different options for each feature. For instance, when we described which notes to select, we tried specifying note names, intervals, and scale degrees. When we considered the rhythm, we talked both in terms of duration ("two beats long") and reference to the piece's timeline ("two beats later"). Finally, we communicated metric information by using the beat pattern ("beat 1") and beat strength ("the downbeat"). Figure 4.2 lays out these different options for each parameter.

Much of the information across the different categories is redundant. If our hypothetical pianist tried to humor this litany of descriptions about the melody, harmony, and duration, they would eventually become frustrated with how much redundant information we're peppering them with. I've highlighted in black the obviously redundant descriptions in Table 4.2. For instance, giving the intervals in a harmony tells the pianist much the same information as does pitch names or scale degrees.

However, if you noticed the pianist's annoyance and started to pare back your descriptions, you'd soon realize that you were leaving out crucial information. You might begin by saying, "the 'maz' of 'Amazing'

TABLE 4.1 The various ways to describe aspects of a musical moment.

What you're specifying:	*Ways to specify:*
Which notes to select for the harmony and melody	Pitch, scale degree, interval
Rhythm	Note value, position in timeline
Meter	Position in measure, beat strength

TABLE 4.2 A (totally inexhaustive!) list of ways one might specify the features of harmony, melody, duration, and meter at the beginning of "Amazing Grace."

Harmony pitch features	Melody pitch features	Duration features	Meter features
The notes are the C below middle C, E and G above that, and middle C	Melody uses middle C (then E and C again)	Harmony lasts three beats	The harmony begins on beat 1 of a three-beat measure The harmony begins on the strongest beat
The note C is lowest			The harmony continues
C major triad (C, E, G)	Melody uses scale degree 1 (then 3 and 1 again)	Melody lasts two beats (then uses two quicker half-beat notes)	until the next measure's beat 1 (or, to the next downbeat)
Major triad above scale degree 1 (I chord) scale degree 1 is lowest scale degree 1 is lowest, and there's a third, fifth, and octave above it A bass note with two stacked thirds above it	Melody is the octave above lowest note (then rises a third and falls back to original pitch)	The event begins on the second beat of the piece and continues until the fifth beat	The melody begins on the downbeat and continues to the measure's third beat (then divides the third beat into two quicker parts)

begins on the downbeat, and the next melody note starts on beat three." Realizing that there are two beats between beats 1 and 3, you might censor yourself from adding that the second melody note lasts two beats. But these aren't *exactly* redundant pieces of information. If you left out the latter dictum, your pianist wouldn't know how long to hold each note. Do they hold the first note until the next note ("A-maaaaaz-ing"), or do they quickly silence that note and let a moment of empty space ring before the following note ("A-ma-….-zing")?

Situations of this sort abound. Scale degrees and note names express nearly—but not exactly—the same information. If you wanted to make sure that a melody fits into a singer's range, for instance, you'd need to specify exactly which notes are being sung. Providing specific pitches *and* scale degrees gives your pianist a lot of information about the intervals used in a musical sequence, but it doesn't give *all* the intervals needed to construct chords and melodies. Such overlaps and redundancies abound.

Balancing the general, the specific, and the redundant in musical tokenization: an example

And now we return to juggling the ungainly firehose of features associated with each musical moment, and how to neatly package that overflowing deluge into tidy packets. How do you *represent* a musical moment to a computer? Do you give it all the detailed information, and allow for large amounts of redundancy to populate an enormous, highly detailed, and specific system? Or do you lean toward more general representations and tokenizations, choosing some subset of this detailed information, and hope your AI can still reliably produce new musical content?

This is the problem of musical tokenization. If text-based tokenization can be analogized to the discrete ingredients in a recipe, musical tokenization is better analogized to the dynamics of a honeybee colony. In principle, it seems like you should be able to isolate each individual worker, drone, and queen bee and consider that insect's unique contribution to the hive. However, and famously, each honeybee's behaviors are tied into a logic much larger than the sum of its parts. The behavior of a single bee makes little sense without reference to larger trends of behavior within the hive, or to the emergent goals of the hive as a whole. Isolating any single insect from the rest of the hive would be fatal to that bee, detrimental to the collective, and simply wouldn't make sense to anyone studying the motivations and procedures of a honeybee hive. Musical tokenization is more like bees than baking powder. Any single element in the system is both functionally independent and, simultaneously, fatally dependent on the dynamics of the larger system.

To illustrate a concrete example of musical tokenization, I'll show several ways we might represent three short musical moments in "Amazing Grace." I'll also show how these choices relate to, and divide up, training data in which you might find that hymn. This tour will illustrate some issues of tokenization as we make decisions about exactly what musical information the computer "sees" when it engages with the music, and what information will constitute its artificial "mind."

When I initially teach my students how to apply machine learning to chord progressions, I start with a relatively small dataset of hymns that I've collected from several online sources.[13] The tunes are all written in the four-voice, soprano–alto–tenor–bass style of traditional protestant church choirs and digitally notated in MIDI format. In this hymn dataset, there are 427,288 instances where pitches change, either through a change in harmony or a transition to a new melody note. Figure 4.4 illustrates the first full measure of "Amazing Grace," segmented into the three distinct moments that pitches change, which I'll refer to as "slices." To show these discrete slices, I have divided the underlying chord into segments that correspond to each individual melody note. (But, because the actual harmony extends between these slices, ties indicate that these harmony notes are sustained throughout in the actual music.) In the figure, I show three characteristics: 1) combined harmony and melody, 2) the chords' inner intervals, and 3) rhythm and meter. Under each domain, I've laid out various, more exact methods for describing the slices, and I've arranged these such that the most specific are at the top of the figure, and the most general are at the bottom. Under each of these methods, the figure demonstrates how each of the three slices would be represented by a computer.

I've labeled the most specific option for capturing the combined harmony and melody of this passage as "Pitches." This straightforward approach captures exactly the notes occurring at each moment, but it presents some difficulties in terms of the efficiency in using the dataset. For example, this method will consider slices containing any minute variations as different tokens. If the same slice was transposed from C major to the key of D major, or if a high C was substituted for a middle C, a computer would label the resulting event as a completely different token. Further, this method is not particularly helpful in balancing specificity and generalization. Because this representation is so minute and specific, it doesn't narrow down the options within the dataset. Applying this method to my hymn training data, we find that it contains 33,291 different pitch sets. In other words, there would be 33,291 different tokens in this approach. This is not a particularly good generalization of the initial 427,288 events—a machine learning method would need to keep track of these tens of thousands of different chord tokens, their behaviors, and their relationships with one another.

Continuing down the harmony/melody column: in the "Scale degree and intervals" approach, the bass note is designated as a scale degree, and additional notes within each slice are identified by their intervals relative to it. In the hymn dataset, there are 5,284 different tokens using these sorts of combinations. As we have seen, using scale degrees allows us to generalize across different keys: events in C major would now be represented the same way as corresponding events in D major, or in any other key. While this representation is more general, the universe of tokens is still somewhat large. Any time a scale degree changes, or the arrangement of a chord's inner notes is altered even slightly, the computer will tally a totally new and different token.

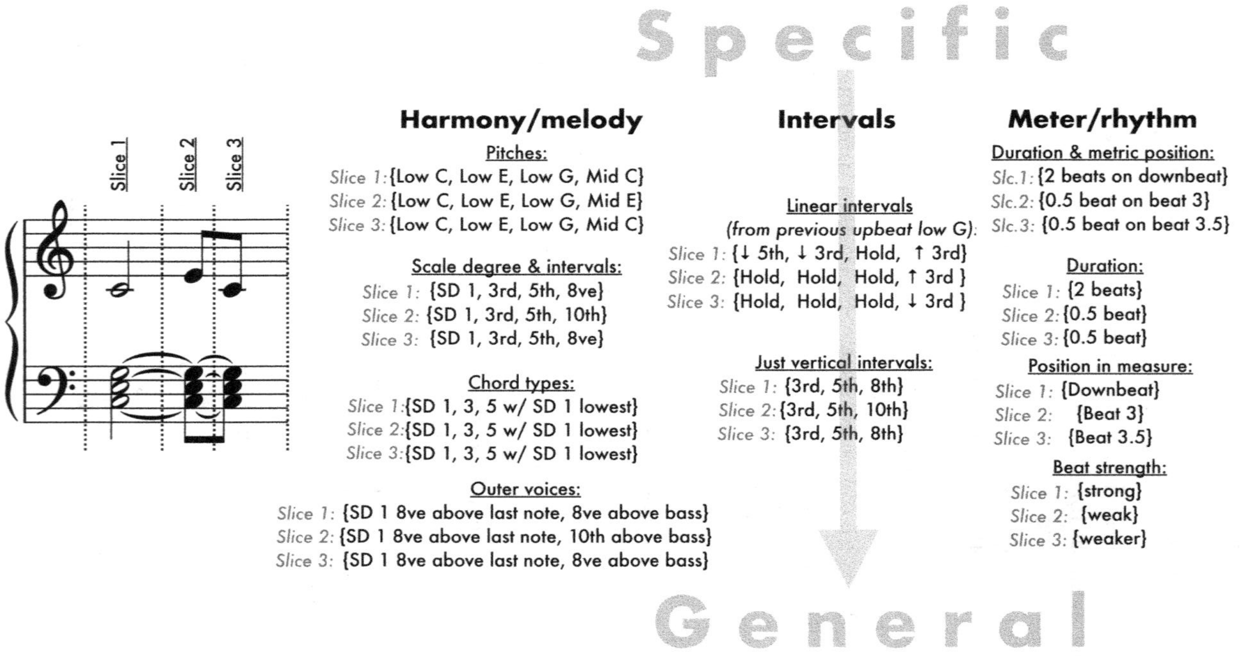

Specific

General

Harmony/melody

Pitches:

Slice 1: [Low C, Low E, Low G, Mid C]
Slice 2: [Low C, Low E, Low G, Mid E]
Slice 3: [Low C, Low E, Low G, Mid C]

Scale degree & intervals:

Slice 1: {SD 1, 3rd, 5th, 8ve}
Slice 2: {SD 1, 3rd, 5th, 10th}
Slice 3: {SD 1, 3rd, 5th, 8ve}

Chord types:

Slice 1: {SD 1, 3, 5 w/ SD 1 lowest}
Slice 2: {SD 1, 3, 5 w/ SD 1 lowest}
Slice 3: {SD 1, 3, 5 w/ SD 1 lowest}

Outer voices:

Slice 1: {SD 1 8ve above last note, 8ve above bass}
Slice 2: {SD 1 8ve above last note, 10th above bass}
Slice 3: {SD 1 8ve above last note, 8ve above bass}

Intervals

Linear intervals
(from previous upbeat low G).

Slice 1: {↓ 5th, ↓ 3rd, Hold, ↑ 3rd}
Slice 2: {Hold, Hold, Hold, ↑ 3rd}
Slice 3: {Hold, Hold, Hold, ↓ 3rd}

Just vertical intervals:

Slice 1: {3rd, 5th, 8th}
Slice 2: {3rd, 5th, 10th}
Slice 3: {3rd, 5th, 8th}

Meter/rhythm

Duration & metric position:

Slc.1: {2 beats on downbeat}
Slc.2: {0.5 beat on beat 3}
Slc.3: {0.5 beat on beat 3.5}

Duration:

Slice 1: {2 beats}
Slice 2: {0.5 beat}
Slice 3: {0.5 beat}

Position in measure:

Slice 1: {Downbeat}
Slice 2: {Beat 3}
Slice 3: {Beat 3.5}

Beat strength:

Slice 1: {strong}
Slice 2: {weak}
Slice 3: {weaker}

Slice 1 Slice 2 Slice 3

FIGURE 4.4 The first three slices of "Amazing Grace" and several ways to tokenize them.

Moving one step down in the figure to the more general "Chord Types" representation, only the scale degree content of each moment is represented. The effects of this generalization are immediately evident in the figure. Because the three slices involve scale degrees 1, 3, and 5 exclusively, each slice becomes identical. This method effectively reduces the complexity of the data, condensing the number of unique representations into a more manageable vocabulary of 3,199 tokens.[14] I also show a fourth, even simpler approach with the "Outer voices" version. Here, only the bass and melody notes are considered, using only the lowest scale degree and the interval of the melody over that bass note. Using this information vastly shrinks the number of tokens. In my hymn dataset, there are only 772 discrete melody/bass pairs.

But these generalizations come at a cost. With the smaller number of tokens—and the corresponding much more general information—it would certainly be easy for a deep learning system to identify how chord types or melody/bass pairs behave. However, these tokens erase a lot of information crucial to writing music. In the "Chord types" approach, information about the melody is deleted, as are the intervals inside individual chords. Just as our proverbial baker would not know the actual quantity of eggs, sugar, and butter to use if a recipe simply listed "creamed sugar," a music writing AI that uses only chord types wouldn't know which note to use in the bass, or how to order the remaining scale degrees. Similarly, in the "Outer voices" approach, the model knows only the skeleton of a passage's bass and melody lines. If a model were to write music using this representation, it wouldn't know how to fill in the inner harmony notes.

A computer program could indeed enhance these approaches by incorporating additional tokens or procedures that add information about melodies or the inner notes of chords. Figure 4.4's middle column shows two ways to tokenize some additional supplementary information about chords, bassline, and melody. The "Linear intervals" representation tracks the distance between the notes of a slice and those of surrounding slices. For instance, the initial upbeat of "Amazing Grace" contains only a single G. With this representation method, the program would measure the interval between that G and each note that follows it. This method will capture every individual pitch in the music by constantly tallying the distances between members of each slice in the piece. Alternately, the "Just vertical intervals" method reckons the distance each pitch sits from the chord's lowest note. In my hymn dataset, there are just over 4,000 unique sets of interval combinations with either approach. These few thousand interval-based tokens could then be combined with the "Chord types" or "Outer voice" tokens to add more information to the general harmony/melody representations.

However, as we saw in our communications with the hypothetical pianist across the room, any interval-based information will replicate some portion of the pitch or scale degree information. Consider the scale degrees within the "Chord type" tokens. If we know that a chord type contains scale degrees 1, 3, and 5, we already know the extent of intervals available to that chord. The chord will inevitably use some shuffled version of those scale degrees, and there's a limited number of permutations between those three scale degrees. The interval of a 2nd, for instance, could never occur in that chord type, because none of those scale degrees are directly adjacent to one another in the scale. Once again, our tokenization process produces potentially redundant information. While information from the Harmony/melody column doesn't *entirely* replicate information from the Intervals column, there's a good amount of overlap between the two approaches.

And what of rhythm and meter? The righthand side of Figure 4.4 illustrates four methods for representing rhythmic and metric aspects of this short passage. The "Duration and metric position" method details the slices' positions within the measure and the duration of each. Decreasing in specificity, the next two representation methods use only metric *or* duration information. The most general representation uses only beat strength, ranking slices occurring on downbeats as the strongest events, followed by slices at a measure's halfway point, quarter point, and so on. In my hymn dataset, there are 16 different metric positions, 17 distinct note durations, and 189 combinations of the two. There are five possible beat strengths.

To get a full representation that captures exactly what notes are happening and when, we would need to create some combination of the harmony/melody, interval, and metric/rhythmic information. We could combine information from the first and third columns into a single token. We might distinguish between "Scale degree and intervals" sets that appear at different positions in the measure. Here, pitch and metric information would be combined into a single token, with the same chord appearing at different positions in the measure represented as different tokens. For instance, {SD1, 3rd, 5th, 8ve} + {two beats on downbeat} would be tokenized differently from {SD1, 3rd, 5th, 8ve} + {0.5 beat on beat 3}.

This solution, however, will explode the number of unique tokens. If there are 16 metric positions and 5,284 scale degree/interval sets, there are 16 x 5,284 combinations, or 84,544 potential tokens. Alternately, we could just treat meter and rhythm as an independent token. Like an adjective modifying its adjacent noun, these tokens would tell a computer the rhythm and metric position of a slice. The issue here, however, is that the training data becomes twice as long and twice as complex.

With a metric modifier appended to each of the 427,288 moments that pitches change in the hymn dataset, you'd double the size of the dataset to 854,576 tokens.

We could also add separate procedures into the deep learning and subsequent generative processes. We could, for instance, train a neural network on very general information like the "Chord types" and "Beat strength" tokens, and then train additional networks on how these chord types and beat strengths connect to particular intervals, melodies, and rhythms. In this situation, new music would be generated by creating chord progressions first, then musical specifics would be layered on top of that harmonic skeleton.[15] This approach will simplify the initial stages of data handling and reduce the complexity of the first harmonic model, but this initial simplicity will be counterbalanced by the addition of a second model that essentially doubles the size of the entire computational process.

And, of course, the addition of moving parts means more decisions for the model's engineers and programmers. Does the model learn beat strength alongside chord progressions? Or does it learn position in a measure? Or perhaps duration and metric position? And at which point is melody introduced into the texture? Are linear or vertical intervals used? The list goes on.

This example shows how difficult it is to balance the general with the specific in musical tokenization. Each time we generalize, we lose information that's crucial to writing and producing actual music. However, adding specific information to our tokens creates huge numbers of differentiated tokens, and these differentiations make it more difficult for a deep learning system to draw reliable patterns and tendencies from its dataset. Additionally, using multiple domains of information domain consistently results in redundancy. Tokens that clarify a particular musical characteristic often replicate information about other musical characteristics without fully determining or exactly overlapping with them.

From where I sit, there's no obvious answer to these issues. In experiments conducted in my own lab with this training data, we've found that different combinations of tokens have different strengths and weaknesses. For instance, combining "Scale degrees and intervals" with "Position in measure" creates very convincing short chord progressions, while using "Outer voices" and "Duration and metric position" together produces better melodies. Before diving into the broader implications arising from the variety of choices available—and the lack of obvious answers—I will first outline additional methods that researchers have explored to address the challenges of musical representation and tokenization.

The vast landscape of musical tokens

My short example illustrates only a fraction of the ways that researchers have attempted to tokenize music for machine learning. For instance, AI researchers like Tsung-Ping Chen and Li Su have been experimenting with using chord symbols and Roman numerals as descriptions of musical moments in much the same way that words and descriptors have been connected with images and objects in visual AI. Just as visual AIs connect a diversity of images with the description "Teddy Bear," these researchers treat a label like the Roman numeral "I" as a connector for the diverse ways this chord can appear in music. On another front, Google's *Bach Doodle* has had success creating hymn-like music in the style of Johann Sebastian Bach by focusing primarily on the intervals between notes. Other researchers focus primarily on melody, with work from Bob Sturm's lab training models on the melodic shapes, rhythms, and metric structures of folk tunes.

Researchers and engineers who use audio data grapple with similar issues of representation. In my last chapter, I outlined the difficulty of converting sound waves into reliable digital information. There, I showed that the combination of fundamental tones with overtones and non-pitched noise can make identifying individual notes in a sound signal very challenging and prone to error. However, should sound engineers successfully extract pitch information from the total sound mass, they would still be presented with the same problems I've outlined throughout this chapter as they puzzle about how to create tokens that adequately capture musical equivalences and differences.

Audio engineers have introduced several potential solutions to this sound-signal work that sidestep the problem of pitch extraction. One approach involves using image-based AI. These models study datasets of spectrogram images and learn how these visual representations of soundwaves look and behave. In other words, these models treat spectrograms as *visual* images and learn the contours, structure, and norms of these images just as any other image-based AI. Then, just as other image-generating AIs produce pictures of teddy bears and skateboards, these models output new spectrogram images, which are then subsequently converted into sound to create music.[16] Other researchers convert waveforms—a manner of graphing sound that focuses on the periodic fluctuation of sound waves—into series of simplified numerical values from which a model can learn patterns. Those numerical patterns can subsequently be used to produce music.[17]

However, any of these approaches will still be dogged by the issues of complexity and redundancy. Even a single instrumental line can have a mindboggling amount of variation within the overtones from note to note. Imagine a violinist playing a romantic solo passage in the key of C. Every time the violinist returns to the note C, for instance, the quality of the note will have a different shade. At one point, the violinist may play the C excitedly, at another point, the note may sound more tense. Even subtle differences like this are the product of changes in the overtone series. Removing those differences and treating all the sound waves as one token might help a neural network learn how a note behaves in its dataset, but it also removes some of the most expressive information available in the sound signal. Similarly, when a model simplifies waveforms to a series of numbers, it's harder to convert those numbers into convincing music.[18]

The resource problem of many possible solutions

In antiquity, when generals of the Roman Empire would arrange their phalanxes for battle, they would place more lines of soldiers at points expected to receive heavier engagement from the opponent. The deeper columns created a stronger barrier against defensive counterattacks, and the rows' increased momentum made it easier to break through the enemy line. However, if the commanders were unsure about where the strongest counteroffensive would occur, they would distribute their forces more evenly across the entire field. This even allocation ensured that the army would be prepared for any eventuality, but a Roman victory would take more time; a more diluted Roman line wouldn't be able to overwhelm the opposing force nearly as quickly as a strategically distributed one. Additionally, if the opponent advanced on only one part of this thinner line, more distant parts of the army would be unable to contribute to the concentrated fighting, with many soldiers not even seeing combat. In this scenario, much of the army's resources remained unused.

The problems of representation and tokenization spread musical AI's resources relatively thin. There is little consensus about the best way to represent music to a machine learning system, and there are many options. Just like the ancient Roman army unsure of exactly where it will engage its foe, researchers are working in many separate spaces. As it stands, teams around the world are making advances within their own particular approaches to musical AI. But because much of this work differs in the fundamentals, a breakthrough for one group of researchers does not necessarily offer immediate benefit to the field as a whole. Certainly, musical AI is advancing. But because resources aimed at answering the problems of tokenization are not concentrated on any single area, it is less likely that a major advance will trigger a paradigm-shifting victory for generative musical AI.

Tokenization in music versus other media

Bernstein's lectures on the overlap between music and language have been met with skepticism from both the linguistic and musical academic communities.[19] Critics frequently argue that Bernstein overly simplifies musical concepts to fit into his linguistic analogies. So much of music's grammar and so many of listeners' expectations are deeply complicated, subtle, and multifaceted, and Bernstein's clean connections between musical and linguistic ideas does justice to neither category. Music is just too complex a knot to untie with linguistic metaphors.

My hunch is that music is more complex than other media, and that music therefore faces a greater number of problems and decisions surrounding computational tokenization.

But I don't *really* know. As I've outlined in this chapter, each musical moment is made up of many interwoven factors constantly overlapping with and influencing one another. This makes it very difficult to figure out how to efficiently represent music to a computer. To me, this seems to contrast with the ways we can carve up a text into discrete words and segments or divide images into their constituent objects. This difference between music and other domains seems to be reflected in the diversity of approaches taken in academic publications and industrial designs.

However, it's also possible that these other domains only seem simple because researchers have already solved their tokenization problems. It could easily be the case that other media are exactly as multifaceted and complicated as music, and that we've simply found better and more efficient ways to approach those media. Musical tokenization might seem so tricky because less time and fewer resources have been allocated to this problem (Chapter 2), or because the available datasets aren't large and consistent enough to support robust testing of different tokenization methods (Chapter 3).

Both explanations are likely true. Music probably does have some unique challenges, and these challenges haven't been given the same time and attention as, say, chatbot technology or facial recognition. But in a lot of ways, it doesn't really matter *why* music faces a tokenization problem, only that it *does*. At present, the question of how to package musical information for a computer presents a steep hill for music researchers. The hill might seem steep because music begins from a disadvantaged position on lower ground. Or the steep slope might be due to the height of the hill itself. Either way, the hill is hard to climb.

However, it is not insurmountable, and breakthroughs are far from impossible. The fact that music poses complicated problems for tokenization does not mean these problems can't or won't be solved. Indeed, several companies appear to be making progress on this front. Here, I'm thinking of the impressive audio output of startups like Udio and Suno mentioned in Chapter 2. Music's tokenization problem is being solved, but it is a still a problem.

Summary

For a machine learning system to process and learn from a dataset, the dataset's contents—its text, images, or music—must be converted into computer readable, discrete elements, or tokens. Tokens are the basic components of a generative AI's learning process. They constitute the building blocks that the model uses when it creates new content. In models that generate text, these tokens can be words, word components, or even letters. In visual models, they can be objects, shapes, or colors. Tokens are the tool through which an AI *represents* some medium in its computational "mind."

Tokenization attempts to balance *generality* with *specificity*. Ideal tokens capture a lot of information about some medium, and they do so efficiently. On the one hand, tokens need to be able to capture information that's specific enough to allow an AI to learn all the subtleties and details necessary for creating convincing content. On the other hand, tokens also need to capture information that is general enough to allow a deep learning process to learn the broadest possible trends and patterns within a dataset.

In music, it's difficult to balance the general with the specific. Musical moments can be described in many different and complementary ways, and it's difficult to select characteristics that don't replicate information from other tokens without excluding crucial data. For instance, a melody note can be discussed in terms of its note name, its position in a scale, its interval above the bass line, its position in a measure, its duration, and so on. Many of these characteristics partially—but not completely—overlap with one another. If you know that melody notes occur on beats 1 and 3 of a measure, you know *something* about those notes' durations, namely that they are separated by two beats. However, you don't know the exact duration of the first note. Should you sing it for the whole two beats? Should you sing it for only one beat and then take a one-beat breath?

Because these pieces of information are overlapping, a computational token *could* simply represent the beats on which these notes occur. But to capture every aspect of a passage, a token *could* also include durational information. In the former, more general case, the tokens would be easier for an AI to learn, but they might lead to errors and imprecision when generating music. In the latter, more specific case, the tokens would produce strictly defined musical durations, but they would pose more difficulties for a deep learning process. Similar issues apply to many aspects of musical construction, including harmony, meter, chord construction, and even audio signals. It's simply not obvious how to represent music in a way that is general enough for successful machine learning and specific enough to capture the nitty-gritty details of musical composition.

Finally, I suggested that these questions pose a problem for research and development of musical AI. When there's a clear way to solve a problem—when there are only a handful of plausible solutions—researchers can focus their time and talent on those limited possibilities. However, because music offers so many possible tokenization options, engineers, researchers, and developers spread their time and attention thinly across these many possibilities. Because musical AI's resources are dispersed, research in any particular area will be slower, and breakthroughs will have less influence over the wider field.

This chapter focused on how music can be converted into representations that a machine learning system can successfully use to build a generative AI. However, when we broaden our perspective to consider larger aspects of how music is composed, musical AI encounters additional challenges. In the next chapter, I will address how music's compositional structure presents unique difficulties for computer learning.

Notes

1 Readers can play around with their own text with OpenAI's tokenizer at platform.openai.com/tokenizer.
2 I am being a bit ungenerous. There are certainly ways to embed some complex relationships into computational tokens. Instead of simply learning contextual similarities, a chatbot can learn features like letter similarity. However, this must be an intentional choice made by engineers. A machine learning algorithm needs to be told what similarities to connect to its abstract tokens.
3 The fact that abstract computational tokens become disconnected from the source material has implications for whether these models represent true intelligence, and whether their processes are genuinely creative. I return to this issue in Chapter 6.
4 What is considered a token can change between datasets and vary according to different models' priorities. In the 1800s, baking powder was not an independent product with reliable ingredients and ratios, and cookbooks would often list the different chemicals that bakers would need to purchase from their local pharmacist to use as leavening agents. Similarly, a different dataset might use "dew" so infrequently or unreliably that a model would be better served by dividing the word into its constituent components.
5 Music scholars have long grappled with the nature and constituency of musical objects (see Goodman 1969). Unlike objects that have some kind of permanent existence, music floats between score, sound, and live performance, and each facet has its own claim to being what music *is*.
6 I do not mean to imply that other media are necessarily *easier* to tokenize than music. There are many levels of complexity at play in language, and I do not want to downplay those. I only want to illustrate why music is hard to tokenize, not necessarily why music is hard*er* than other domains.

7 The tendencies of scale degrees in different types of scales—major, minor, etc.—are not necessarily the same. Here, the qualifier "parallel" means that the keys in question are all of the same basic type.

8 If this is unfamiliar territory for you, you might try counting "ONE–two–three" to yourself while listening to or singing the song.

9 A quarter note is identified by the fact the notehead is filled in and has a stem attached to it.

10 As we saw earlier, half notes appear as open note heads with an attached stem.

11 Unlike scales and scale degrees, intervals don't necessarily repeat beyond the octave. A "tenth" is an interval greater than an octave, and like all intervals, it follows the basic criteria for intervals and their labels that I described earlier in the chapter.

12 Dotted half notes look just like the more basic half note, but they are followed by a little dot. Any time a little dot follows a note, it indicates that the performer should increase the duration by half of its original value. A half note is held for two beats; half of two is one; add the one to the original two; and we find that a dotted half note is held for three beats.

13 We describe this dataset in Cosme-Clifford *et al.* (2023).

14 Musicians might notice that "Chord types" are akin to Roman numerals and, therefore, might be surprised that the number of tokens is not lower. However, this approach will count every added dissonance (any 7th, 9th, 13th, etc.) and every inversion as a separate chord type. It also considers incomplete chords as separate from complete chords. For example, a I chord without a fifth has different scale degree content than a complete triad and is therefore a distinct "chord" in this approach. However, most of these chord types occur very infrequently. There are only 18 chord types that occur more than 1% of the time, and these correspond to the classic Roman numerals and inversions found in any harmony textbook.

15 See Sturm *et al.* (2018), Fernández and Vico (2013), Bodily and Ventura (2022), and Civit *et al.* (2022).

16 See Choi *et al.* (2016), Dhariwal *et al.* (2020), Lee *et al.* (2018), Gourisaria *et al.* (2024), and Joung and Lee (2024).

17 See Briot and Pachet (2018), Dhariwal *et al.* (2020), Copet *et al.* (2023), and Agostinelli *et al.* (2023).

18 Cosme-Clifford (forthcoming) discusses this issue in some detail.

19 Keiler (1978) and Baber (2019).

References and Further Reading

Agostinelli, A., T. I. Denk, Z. Borsos, J. Engel, M. Verzetti, A. Caillon, Q. Huang, A. Jansen, A. Roberts, M. Tagliasacchi, M. Sharifi, N. Zeghidour, and C. Frank. 2023. "MusicLM: Generating Music from Text." arXiv. https://arxiv.org/pdf/2301.11325.

Baber, K. 2019. *Leonard Bernstein and the Language of Jazz.* Champaign, IL: University of Illinois Press.

Bodily, P., and D. Ventura. 2022. "Steerable Music Generation which Satisfies Long-Range Dependency Constraints." *Transactions of the International Society for Music Information Retrieval* 5(1): 71–86. https://doi.org/10.5334/tismir.97.

Briot, J.-P., and F. Pachet. 2018. "Deep Learning for Music Generation: Challenges and Directions." *Neural Computing and Applications* 32(4): 981–993.

Choi, K., G. Fazekas, and M. Sandler. 2016. "Explaining Deep Convolutional Neural Networks on Music Classification." arXiv. https://doi.org/10.48550/arXiv.1607.02444.

Copet, J., F. Kreuk, I. Gat, T. Remez, D. Kant, G. Synnaeve, Y. Adi, and A. Défossez. 2023. "Simple and Controllable Music Generation." arXiv. https://arxiv.org/abs/2306.05284.

Cosme-Clifford, N., J. Symons, K. Kapoor, and C. Wm. White. 2023. "Musicological Interpretability in Generative Transformers." In *Proceedings of the 4th International Symposium on the Internet of Sounds*. IEEE Xplore. https://ieeexplore.ieee.org/xpl/conhome/10335168/proceeding.

Cosme-Clifford, N. forthcoming. "Filter Convolution, Wavelets, and Deep Neural Networks: Building Deep AI Tools for the Analysis of Large Collections of Musical Audio." PhD diss., Yale University.

Civit, M., J. Civit-Masot, F. Cuadrado, M. J. Escalona. 2022. "A Systematic Review of Artificial Intelligence-Based Music Generation: Scope, Applications, and Future Trends." *Expert Systems with Applications* 209. https://doi.org/10.1016/j.eswa.2022.118190.

Dhariwal, P, H. Jun, C. Payne, J. W. Kim, A. Radford, and I. Sutskever. 2020. "Jukebox: A Generative Model for Music." arXiv preprint. arXiv:2005.00341.

Fernández, J. D., and F. Vico. 2013. "AI Methods in Algorithmic Composition: A Comprehensive Survey." *Journal of Artificial Intelligence Research* 48(1): 513–582.

Goodman, N. 1969. *Languages of Art: An Approach to a Theory of Symbols.* Oxford: Clarendon Press.

Gourisaria, M. K., R. Agrawal, M. Sahni, and P. K. Singh. 2024. "Comparative Analysis of Audio Classification with MFCC and STFT Features Using Machine Learning Techniques." *Discover Internet of Things* 4(1): 1.

Joung, H., and K. Lee. 2024. "Music Auto-Tagging with Robust Music Representation Learned via Domain Adversarial Training." arXiv preprint, arXiv:2401.15323.

Keiler, A. 1978. "Bernstein's 'The Unanswered Question' and the Problem of Musical Competence." *The Musical Quarterly* 64(2): 195–222. https://doi.org/10.2307/741445.

Lee, J., J. Park, K. L. Kim, and J. Nam. 2018. "SampleCNN: End-to-End Deep Convolutional Neural Networks Using Very Small Filters for Music Classification." *Applied Sciences* 8(1): 150.

Park, H., J. Kim, J. Nam, and J. Park. 2019. "A Bi-Directional Transformer for Musical Chord Recognition." *Proceedings of the 20th International Society for Music Information Retrieval Conference*, Delft, The Netherlands, 798–803.

Quinn, I., and P. Mavromatis. 2011. "Voice-Leading Prototypes and Harmonic Function in Two Chorale Corpora." In *Mathematics and Computation in Music*, edited by Carlos Agon et al., 230–240. Berlin: Springer.

Rashkovsky, S. 2012. "An Assessment of the Validity of Bernstein's Linguistics in *The Unanswered Question* (1973) and the Boundaries of His Quasi-Scientific Approach." *S2CID* 26396270.

Sturm, R. L., O. Ben-Tal, U. Monaghan, N. Collins, D. Herremans, E. Chew, G. Hadjeres, E. Deruty, and F. Pachet. 2018 "Machine Learning Research That Matters for Music Creation: A Case Study." *Journal of New Music Research* 48(1): 36–55.

Tsung-Ping, C., and L. Su. 2019. "Harmony Transformer: Incorporating Chord Segmentation into Harmony Recognition." *Neural Networks* 12: 15.

Tsung-Ping, C., and L. Su. 2021. "Attend to Chords: Improving Harmonic Analysis of Symbolic Music Using Transformer-Based Models." *Transactions of the International Society for Music Information Retrieval* 4(1): 1–13.

Xu, S. W. Zhao, and J. Guo. 2021. "RefineGAN: Universally Generating Waveforms Better Than Ground Truth with Highly Accurate Pitch and Intensity Responses." arXiv preprint, arXiv:2111.00962.

5
MUSICAL STRUCTURE IS HARD TO LEARN

"It's taken me all my life to learn what not to play."

Dizzy Gillespie

"Life is selection... The work of the gardener is simply to destroy this weed, or that shrub, or that tree, and leave this other to grow."

Ralph Waldo Emerson

When I was in graduate school, I attended a talk by David Cope, one of the first composers to make AI the cornerstone of their musical output. He began working on his program EMI, Experiments in Musical Intelligence, in the 1980s. According to Cope, the project began as a desperate attempt to overcome a crippling case of writer's block, and he wondered if he could use a computer to provide him with compositional ideas. As a proof of concept, Cope set out to replicate the style of Johann Sebastian Bach's four-voice chorales. To do this, Cope transposed all Bach's chorales into the key of C. From there, he tallied the probabilities of every chord type in the corpus, progressing to every other chord type. To produce a new chorale, Cope would have EMI select a chord that it had seen begin a chorale and then select a chord that it had seen follow that chord. It would continue selecting subsequent chords in the same fashion until it completed a chorale. By chaining chords one after another, EMI should create new, Bach-like strings of harmonies.

Cope described this procedure in his talk and—to my delight—took out his computer to produce a new chorale live on the spot. The result was terrible. While each pairing of chords exhibited some harmonic logic,

DOI: 10.4324/9781003587415-5

longer sequences had little coherence. They would meander to surprising—and very un-Bach-like—harmonic areas. However, as Cope talked through this music, he pointed out several short passages that *did* make musical sense. He noted that one of these moments might work well as a phrase's beginning, while some other snippet might serve as that phrase's climax. He then generated another chorale, with similar results.

At this point, I realized that Cope wasn't treating his AI as an independent computational composer. Rather, he viewed it as a tool to generate musical material that he could curate and assemble. The machine would produce a pile of music, and Cope would cut and paste the best parts of that pile into a final product. What Cope specifically added to the music—and what EMI could not comprehend—was *structure*. While individual moments made musical sense, it was up to Cope to sew these individual patches into a larger, coherent, flowing, and sensible musical quilt.

Contemporary AI technology is much more sophisticated than Cope's 1980s programming, but it still suffers from many of the same problems. Flipping through the academic literature on AI tools for music composition, one is struck by how many are designed to be used to produce small musical building blocks that a human composer can arrange into a larger whole.[1] As I mentioned in Chapter 1, the Beethoven X project developed an AI not to compose a symphony in the style of Ludwig Beethoven, but to generate something equivalent to *sketches*, musical fragments drafted by a composer to assemble into a larger musical work. The researchers and composers behind the Beethoven X project then took these AI-made sketches and stitched them into a new Beethoven-like symphony. The same dynamics can be found in hip-hop and EDM production. One recent YouTube video introducing MelodyStudio's beat-generating bot yielded several comments noting that the AI's beats work best when a producer—in the words of user @dakidd264—"adds his own vibe."[2]

Even state-of-the-art AI music bots struggle with structure. In a 2024 post purporting to "crown the best AI music generator," blogger Nigel Powell describes the bots Udio and Suno. "All you have to do is use your ears to curate the best results, and stitch clips together to make a full track," Powell writes. The human is not only the final judge of quality, but—similar to Cope's process back in the 1980s—the human connects AI-generated components to create the end result.[3]

This short tour shows humans consistently sculpting and organizing AI-generated musical materials. In other words, humans are adding the structure that the raw AI-made material seems to lack. In this chapter, I show that machine learning tends to work best with data types that exhibit nested, determined proximities, a concept I introduced in Chapter 1. I then show how music is often constructed in ways that are neither nested, nor determined, nor proximate. These musical properties make it difficult for machine learning to capture crucial aspects of musical organization, and it is unsurprising that humans often need to add structure to AI's musical creations. To show the gap between human-made structures and AI-made music, I provide some analyses of human-made tunes and contrast them with AI-generated music. This analysis will identify various levels of sophistication in how AIs learn musical structure. From these different levels of structural "maturity," I outline *Toddler*, *Child*, and *Adolescent* models, showing the deficits in the understanding of each, and how—like their namesakes—they fall short when compared to "adult" (i.e., expert human) musical composition.

Proximities and the problem of combinatorics

Machine learning models of language will learn which words and phrases tend to follow other words and phrases in the models' training data. Image-based programs make connections between colors and shapes. Voice imitators identify how particular sound colors accompany various spoken syllables. Musical AIs learn how melodies and harmonies fit together to create musical phrases. All of these associations, connections, and building blocks are easier to learn the closer they are in space or time. Shapes and colors are easier to connect if they are adjacent to one another than if they are on far-flung parts of the page. Words in the same sentence are easier to connect than words in different paragraphs. Vocal inflections will be easier to link to a specific consonant when they immediately precede or follow that consonant. And sequential, adjacent chord progressions are easier to associate than chords separated by large swaths of music.

This might seem obvious. *Of course,* it's easier to notice and remember associations between events that occur right next to one another. However, this fact has cascading effects on how machine learning algorithms learn and behave.

Recall from Chapter 2 that machine learning models learn to predict sequences of events using mathematical probabilities. Sequences that happen more often in a model's training data will be more probable (they'll have higher probabilities), and those that happen less often will be less probable (they'll have lower probabilities). In a system like Cope's EMI, for instance, the AI will learn all the individual chords in the Bach chorales, and it will calculate how many times each occurs. When it makes new chord progressions, it will then favor those chords that occur more often—those that are more probable. Probabilities are applied to sequences as well. If chord A moves to chord B 90% of the time in the dataset, when the AI writes chord A, roughly nine times out of ten it will subsequently write chord B. Chord B is highly probable in that context.

The use of probabilities in machine learning systems extends far beyond Cope's relatively simple EMI. For example, deep learning networks use probabilities in a similar way when making connections between their nodes. Events connected with higher probabilities will be generated more often than those with lower probabilities. The architecture of a neural network—or any deep learning model—captures these probabilities with the connections embedded within its computational memory, with stronger connections devoted to higher probabilities. In Chapter 2, I described the strength of neural networks as their ability to make connections between longer periods of time and between larger/longer chunks of their training data due to their more sophisticated and complex computational architectures.

But regardless of the complexity of the architecture, it is always easiest to notice trends and norms in a dataset when they involve events that are close to one another, with the easiest patterns being based on directly adjacent events. For instance, in Chapter 2's deep dive into "Amazing Grace," the notes D and A tended to be adjacent to the notes C, E, and G. These adjacencies encouraged the neural network to associate one group of notes with one series of nodes, and another group of notes with a separate series of nodes. It was easy for a neural network to learn this grouping because the pattern involved events close to one another within the training data or *proximities*.

As another example, consider how shadow works in visual images. Shadows are inherently linked to specific objects and maintain a direct relationship with both the object and its apparent light source, regardless of their separation on a page. When a shadow expands across the ground or a wall, the affected pixels extend in a direct and connected line from the position of the light. Like a sequential flow of notes, shadows operate with some degree of proximity and are relatively easy for a probabilistic machine-learning model to identify.

Mathematically, closer events tend to be easier to connect because of *combinatorics*. Specifically, combinatorics can be used to observe the explosion of possible solutions as you add layers to a problem.

Imagine trying to navigate a series of roads in which you can only turn left, turn right, or continue straight. If your trip is very short, and you only encounter one intersection, you'll have three possible solutions: left, right, and straight. However, if you need to make two different decisions—if there is a second intersection—your options start to immediately balloon. After you make your first choice, you'd come upon the next intersection, where you'd again be confronted with the same left-right-straight trio of options. Your initial decision had three possible routes through the first intersection, and the same will hold true for your next decision. If we are counting the total options possible, we'd count the three left-right-straight options at the first intersection, and a trio of left-right-straight options tacked onto *each and every one of the first three options*. In other words, each of the three initial possibilities presents three additional choices, yielding 3 x 3 possible outcomes. In other words, adding one more intersection doesn't *double* the number of possible routes, it *squares* the possibilities. Because three possible turns follow from each of the three initial options, you'll be presented with nine (3 x 3, or 3^2) options.

The longer this sequence becomes, the larger the universe of possible options. Three turns would offer 27 options (3 x 3 x 3), four turns would have 81 options (3 x 3 x 3 x 3), and so on. The further apart two intersections are, the more extreme the number of other intervening options becomes. By the time you've taken nine turns, 19,682 options have separated your ninth decision from your first decision.

This explosion of possibilities is a major reason that proximities are easier for a machine to learn than events separated from one another. Even if the same sorts of things tend to occur nine events away from one another, so many other intervening options can occur in between that this connection would be hard for a machine to notice.

And the issue becomes even worse when working with probabilities! When a machine learning model tracks how frequently it has seen a long chain of events, it is identifying probabilities at each link in that chain. If our hapless driver were using probabilities to determine their route, they wouldn't need to remember *whether* to turn left, turn right, or continue straight at each intersection, but rather *how often* they've seen each of those choices made in sequence. We can imagine our driver's head starting to spin as they incorporate prior events into their current probabilistic decision, considering questions like: "How frequently do drivers turn right at this intersection if they continued straight at the previous several intersections?," and "Given I turned left five blocks ago, what's the probability I'll also turn left at the upcoming stoplight?" Similarly, a mathematical model will buckle under the weight of calculating the interconnected probabilities of many individual outcomes within long sequences of possible decisions. It will be so much easier for our driver—and for a computer—to remember short sequences of directions and events than long decision chains.

To be sure, many recent innovations in machine learning have responded to this very problem. For instance, one of the benefits of the transformer model—the architecture behind ChatGPT, which I referenced in Chapter 2—is that it allows the model to pay closer attention to regular occurrences separated in time.[4] However, the very fact that engineers are experimenting with these solutions attests to the underlying problem. Any probabilistically oriented model will have a combinatoric issue with separated events, and it will be easier for these machines to connect proximate events than those separated within their dataset.

Determined events and the importance of high probability

Not all probabilities are created equal within machine learning systems. We refer to highly probable events as *determined*, and they often have special roles in any system that relies on probabilities. Specifically, probabilistic machine learning systems thrive on determined events, as they can be easily detected. For instance, if chord B follows chord A 90% of the time within a dataset, it will be easy for a machine learning system to notice that connection, simply because it occurs a lot. If, on the other hand, chord A moves to chord B 55% of the time and to chord C 45% of the time, it will be more difficult for the model to recognize these patterns. Since the chord progressions are less determined, it will take longer for a probabilistic model to notice and learn them.

We can look at shadows again for an example of highly determined processes. The physical properties of light create predictability and consistency within images. Once a shadow pattern is established in one part of an image, it's almost certain that similar shadowing will occur throughout the rest of that image. The relationship between the light source and the shadows it casts is strict and consistent, and it will be repeated across an entire dataset of various images. Such predictable relationships are straightforward for machine learning algorithms to identify and learn.

At their core, these concepts are intuitive. If a red car drives past your kitchen window six out of seven mornings every week, it's easier to notice the driver's travel pattern than if they only pass by your window two mornings per week. The 6/7 (86%) probability is easier to notice than the 2/7 (29%) probability.

Once again, this basic intuition has strong implications for the engineering of neural networks. Because they generate content by tracing pathways through their hidden nodes, if there are no obviously strong pathways between nodes, the output of neural networks will be completely random. The new texts, images, or music they produce will be random, haphazard, and incoherent. If a machine-learned neural network trains on a dataset without highly determined events, none of its pathways become well worn. However, datasets with highly determined sequences give the model a chance to create strong pathways between its hidden nodes, leading to more structure and organization in its outputs.

Nesting, and how events are connected and grouped

Shadows originate from a light source. Identifying this source allows you to understand the common logic behind the various shadows in an image. Knowledge about the source makes the behavior of individual shadows predictable, and it also allows the shadows to be grouped and linked under a single, overarching influence. Because the entire sequence of shadows is governed by a single light source, the individual shadow patterns are *nested* within the broader dynamics of the source.

Neural networks are innovative primarily because of their ability to learn connections between events and patterns on a larger scale than a simple moment-to-moment model can afford. The lefthand side of Figure 5.1 shows a melody with two repeated licks: C–E–G–G–A and G–C. These licks tend to alternate. Sometimes they are immediately connected, but they also appear separated by other pitches. While the whole sequence *can* be represented by a note-to-note grammar—it is, after all, not wholly dissimilar to my earlier "Amazing Grace" example—the most salient aspects of the melody are best described by the larger groupings.

In the righthand side of the figure, I show one possible way that a modified version of the neural network from Chapter 2 might learn these larger groupings. Here, the input only shows the first nine notes of the melody. As the neural network learns the melody, the C–E–G–G–A motif develops a strong connection to the dark gray node, while the G–C lick creates a strong connection to the light gray node. If we expand this to include the rest of the melody, the intervening pitches will be seen to act in less regular ways, establishing no strong connections. All the behaviors are then embedded into the deepest black node.

These larger groups are nested within a single overarching rule for the AI: once you write the motif, you'll write the second motif and then return to the first. Just like an image's shadows all emanating from a light source, this sort of rule allows for individual musical decisions to be nested inside one overarching stricture. When the model writes the five-note sequence C–E–G–G–A, it's not making five decisions. It's only making one. When it subsequently writes the C–G motif, it does not relate each of those notes to all the events that have occurred before. Rather, it only needs to relate this motif to the prior group of notes. The model simplifies its learning and its decision-making process by nesting individual notes into larger groups and determining the rules that govern them.

The most successful deep-learning models of text, speech, and images magnify this capacity. In a written language, certain words tend to follow one another, and when these proximate events are determined, they can

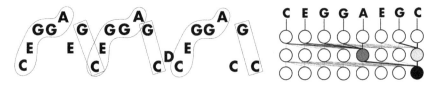

FIGURE 5.1 A melody with note groupings and its representation in a hypothetical neural network.

be easily noticed by a machine learning algorithm. For instance, nouns will almost always follow adjectives in English texts—such a connection would be a "determined proximity." But words are also grouped and connected by their meaning, the style of writing, or the topics being discussed. A paragraph about pies would be governed by the rules of grammar, but it would also use themes associated with that specific topic. Words like "cherry," "pumpkin," or "meat" would likely occur before and around the word "pie," and those modifiers would in turn influence other words in the sentence. If the grammar governing a paragraph about pies could be described as *determined* and *proximate*, the overall "pie" theme *nests* all these words under a single topic.

Images work similarly, with particular images regularly occurring in tandem with one another. If an image of a pumpkin pie sits on top of an orange-and-red checkered tablecloth, some autumnal or turkey-themed table decorations would not seem out of place in the image. These strings of associations are *nested* connections, here nested under a Thanksgiving holiday theme. The motives of Figure 5.1 act analogously. When an image-generating bot includes pumpkin pie, autumnal colors, and Thanksgiving decorations within the same picture, it's not making many different decisions, but one holiday-themed decision, just as C–E–G–G tends to precede G–C in my melody because of the larger thematic organization of that excerpt.

Nested, determined proximities, and what an AI prioritizes

Machine learning systems, deep learning models, neural networks—all these procedures certainly *can* extract features from datasets when those features aren't nested, determined, or proximate. Indeed, as I noted above, many 21st-century AI models have exhibited increasing facility with this very task, with new machine learning models capable of making subtle connections between events in far-flung portions of their training data. However, because events that are close within a sequence, are highly probable, and are connected to some general principle will be learned more easily, they'll often be learned *earlier* within a machine learning procedure. Because nested, determined proximities are simply mathematically simpler for a probabilistic machine to notice and process, these sorts of events can often be prioritized as an AI learns about its training data. These priorities will then be subsequently reflected in the kinds of material that a generative AI will produce.

Recall that models like neural networks iterate through training data, cycling over and over some dataset as they hone their predictions, connections, and probabilities. If a model internalizes nested, determined, and proximate predictions quickly, then these connections will become the first to be strengthened in a deep learning network. Further iterations will elaborate, expand, and add sophistication to these connections, but these first observations will likely serve as the basic arteries of the network. Just as the foundations of a house determine the kinds of structures that can be built above it, so too will nested, determined, and proximate probabilities influence the sorts of features that any iterative probabilistic process can draw from its training data.[5]

The problem of hands and keyboards

As the increased sophistication of AI-generated images captured the public's imagination in early 2023, commentators began noticing a consistent shortcoming among the algorithms. They couldn't draw hands or piano keyboards. In Figure 5.2, I show two images I generated in early 2024 using Hotpot's AI Art Generator (left) and DALL-E4 (right).[6] In both, the players have an unusual number of fingers, and the alternating pattern of black and white keys isn't correct.

The AIs have clearly internalized some amount of proximate knowledge about hands and keyboards. In terms of the keyboard, the programs have learned that black notes are surrounded by white notes. As for fingers, the programs have learned that they come out of hands, that fingernails appear at their ends, that knuckles have a particular placement, and that each finger is separated from the others. But hands and keyboards both exhibit non-proximate structures.

Modern keyboards follow a consistent, repeating pattern of black and white keys: **W–B–W–B–W–W–B–W–B–W–B–W**. As I show in Figure 5.3, this larger pattern contains constituent components. The white/black

FIGURE 5.2 Images of hands on a keyboard generated by Hotpot's AI Art Generator (left) and DALL-E4 (right).

alternations nest together into predictable groups. Pattern 1 contains two pairs ("WBx2") plus an extra white key ("+W"), while pattern 2 consists of three pairs ("WBx3") plus an extra white key ("+W"). Further, pattern 1 and pattern 2 alternate. Should an AI successfully learn keyboard patterns, it would almost certainly *not* learn a full, complex pattern like **W–B–W–B–W–W–B–W–B–W–B–W** as a single chunk. Rather, it would learn by nesting smaller events into larger patterns with highly regular and determined relationships. Figure 5.3 schematizes this approach, showing the structure of a piano's white and black keys as nested, determined, and proximate.[7]

Hands are more difficult. With five digits splaying out from the palm, a hand exhibits proximity, nesting, and determinacy problems. The right-hand side of Figure 5.3 shows a hand in a pointing position. I've noted several aspects of this particular hand, but these features aren't necessarily relations among hands in general. Fingers move somewhat independently of one another. That one finger extends forward, or that the thumb rests on top of the middle finger, doesn't dictate the positions of the remaining fingers. Finger position isn't nested: knowing something about the position of an individual finger doesn't yield much information about the larger whole. Hands can also move in so many different ways that any individual position isn't particularly determined. Every slightly modified ordering of fingers, palms, and wrists introduces a new series of probabilities and connections, making each orientation seem unique. And finally, fingers aren't always directly proximate to one another. The pinky is separated by three other fingers from the thumb, and each pair of fingers may or may not have space between them.

A simple, complicated musical example

In practice, making new music is much more like drawing hands than recreating the melody of Figure 5.1. Figure 5.4 shows the first eight measures

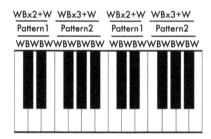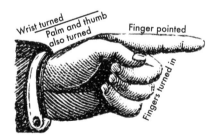

FIGURE 5.3   A keyboard's nested and determined structure and a hand's less nested, less determined structure.[8]

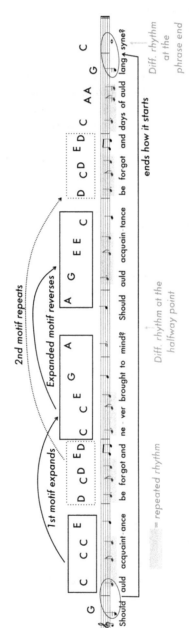

FIGURE 5.4   The melody to the Scottish folk song, "Auld Lang Syne," with structural annotations.

of the New Year's Eve hallmark, "Auld Lang Syne." I've annotated it with a few aspects of the melody's structure that make it easy to sing, coherent, and catchy. As I show with gray boxes, almost every measure starts with the same rhythm, the skipping feel of the long–short–long sequence setting the words "auld acquaint-," "be forgot," and "never brought." The ubiquity of this rhythm makes each measure feel connected to its surrounding measures, but minor variations keep the melody from sounding stagnant. As I show with the light gray annotations, the two measures that do *not* contain this ubiquitous rhythm are the phrase's end and its halfway point. The music comes to rest at these moments, giving singers a natural place to breathe, listeners a momentary reprieve from the driving, dance-like rhythm, and making it clear that the larger eight-measure phrase is divided into two symmetrical four-measure halves.

Above the example, solid boxes show transformations of the opening melodic motif. This motif, with the words "auld acquaintance," reaches up to E. Its first transformation begins with identical notes on the words "never brought to," but the motif is extended, and it ventures higher, up to an A on the word "mind." A subsequent transformation begins the second half of the melodic phrase on the word "Should" in measure 4. Here, the direction of the motif is reversed. Instead of climbing upwards toward the A (C–C–E–G–A), the melody tumbles down from the A (A–G–E–E–C). This yields an overall feeling of a melodic rise into the middle of the phrase followed by a subsequent descent. Additionally, as I show with the circled G–C pairs, the first two notes we hear in the phrase are also the last two notes. Finally, a second motif accompanies both instances of "be forgot and," highlighting the repetition of the text and reminding us that the phrase divides into two symmetrical halves.

Some of this music involves nested, determined, adjacencies. The eight-measure phrase *does* divide nicely into two halves of four bars. These four-bar chunks are directly next to one another, i.e., they are proximate. Further, the second four measures have almost the same sequence of rhythms as does the first; the latter half's rhythms could be considered a nested consequence of the first half. And, even if it is absent for two measures, the repeated rhythm is nearly ubiquitous throughout the example, making it determined.

But much of this music's rhythms and motifs are not nested determined proximities. The main and secondary motifs don't always alternate. The main motif changes with each iteration, and its reversal happens only once. In contrast, the second motif repeats exactly. Finally, the connection between the first and last two note pairs is separated by eight measures and represents an extremely subtle musical relationship. None of these choices seems to arise from some larger, single overarching principle, and they often connect disparate portions of the melody. Plus, compared to other melodies, the motivic structure of "Auld Lang Syne" is not entirely standard. While the repetitions and thematic variations of the melody are clearly organized, it exhibits only one of many possible organizations that could have been used. The "Amazing Grace" melody I analyzed in Chapters 1 and 4, for instance, had a very different organization. In short, many of the music's most notable events aren't nested, determined, or proximate.

This example shows that even simple melodies pose many potential difficulties for machine learning. Important connections are separated by several measures. The theme's developments and expansions aren't necessitated by, or nested into, any one single principle; and, melodic organization can differ significantly from song to song.

A more complicated musical example

When we consider more than a single-line melody, the situation gets even more complicated. Figure 5.5 shows an annotated passage from the absolutely gorgeous song, "If you love beauty," by Clara Schumann. The piece is in the key of D-flat major and is a setting of a German poem "Liebst du um Schönheit" by Friedrich Rückert. A vocalist—usually a soprano— sings the melody accompanied by piano. After a brief introduction from the piano, the singer's melody begins with a musical "basic idea." This is immediately followed by a second idea that responds to the first theme with contrasting material while still retaining the underlying accompaniment pattern. I have delineated these and subsequent musical subdivisions with gray boxes in the figure. The basic idea and its variation lead into a continuation that develops the initial material and flows into the figure's third line. This structure adds a very intentional pacing to the melody. The melody states an idea, repeats that statement, and then expands and concludes the idea. (*I've written the ensuing discussion for readers interested in a deep dive into musical structure. If this isn't up your alley, feel free to skip to the next section!*)

This small phrase contains several aspects that tie the melody and accompaniment together while still lending the music a sense of development. For instance, in measures 1–6, every single quick, eighth-note pulse is articulated. Note how the piano's lower staff, played by the pianist's left hand, prominently features strings of barred eighth notes. In those instances when the left hand is resting—the squiggly little marks at the beginning of each measure and at the ends of measures 5 and 6 are eighth rests—or playing the longer, beamless quarter notes, the pianist's right hand fills in the eighth-note texture. In measure 7, the piano's gestures change, with the earlier harp-like rising pattern being replaced by a falling motion in both hands. However, this new texture continues to articulate every single eighth-note pulse.

FIGURE 5.5 "If you love beauty" by Clara Schumann (1841), poem by Friedrich Rückert, using my translation from the original German.

There are many more small details throughout this phrase that create a sense of coherence. When the voice first enters in measure 3, it introduces a long–short–short rhythm that pervades the melody in the continuation. Additionally, the voice's first leap, between the repeated notes of "If you love" and "beauty," is an interval of a fourth. That interval is immediately reinforced through the variation of the basic idea, as the melody with "Oh, do not love me" outlines the same fourth, this time descending. In the continuation, the melody once again outlines a fourth, this time extended from the B-flat on "Love" all the way to the F of "hair."

As the first phrase comes to an end, Schumann creates several further musical connections. The phrase ends on the note F. That pitch also serves as the piano's highest and lowest notes. Notably, this is *not* scale degree 1 in D-flat, giving the moment a sense of inconclusiveness. The most immediate fallout of this choice is what I've labeled a "Transition" in the figure. To begin her second phrase on scale degree 1, Schumann needs to reorient our ears back to D-flat, and she does so through this short harmonic transition. The prominent F also has long-term implications. Jumping to measure 19 and the end of the second phrase in, under the word "year," we see the voice once again ending on F, echoing the first phrase's conclusion in measure 10. But now, to exhibit a greater feeling of finality, the piano's lowest note is D-flat, which activates the weight of scale degree 1. The first phrase's unusual and striking F becomes reinterpreted as part of a stable D-flat harmony, creating a large-scale connection between the two phrases.

The second phrase begins in measure 11 by repeating the first phrase's basic ideas. Aside from some slight rhythmic variation in the melody, the music in measures 11–14 is identical to the music in measures 3–6. Yet, in measure 15, the second phrase varies the prior material in some new ways. Now, as I show with a dotted box, the piano's accompaniment evokes the harp-like motion it used during the initial basic ideas. While the piano brings back this familiar pattern, the voice introduces a new quicker version of the Long–short–short pattern and even drops out for a measure.

To this point in the song, the voice has treated D-flat as something of a ceiling: the high notes in measures 4, 5, and 12 all leap up to the same D-flat. However, as the second phrase aims toward a conclusion in measures 17–18, the melody rises to a high E-flat, which I've highlighted with a shaded, solid box. The melody therefore feels like it breaks through its previous limit in measure 17, yielding the sense of a climax right before the phrase draws to a close.

As with my description of "Auld Lang Syne," I've outlined much of what makes this music feel like a cohesive idea. To be sure, some of these observations involve nested and proximate decisions. Some of the events are more like inevitable shadows cast from a single light source than the independent fingers of a hand. For instance, the piano's introduction seems to propagate identical or similar shapes in the ensuing measures. The presentation of a basic idea also triggers its subsequent variation in both phrases. Additionally, once we've heard the basic idea/variation/continuation paradigm in the first phrase, the structure of the second phrase seems a *fait accompli*.

However, many connections within this passage are separated by quite a bit of music. For instance, Schumann makes the unusual decision to draw our ears away from D-flat when she ends her first phrase on F. This choice retrospectively makes sense when F becomes reinterpreted as part of a D-flat harmony at the end of the second phrase, but the listener must wait a full eight measures before hearing F's interpolation into the home key. Such connections between phrases are certainly not determined—there are many more standard ways to end a phrase. And, given the distance separating these moments, the ideas are not proximate to one another. Furthermore, the climax in measure 17 dialogues with the sporadic, separated, and definitely-not-proximate vocal high points in measures 4, 12, and 15.

While these sorts of events feel connected, later events are not *caused* by prior events, at least not in the same logical and predictable ways in which a light casts shadows on a wall. The repeated D-flats in the voice don't cause the voice to rise to an E-flat in measure 17, and if the voice had not leaped to the high E-flat in measure 17, we would not have felt some physical law being broken. When the first phrase ends on F, it did not cause measure 10's transition material. Schumann could have, for instance, continued the second phrase in the key of F, or simply plunged back into the key of D-flat.[9] The melody repeats motifs, inserts contrasting material, and moves to high points in *ad hoc* and unpredictable ways. In other words, the events that foster a sense of unity are not only separated in time, they are unpredictable and don't arise from some larger nesting decision.

My analysis only scratches the surface of the compositional expertise a musical AI would need to learn in order to write music like this. I didn't discuss the music's meter, its larger-scale repetitions, or the performance of the lyrics' meanings. All these topics require making connections between developing events separated in time. When music plays with listeners' expectations, cleverly references other songs, or modifies previously used harmonies, it does not exhibit some mechanical, deterministic series of decisions that flow from a larger organizing principle. No: constructing musical structure is a far more fluid and extemporized process.

The Toddlers, Children, and Adolescents of musical AI

How does AI measure up to human composition? What are music bots capable of learning? What do they fail to learn? And in what order do they learn musical features and concepts?

I think of the range of musical AI as falling into three camps. These represent varying levels of musical learning and sophistication, and I refer to them as Toddler, Child, and Adolescent models. Each of these developmental groups has a different relationship with musical structure, and—taken together—they illustrate which aspects of this structure are easy for the models to learn quickly and which take longer to learn. They range from learning only the most basic nested, determined, and proximate musical connections to experimenting with the structural sophistications that make tunes like "Auld Lang Syne" and "If You Love Beauty" feel so coherent. However, the broader and subtler components of musical structure remain out of reach for even the most advanced AI, making their development far from completely mature. At least as I write this paragraph, a fully Adult model that expresses musical structures akin to those in human-made tunes has yet to be developed.

Toddler models are either the product of straightforward machine learning processes, or they use smaller datasets. In both situations, the AI has a limited opportunity to make complex connections within its training data and develop and identify subtle norms and trends. Because of their limited sophistication and training, they tend to rely on proximate connections. Consequently, the music they create tends to make sense on a very local level, but it quickly moves toward rambling and musical directionless. Figure 5.6 shows an excerpt from a simple model called "MidiGPT," which was developed in my lab. MidiGPT uses a transformer neural network to train on the Lakh MIDI dataset, a computer-readable version of the Million Song Dataset of mainstream music.[10] Here, we prompted MidiGPT to continue the famous opening melody of Ludwig Beethoven's "Für Elise." The prompt itself comprises the first four measures of the piece, which begins with the famous repeated E–D-sharp note pairing before moving on to outline several developing harmonies. Rhythmically, Beethoven's melody is characterized by its ubiquitous use of eighth notes.

The AI's work begins in measure 5. As the example shows, MidiGPT repeated and recycled the most prominent aspects of Beethoven's melody: the E–D-sharp note pair and the eighth-note rhythms. I've highlighted instances of this oscillating eighth-note pair in dotted boxes in the figure. As MidiGPT's melody continues, the AI adds new musical ideas, departing further and further from the initial Beethovenian motifs. By the second staff, the melody contains a greater diversity of notes and rhythms, but it is still holding onto the most salient aspects of the opening prompt. The pitch material still surrounds the note E, and the rhythms continue to feature mostly eighth notes. As that line ends, however, the machine veers downward, ending on the note B.

Just like human toddlers adorably wobbling through the world, AIs of the Toddler variety stumble their way through a basic musical grammar. Also like toddlers, these models embody a very early stage of the learning process. A Toddler model can point out the features of music that are easiest and quickest to learn. Conversely, they can reveal what aspects are hard enough to be excluded in this developmental stage. Specifically, these models show that very local, determined proximities are quite easy to learn and replicate. MidiGPT's near obsession with the E–D-sharp pair is a good example—think of how a toddler will repeat their favorite, newly learned phrases constantly (and often at the top of their lungs). And when the model does depart from this obsession, it usually moves between adjacent notes in the scale. I've highlighted these moments in the example. The AI learned that notes in this dataset tend to move in small distances upwards or downward, and it replicated that very determined and proximate melodic behavior. Finally, it recognized that eighth notes pervade the prompt, and it projected that rhythmic profile into its newly generated music. It constructed a nested rule, "use mostly eighth notes," and

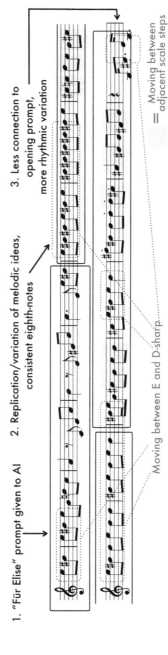

FIGURE 5.6 MidiGPT's continuation of the opening melody of "Für Elise," an example of the Toddler model.

it dutifully applied that stricture. Nearly all of the excerpt's material can be explained by these highly determined, proximate, and nested features.

As one would expect, *Child models* are somewhat more sophisticated than their Toddler counterparts. These models tend to gain sophistication by using larger, more curated datasets, which are often specifically tailored to the type of music the AI aims to reproduce. Child models often rely on more complex computational architecture, use more powerful computing, and may even incorporate human feedback to help hone their final results.[11] Their developmental milestones include the capability to identify some larger nested aspects of musical structure, and the ability to produce music with some basic organizational coherence. However, these tend to be repetitive, predictable, and straightforward.

Boomy.com is a startup supported by Warner Music Group. They offer a generative musical AI that can produce, on demand, a two-minute track in various genres, including Lofi, Electronic Dance Music (EDM), and Relaxing Meditation. Figure 5.7 reproduces an EDM melody I generated using a 2024 version of the bot. My annotations illustrate aspects of the melody's organization. As I show with the smaller boxes, the melody begins with an initial idea that is immediately repeated. The larger boxes show how these smaller repetitions are followed by subsequent pairs of melodic variations. The second variation mirrors its motive, and the third variation ends the melody by stepping upward through the scale to finish on scale degree 1. The melody clearly divides into groups of two or three measures and ends with an apparent concluding gesture.

Just as toddlers represent the first stages of learning, older children embody an advance in learning by beginning to internalize and understand more complex concepts. Boomy certainly acts with some sophistication when it organizes the music into thematic groups. The model has learned to repeat musical material at the measure level and to introduce variations every second bar without fail. It also showcases its developing musical intelligence by maintaining a consistent rhythm throughout the excerpt. This requires a layered understanding of how to apply melodic variations within each measure.

However, the bot treats these groups as rigidly and simplistically as the Toddler model treats its note-to-note progressions. The repetitions are constant, and each of Boomy's variations persistently revolves around scale degree 1, lacking any clear directional movement. Plus, the music is boring! The triple repetition becomes incredibly monotonous, and the unchanging rhythm is too ubiquitous, diminishing any sense of musical action or development. The mirroring motion in the third variation provides novelty, but it does so with no perceptible motivation. The specific variation doesn't feel connected to earlier or later melodic ideas, and it doesn't contribute to a sense of progression. While the final three bars

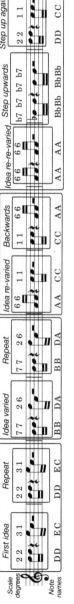

FIGURE 5.7   An EDM melody generated by the Boomy music bot, a prototypical Child model.

show some logical movement as they ascend through the scale, this three-measure gesture emerges from a predominantly two-bar pattern, creating a disjointed imbalance.

Child models certainly learn important aspects of musical structure, but they still fall short on several fronts. Observing where these systems succeed and fall short can help us identify intermediate aspects of musical structure. While Boomy learns to repeat themes, for instance, it does so in a very predictable and pedantic way. As a Child model, it relies on determined sequences; any variation that Boomy uses directly relates to the surrounding material. It seems incapable of invoking any overarching process or development. It has learned to connect directly proximate themes, but it has not learned to make broader connections. And, once again, the single pervasive rhythm casts a nested shadow over the entire excerpt. The model has learned to rely on consistent rhythmic cells, but it has not learned how to create subtle and convincing rhythmic modifications or variations.

Adolescent models exhibit even more sophisticated behaviors, but they still have room to grow and mature. Companies such as Suno, ElevenLabs, and Udio have produced Adolescent models that can generate music from textual prompts specifying a user's desired genre, instrumentation, mood, tempo, or thematic content. These bots tend to produce snippets of music which users can then extend by adding sections before or after the initial output.

Just as teenagers are all-but-adults in many respects, these bots produce music that's quite convincing in certain circumstances. Their machine-generated vocal and instrumental sounds are excellent, and they often produce melodies and harmonies that chain together to create very effective phrases. Indeed, these technologies were good enough for the restaurant chain Red Lobster to use an AI-generated jingle in a 2024 advertising campaign![12]

Figure 5.8 illustrates an excerpt of several phrases generated by Udio on my prompt to write a sung hymn. My annotations show its capacity to generate sophisticated organizational structures. The initial phrase employs a concise basic idea, repeats it, and then transitions to new material. Additionally, the first two phrases maintain a large-scale relationship, with the second phrase echoing the material of the first but with a different conclusion. The third phrase demonstrates a balanced symmetry with an initial rising motion, a complementary descent, and a pause punctuating the midpoint.

However, several elements within this passage show the Adolescent AI's limitations. While the first two phrases begin promisingly, they start to ramble after setting out their basic ideas. After reaching a natural conclusion in the fourth measure, the melody is extended with a further

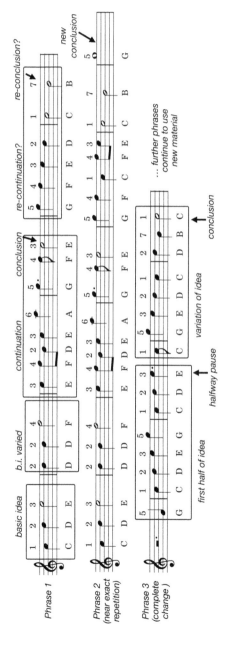

FIGURE 5.8   My annotated transcription of a hymn tune created by Udio's Adolescent model.

continuation and conclusion, making the phrase feel like it's coming to a close twice. The phrase's six measures are grouped into three groups of two, and—at least to my ear—each pair feels disconnected from the others. In particular, after the repetition of the first basic idea, very little material is reused or reworked in subsequent pairs of measures. Furthermore, the fact that these two phrases are six and seven measures long, respectively, is very unusual for this style, as the overwhelming majority of hymn phrases (and phrases in Western tonal music overall!) involve four or eight measures, and pairs of phrases tend to be the same length. Then, instead of reworking the first phrase to achieve a more impactful ending for the second phrase, the AI merely shifts a few notes around and appends new notes to the end. The third phrase appears disjointed from the first two, reintroducing neither the theme nor the characteristic rhythms. Furthermore, the subsequent music—which I haven't notated here—continues to introduce entirely new material. Those initial musical ideas never return. Once again, the transitions between notes predominantly involve simple scale steps, and the rhythm employs a very straightforward series of note values.

Adolescent models show sophistication in their ability to make connections across broader musical structures, yet these connections once again rely primarily on nested determined proximities rather than more subtle, variable, and long-term features. In the hymn tune generated by Udio, the model seems to treat the first two phrases as two adjacent blocks, generating the second phrase by simply tacking on a few new ideas onto the initial paradigm. Similarly, while each phrase's constituent two-measure blocks do create feelings of continuation and closure, their musical themes are minimally related, and the trajectory and direction feel halting. The very fact that the phrase is six measures also would seem to indicate a lack of long-range thinking. Instead of constructing a stylistically expected four-measure phrase, it awkwardly glues together three two-measure chunks. There is also limited thematic recall after the first two phrases—the bot fails to reintroduce melodic ideas from the first two phrases in the third. This would seem to reinforce the idea that the model's intelligence is limited to linking immediate phrase pairs rather than extending to encompass the entire musical complex. The rambling ends of the first and second phrases highlight another limitation: the AI struggles to effectively pace the structure of a phrase from its beginning to its end. It seemingly forgot that it had already concluded its phrase in the fourth measure and disrupts the musical flow by re-continuing and re-concluding the phrase.

Figure 5.9 shows my recomposition of the melodic material generated by Udio. In this version, I have eliminated the final two measures of each melody to tighten the structure. I've also introduced more fluidity and development between the first and second phrases by varying the middle

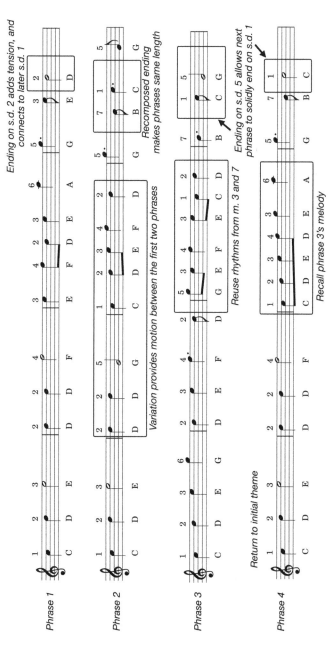

FIGURE 5.9 My "Adult" recomposition of Udio's melody.

of the second line. I've added a fourth phrase that recapitulates the themes, bringing a sense of global return and closure to the composition. The third phrase also no longer ends on scale degree 1, making it feel less stable and producing more drive into the recapitulatory final line. Additionally, the third phrase now includes rhythms that echo the initial melody, enhancing thematic continuity. This restructuring not only improves thematic integration but also gives the piece a more rounded and complete narrative arc.

My recomposition might not be groundbreaking—it's not going to win a Grammy any time soon—but it demonstrates the kind of interweaving structural connections that give music its overall structure and coherence. These connections span various time scales and different musical components, intertwining measure-to-measure connections, thematic development, phrase interplay, and variations between phrase groups in unpredictable yet satisfying ways. While Toddler, Child, and Adolescent models do establish some connections, their music often relies on rigid and predetermined linkages between adjacent musical events. In contrast, an Adult composition integrates variation and repetition across a broad spectrum of structural levels, creates links between diverse musical contexts, and exercises more freedom in its use of these elements.

Music as hands

Toddler, Child, and Adolescent AI models primarily produce music characterized by local connections, frequent repetitions, and block-like structures. They often lack internal thematic development and large-scale connections, which are essential to a lot of human-composed music. The human compositions I've analyzed exhibit much more complex interactions between musical elements. They feature developments and connections that aren't rigidly dictated by previous events, nor are their repetitions and variations always directly adjacent to the themes they reference. Furthermore, these smaller events aren't always strictly nested within a larger framework. Instead, human-made musical connections engage in a dynamic dialogue. They weave together to form a coherent and fluid whole. This level of large-scale interconnectivity is notably absent in AI-generated compositions. To achieve a truly Adult level, it would be essential for AI music models to incorporate these expansive and interconnected musical structures.

The challenges music presents to machine learning are akin to those posed by hands and fingers to image-based AI. Like flailing independent fingers, musical coherence relies on connections that span significant distances, with musical gestures often recalling and elaborating elements from earlier moments. Like a turn of the wrist affects both the pinky and the thumb, a melody interacts with its immediate surroundings, but it can also echo themes from far-flung phrases. These large-scale relationships develop through the recycling and variation of rhythms, musical contours, and note patterns, yet they aren't dictated by any fixed, predictable forces. A dip in the melody in one measure doesn't automatically mean there will be a rise in the next. And, like the nearly infinite variation of hand and finger positions, musical connections and organizations can manifest in a truly cosmic number of ways.

Certainly, some musical styles will be easier for machine learning models to absorb than others. Music that features a verse/chorus structure with identical melodic repetitions will be easier for an AI to learn than strings of improvised jazz solos. The melodic repetitions in a verse/chorus form are both entirely determined and proximate. In contrast, a jazz improvisation will recall, vary, and develop numerous musical ideas across multiple time scales. Such truly sophisticated musical AI model would need to master its subtle, large-scale developments and interconnections. These are the non-nested, undetermined, and nonadjacent connections that make music sound fluid, coherent, convincing, and creative.

Musical structure is also hard for humans to learn

Notably, humans experience many of the same difficulties in internalizing musical structures as deep learning systems. To boot, these difficulties reflect the unique ways that music is learned compared to other media.

Music's distinctive dynamics are especially stark when compared to spoken language. Consider the fact that nearly every reader of this book will be able to write and speak fluent and meaningful sentences in the English language. After all, you're reading a book in English, and almost everyone who can read a language can also write and speak that language. In general, being "fluent" in a language entails both producing and understanding that language. There's an equation between what it means to produce and comprehend English.

This equation is foundational to the theory behind machine learning, and it's a theme that has subtly permeated my previous chapters. Recall that generative machine learning systems, especially neural networks, iterate over datasets to identify recurrent patterns. These patterns are then used to generate new content. A model learns to create content by consuming content. It computationally listens to, reads, or watches a dataset of media, and then it generates new content based on the information it has consumed. In the context of language, this approach makes complete sense. We learn to speak by being spoken to, and we improve our writing skills by reading.[13] Both in human and machine learning, the information gleaned from *consuming* language can usually be used to *produce* language.

Music does not work this way. Most people who consume music cannot produce it. In his 2010 book, *The Geometry of Music*, Dmitri Tymoczko describes this as the "magician's paradox" of musical learning and listening.[14] In Tymoczko's assessment, music performances are akin to magic shows. In both, the audience is unaware of the nuts and bolts behind the show they're (hopefully) enjoying, while the magician and composer are (hopefully) deeply aware of how to construct music and magical illusions. Audiences do not usually share the expertise of the musical or magical entertainer. Instead, they're happy to simply be amazed by the artistry and expertise on stage. This metaphor puts one of the primary differences between music and language into stark contrast: people can be thoughtful, informed, and intelligent musical listeners without having any knowledge about how to compose or produce music.

Now, to be sure, listeners gain a lot of musical knowledge just by listening to music, and music psychologists have provided mountains of evidence that listeners internalize harmonic and melodic expectations through exposure to music alone.[15] And, folks can often hum a tune just by listening to it, and many non-musicians can fabricate their own melodies. My son, for instance, often runs around the house singing silly melodies of his own invention based on those learned in school.

But, there's an imbalance in these musical examples. While someone speaking English has roughly the same level of linguistic sophistication as a fluent English listener, humming a tune or inventing a fun melody isn't quite the same thing as constructing a complete song or composing musical phrases of the same complexity as those that we hear in concerts and on radios and streaming services. We don't learn the inner workings of music construction just by being exposed to it, at least not as thoroughly as spoken language.

To compose music, musicians tend to undergo additional training, be it the self-driven learning of painstakingly picking apart songs with a guitar on your lap, private lessons at a piano, or the formal learning of a music theory or composition classroom. A quick look at any college course catalog illustrates this point clearly. Music majors often complete several semesters of music theory and ear training to (hopefully) grasp the basics of musical grammar. In contrast, I am unaware of any creative writing curriculum that mandates a course in basic English grammar.

Additionally, musical structure is often the hardest thing for pedagogues to teach, and for young musicians to learn. In 1782, the German composer and theorist Heinrich Christoph Koch wrote an exhaustive multivolume treatise on how to write melodies and chord progressions. He placed particular focus on developing melodic structures. He wrote about how to chain together small melodic ideas into phrases and how to group those phrases together into larger, coherent units. However, when Koch starts to consider how melodic ideas might flow throughout a larger section of music, or how to create large-scale musical motion and coherence, he throws up his hands and declares that principles of high-level structure are the realm of "intuition." These broader concepts, Koch admits, are extremely difficult to learn and nearly impossible to reduce to predictable rules and textbook principles.[16]

Koch's eighteenth-century frustrations with teaching formal coherence in music echo the challenges that deep learning faces today in acquiring the ability to produce human-like musical structures. Learning the subtle flow of large-scale structure—the things that make "Auld Lang Syne" and "If You Love Beauty" sound so coherent and organized—is not only difficult for AI, it is also difficult for human musicians to learn. These skills are only internalized after years of careful study and cannot be expressed by straightforward (i.e., nested, determined, and proximate) rules.

If this skill is so challenging for humans, why should we expect it to be any easier for AI? If a person can listen to music all their life but can't compose a melody, should we be surprised when a machine learning algorithm stumbles? If musicians so often benefit from the assistance of teachers, why should we expect a neural network to learn to write sophisticated, complex, and compelling music by observing a dataset— by simply "listening" to music?

Summary, and the future of musical structure in AI

I began this chapter with an anecdote about David Cope and his 1980s-era experiments in musical AI. Decades ago, it seemed plausible that music would progress along a trajectory similar to other media in computer analysis and machine learning: more data, better models, and bigger computers would eventually lead to breakthroughs in musical production. However, many of the shortcomings that plagued Cope's models still haunt musical AI today.

This chapter outlined one of these perennial challenges: musical structure. I discussed how models based on mathematical probabilities—and this includes the deep learning systems at play in 21st-century AI—excel at learning frequent events, successions that follow clear rules or patterns, and connections in close proximity, characteristics I called *nested, determined proximities*. I suggested that AI models will tend to learn these sorts of patterns first in their iterative learning processes and will subsequently privilege these nested, determined proximities when generating new content.

Yet, as we have seen, musical structure consistently deviates from very nested and adjacent patterns. To illustrate this issue, I showed musical AIs with varying levels of sophistication. I termed these Toddler, Child, and Adolescent models, and I compared their outputs to human-created music. My analysis suggested that AI models have not reached the ability to consistently generate subtle, long-term, coherent musical content. To my ear, none of these AIs have yet matured into Adult models.

Humans frequently play a crucial role in the final curation of AI-generated musical content, focusing especially on refining its structure and design. Just as Cope would selectively paste together successful snippets generated by his AI to create a final product, modern music bots like Udio and Suno engage users in a creative process, encouraging them to select and assemble musical elements into a cohesive whole. For instance, a user analyzing the music in Figure 5.8 might prompt the program to generate new variations until the bot produces a version that achieves a more robust large-scale coherence. Since deep learning systems often struggle with large-scale structure, coherence, and flow, human intervention remains essential in enhancing the sophistication of AI-generated music.

However, many recent advancements in musical AI have been supremely impressive, and generative musical machines create better and better music every day. While it may not have advanced as quickly as other media, the progression of musical AI is still impressive. Even though they may be more separated, less determined, and less nested, musical connections do exhibit a learnable consistency and logic, and they are likely learnable by a sufficiently sophisticated musical AI. Like a guitarist meticulously analyzing her favorite songs to learn or how to write her own music, or a composer studying scores under the guidance of a teacher, AI can leverage its data in combination with human feedback to refine its musical output, and it is getting better and better at this task every day.

But audiences might still be disinterested in AI-generated music, even if it were perfectly constructed. Even if engineers overcome every hurdle and begin to construct music that is indistinguishable from music composed by humans, the music might simply not be compelling to audiences. In my next chapter, I address the final suite of issues facing musical AI: how listeners interpret music they know has been created by AI.

Notes

1 See Deruty *et al.* (2022), Aouameur *et al.* (2019), Briot *et al.* (2020), Clark *et al.* (2018), Gioti (2021), Gotham *et al.* (2022), Knotts (2021), and Shneiderman (2007).
2 youtube.com/watch?v=Xrbmb0yZJY0. Accessed October 23, 2024.
3 www.tomsguide.com/ai/suno-vs-udio-7-prompts-to-find-the-best-ai-music -generator. Accessed October 1, 2024.

4 These are "attention heads," as described in Vaswani *et al.* (2017). In transformers, they function something like medium-to-long-term searchlights, panning over events separated over time to search for consistencies.

5 I've discussed these dynamics as they regard musical corpus analysis in White (2022, Chapter 4), and detailed them within a transformer's learning process in my collaboration with Cosme-Clifford *et al.* (2023).

6 See Hughes (2023). DALL-E's Content Policy and Terms specify that the user has copyright over the generated images, and I purchased a commercial license from Hotpot for use of this image.

7 The difficulties image-generating AIs have with keyboards are probably interrelated to their problems with hands. If an AI had a training dataset filled with clear images featuring only keyboards, I suspect that AI would quickly learn the broader organizing patterns of white and black notes. However, in actual images, fingers and hands are often overlain upon keyboards, and so these machine learning models tend to be learning about keyboards *while also* learning about hands. It's possible that the fact that image-generating bots are figuring out keyboard organization while simultaneously struggling with AI's most intractable body part is what makes the layouts of pianos and organs so difficult. Many thanks to Eric Elder for suggesting this explanation.

8 Both of the images in the figure are in the public domain and can be found at commons.wikimedia.org/wiki/File:Cartoon_Piano_Keyboard.jpg and publicdomainfiles.com/show_file.php?id=13972453814748, respectively. Accessed May 1, 2024.

9 Richard Cohn (1992) identifies this as the "autonomy" of thematic material in music. Melodies and musical motifs are not developed as the necessary results of some process initiated by the composer. Rather, they are the product of a series of flexible, indeterminate choices.

10 See Raffel (2016) and Bertin-Mahieux *et al.* (2011). I discussed this dataset a bit in Chapter 3.

11 Human feedback is crucial to many sophisticated AI models. Many image-based models, for instance, rely on human beings to initially identify the objects in the pictures they are training on. Neural networks can even rely on humans to outline the boundaries of objects in those images, which provides guidance for learning the shapes, contours, and variations within objects like teddy bears and skateboards. See Liu (2023) and Dzieza (2023) for discussions on human tagging. Child and Adolescent music-based machine learning models *likely* incorporate similar human input. The human feedback and tagging *likely* tells the model where musical motifs or phrases start, end, and repeat, and this information *likely* becomes incorporated into the model's understanding of musical structure. I use "likely" because most models above a Toddler's pay grade, so to speak, are proprietary. One exception to this is the work being done in Bob Sturm's lab. Sturm has found targeted corpora, human guidance, and structural guidelines useful for sophisticated musical AI. See Sturm *et al.* (2016, 2018), and Ben-Tal *et al.* (2020).

12 Again, we do not know exactly how proprietary models from companies like Udio, ElevenLabs, and Suno work. My analyses employ some educated guesses based on the behaviors I've observed in the machines. These companies have been tight-lipped about their engineering and their training data. I'll cover some of these issues in more detail in Chapter 6.

13 This assumption was present even in the earliest computer models of language. See Shannon (1948), Shannon and Weaver (1949), Meyer (1957), and Cohen (1962). I also have a discussion of this historical dynamic in White (2022). There are also plenty of contrasting marginal cases that serve as exceptions.

My grandmother, for instance, was the daughter of immigrants fleeing conscription into the German army. While she could always understand German, she could never speak German. And as so many young students of Hebrew might tell you after their bar mitzvahs, reading a language doesn't ensure fluency in listening and speaking that language. To my mind, however, these are exceptions that prove the rule.

14 This phenomenon has been identified by many scholars. Fred Lerdhal (1992) distinguishes between what he calls "compositional" and "listening" grammars, and Nicholas Cook (1992) discusses different "modes of listening."

15 This research is far ranging. Huron (2006), Vuvan and Hughes (2019), and Schwitzgebel and White (2021) address how listeners learn about harmonic and melodic organization in certain styles. Krumhansl (1990), Albrecht and Shanahan (2013), and Temperly and Marvin (2008) examine how we hear musical keys. Gjerdingen and Perrott (2008) look at genre identification through the typical use of various instruments. Iversen and Patel (2008) and Jacoby *et al.* (2024) even explore how we locate downbeats. Listeners who are familiar with a style have learned a bevy of musical knowledge about what to expect and when, and these expectations contribute to their experience and enjoyment of the music. Additionally, this learning is done implicitly. Just as babies learn language by listening to the speech around them, we can garner musical expectations simply by listening. For more on this, see Saffran *et al.* (1999, 2000).

16 See Koch (1782), Ito (2013), and Mirka (2009).

References and Further Reading

Albrecht, J. D., and D. Shanahan. 2013. "The Use of Large Corpora to Train a New Type of Key-Finding Algorithm: An Improved Treatment of the Minor Mode." *Music Perception* 31(1): 59–67.

Aouameur, C., P. Esling, and G. Hadjeres. 2019. "Neural drum machine: An interactive system for real-time synthesis of drum sounds." In *Proceedings of the Tenth International Conference on Computational Creativity*, edited by Kazjon Grace, Michael Cook, Dan Ventura, and Mary Lou Maher, 92–99, Charlotte, North Carolina, USA. Association for Computational Creativity.

Ben-Tal, O., M. Harris, and R. Sturm. 2020. "How Music AI Is Useful: Engagements with Composers, Performers and Audiences." *Leonardo* 54: 1–13. https://doi.org/10.1162/leon_a_01959.

Bertin-Mahieux, T., D. P. W. Ellis, B. Whitman, and P. Lamere. 2011. "The Million Song Dataset." In *Proceedings of the 12th International Society for Music Information Retrieval Conference*, edited by Anssi Klapuri and Colby Leider, 591–596. Miami: University of Miami.

Briot, J.-P., G. Hadjeres, and F.-D. Pachet. 2020. *Deep Learning Techniques for Music Generation*. Cham, Switzerland: Springer.

Clark, E., A. S. Ross, C. Tan, Y. Ji, and N. A. Smith. 2018. "Creative Writing with a Machine in the Loop: Case Studies on Slogans and Stories." In *23rd International Conference on Intelligent User Interfaces*, edited by Shlomo Berkovsky, Yoshinori Hijikata, Jun Rekimoto, Margaret Burnett, Mark Billinghurst, 329–340. New York: Association for Computing Machinery.

Cohen, J. E. 1962. "Information Theory and Music." *Behavioral Science* 7(2): 137–163.

Cohn, R. 1992. "The Autonomy of Motives in Schenkerian Accounts of Tonal Music." *Music Theory Spectrum* 14(2): 150–170. https://doi.org/10.2307/746105.

Cook, N. 1992. *Music, Imagination, and Culture*. New York: Oxford University Press.

Cosme-Clifford, N., Symons, J., Kapoor, K., & White, C. 2023. "Musicological Interpretability in Generative Transformers." *Proceedings of the 4th International Symposium on the Internet of Sounds in Pisa, Italy*. https://ieeexplore.ieee.org/xpl/conhome/10335168/proceeding.

Deruty, E., M. Grachten, S. Lattner, J. Nistal, and Cyran Aouameur. 2022. "On the Development and Practice of AI Technology for Contemporary Popular Music Production." *Transactions of the International Society for Music Information Retrieval* 5(1): 35–49. https://doi.org/10.5334/tismir.100.

Dzieza, J. 2023. "AI Is a Lot of Work: As the Technology Becomes Ubiquitous, a Vast Tasker Underclass Is Emerging—and Not Going Anywhere." *The Verge*, June 20. https://www.theverge.com/features/23764584/ai-artificial-intelligence-data-notation-labor-scale-surge-remotasks-openai-chatbots.

Gioti, A.-M. 2021. "Artificial Intelligence for Music Composition." In *Handbook of Artificial Intelligence for Music*, edited by Eduardo Reck Miranda, 53–73. Cham, Switzerland: Springer.

Gjerdingen, R. O., and D. Perrott. 2008. "Scanning the Dial: The Rapid Recognition of Music Genres." *Journal of New Music Research* 37(2): 93–100. https://doi.org/10.1080/09298210802479268.

Gotham, M. R. H., K. Song, N. Böhlefeld, and A. Elgammal. 2022. "Beethoven X: Es könnte sein! (It could be!)." In *Presented at the 3rd Conference on AI Music Creativity, AIMC*. https://zenodo.org/records/7088335.

Hughes, A. 2023. "Why AI-Generated Hands Are the Stuff of Nightmares, Explained by a Scientist." Science Focus. February 4: https://www.sciencefocus.com/future-technology/why-ai-generated-hands-are-the-stuff-of-nightmares-explained-by-a-scientist.

Huron, D. 2006. *Sweet Anticipation: Music and the Psychology of Expectation*. Cambridge, MA: MIT Press.

Ito, J. P. 2013. "Hypermetrical Schemas, Metrical Orientation, and Cognitive-Linguistic Paradigms." *Journal of Music Theory* 57: 47–85.

Iversen, J. R., and A. D. Patel. 2008. "Perception of Rhythmic Grouping Depends on Auditory Experience." *Journal of the Acoustical Society of America* 124(4): 2263–2271.

Jacoby, N., R. Polak, J. A. Grahn, D. J. Cameron, K. M. Lee, R. Godoy, E. A. Undurraga, T. Huanca, T. Thalwitzer, N. Doumbia, D. Goldberg, E. H. Margulis, P. Wong, L. Jure, M. Rocamora, S. Fujii, P. E. Savage, J. Ajimi, R. Konno, S. Oishi, K. Jakubowski, A. Holzapfel, E. Mungan, E. Kaya, P. Rao, M. A. Rohit, S. Alladi, B. Tarr, M. Anglada-Tort, P. Harrison, M. J. McPherson, S. Dolan, A. Durango, and J. H. McDermott. 2024. "Commonality and Variation in Mental Representations of Music Revealed by a Cross-Cultural Comparison of Rhythm Priors in 15 Countries." *Nature Human Behaviour* 8: 846–877.

Koch, H. C. 2007 (1782, 1787, 1793). *Versuch einer Anleitung zur Komposition*. Reprint. Kirchlengern, Germany: Siebert.

Knotts, S., and N. Collins. 2021. "AI-Lectronica: Music AI in Clubs and Studio Production." In *Handbook of Artificial Intelligence for Music*, edited by Eduardo Reck Miranda, 849–871. Cham, Switzerland: Springer.

Krumhansl, C. 1990. *The Cognitive Foundations of Musical Pitch*. Oxford: Oxford University Press.

Lerdhal, F. 1992. "Cognitive Constraints on Compositional Systems." *Contemporary Music Review* 6(2): 97–121.

Liu, Y. 2023. "The Importance of Human-Labeled Data in the Era of LLMs." In *Proceedings of the Thirty-Second International Joint Conference on Artificial Intelligence*, edited by Edith Elkind, 7026–7032. https://doi.org/10.24963/ijcai.2023/802.

Meyer, L. 1957. "Meaning in Music and Information Theory." *The Journal of Aesthetics and Art Criticism* 15(4): 412–424.

Mirka, D. 2009. *Metric Manipulations in Haydn and Mozart: Chamber Music for Strings, 1787–1791*. New York: Oxford University Press.

López, N. N., C. Arthur, and I. Fujinaga. 2019. "Key-Finding Based on a Hidden Markov Model and Key Profiles." In *Proceedings of the 6th International Conference on Digital Libraries for Musicology*, edited by David Rizo, 33–37. New York: Association for Computing Machinery. https://doi.org/10.1145/3358664.3358675.

Patel, A. 2007. *Music, Language, and the Brain*. New York: Oxford University Press.

Powell, N. 2024. "I Tested Suno vs Udio to Crown the Best AI Music Generator." https://www.tomsguide.com/ai/suno-vs-udio-7-prompts-to-find-the-best-ai-music-generator.

Raffel, C. 2016. "Learning-Based Methods for Comparing Sequences, with Applications to Audio-to-MIDI Alignment and Matching." PhD diss., Columbia University.

Saffran, J. R., E. K. Johnson, R. N. Aslin, E. L. Newport. 1999. "Statistical Learning of Tone Sequences by Human Infants and Adults." *Cognition* 70: 27–52.

Saffran, J. R., M. M. Loman, and R. R. W. Robertson. 2000. "Infant Memory for Musical Experiences." *Cognition* 77(1): 1–9.

Shannon, C. E. 1948. "A Mathematical Theory of Communication." *Bell System Technical Journal* 27: 379–423, 623–656.

Shannon, C. E., and Warren Weaver. 1949. *A Mathematical Model of Communication*. Urbana: University of Illinois Press.

Schwitzgebel, E., and C. W. White. 2021. "Effects of Chord Inversion and Bass Patterns on Harmonic Expectancy in Musicians." *Music Perception* 39(1): 41–62.

Sturm, R. L., O. Ben-Tal, U. Monaghan. N. Collins, D. Herremans, E. Chew, G. Hadjeres, E. Deruty, and F. Pachet. 2018. "Machine Learning Research that Matters for Music Creation: A Case Study." *Journal of New Music Research* 48(1): 36–55.

Sturm, R. L., J. F. Santos, O. Ben-Tal, and I. Korshunova. 2016. "Music Transcription Modelling and Composition Using Deep Learning." arXiv preprint. arXiv:1604.08723.

Shneiderman, B. 2007. "Creativity Support Tools: Accelerating Discovery and Innovation." *Communications of the ACM* 50: 20–32.

Temperly, D., and E. W. Marvin. 2008. "Pitch–Class Distribution and the Identification of Key." *Music Perception* 25(3): 193–212.

Tymoczko, D. 2011. *A Geometry of Music: Harmony and Counterpoint in the Extended Common Practice*. New York: Oxford University Press.

Vaswani, A., N. Shazeer, N. Parmar, J. Uszkoreit, Llion Jones, Aidan N. Gomez, Łukasz Kaiser, and Illia Polosukhin. 2017. "Attention Is All You Need." In *Proceedings of the 31st International Conference on Neural Information Processing Systems*, edited by Ulrike von Luxburg, Isabelle Guyon, Samy Bengio, Hanna Wallach, and Rob Fergus, 6000–6010. Red Hook, NY: Curran.

Vuvan, D. T., and B. Hughes. 2019. "Musical Style Affects the Strength of Harmonic Expectancy." *Music & Science* 2: 1–9.

White, C.W. 2022. *The Music in the Data: Corpus Analysis, Music Analysis, and Tonal Traditions*. New York: Routledge.

6

INTERPRETING MUSICAL ARTIFICIAL INTELLIGENCE

"The purpose of life, after all, is to live it, to taste experience to the utmost, to reach out eagerly and without fear for newer and richer experience."

Eleanor Roosevelt

"Oh, I see," said the Tin Woodman. "But, after all, brains are not the best things in the world."
"Have you any?" inquired the Scarecrow.
"No, my head is quite empty," answered the Woodman. "But once I had brains, and a heart also; so, having tried them both, I should much rather have a heart."

The Wonderful Wizard of Oz, L. Frank Baum

In a brief scene in George Orwell's *1984*, the protagonist nonchalantly reports that the tune currently topping the novel's dystopian pop charts was generated by a computational instrument "without any human intervention"— it was created by AI. The character's description of the song is not positive. In his estimation, the music is sugary, vapid, shallow, and devoid of authentic emotional content.

However, as he walks along the streets of London, Orwell's protagonist hears a woman absentmindedly singing the tune while she hangs laundry. The experience immediately transforms the song in his mind. In her "powerful contralto... the woman sang so tunefully as to turn the dreadful rubbish into an almost pleasant sound." The previously vacant tune becomes meaningful and expressive. Her humanity flips the song

DOI: 10.4324/9781003587415-6

from a background saccharine sound wash to something artistic and enjoyable.

There are two explanations for why the woman's rendition of the song was more enjoyable than the AI's version. For one, she could have manipulated the tune to make it sound better. Perhaps she added some lilting rhythmic freedom that was missing in the original. Perhaps she shaped the melody to highlight the contours of the phrase, making high points louder and low points softer. Perhaps her voice just sounded better than whatever mechanized voice came out of Orwell's imagined AI. Or perhaps she even added her own edits to the melody, making it a more elegant sequence of notes.

My previous chapters have been addressing this first explanation. My discussions have all focused on how and why it's hard for an AI—and specifically machine-learned LLMs—to make musical content that's as convincing as that created by human musicians. In *1984*, we could imagine Orwell's AI suffering from these same shortfalls, being simply worse at making music than the singing laundress.

But there's a second explanation, and it's the one I imagine at play in this dystopian scene. I imagine the AI producing flawless artistic content. I imagine it's impossible to distinguish between human-written and machine-made music in Orwell's world. In this reading, *1984*'s protagonist found AI-composed music dull, gray, and emotionless simply by virtue of the fact it was made by something that wasn't human—a computer. However, when he saw a flesh-and-blood human singing the song's words and melody, the tune was transmogrified into something expressive. The very fact that a human entered the artistic process allowed Orwell's character to find meaning and enjoyment in the performance.

If AI overcomes all the obstacles outlined in the previous pages—if computers compose music entirely indistinguishable from human-made music—I believe we still won't enjoy it as much as we enjoy human-made content. As listeners, we won't emotionally connect with music that we know was made by a computer, and we'll yearn for music that definitively connects to the human experience. This chapter explores the human component of music and its implications for AI's development.

I suggest that there are two main reasons we won't connect with AI-generated music: 1) AI programs are not truly creative, at least not in the same way that humans are, and 2) AI does not experience the human world. I'll argue that for music to be heard as meaningful and expressive—for it to be understood as *Art*—it needs both these components, and machine learning systems are not capable of incorporating these components. Both points have been argued for decades or even centuries, and I'll lay out some of the historical background behind each thread. I'll discuss two main retorts that scholars and engineers have often used against these arguments. First, that deep learning models will soon be able to reliably create content so impressive that it will be indistinguishable from human creativity, and second, that future machines will be so sophisticated that they truly can experience the world like a human. In response, I'll argue that a particular type of creativity—what I'll dub *intentional artistic creativity*—is tethered to human-to-human connections and lived bodily experiences, and these relationships can't be replicated. In particular, I'll suggest that debates about generative AI often fail to take the connection between audience and creator into account, and that this connection is particularly evident in music. When we focus on the role that human-to-human contact plays in musical expression, and creativity in general, we start to see clear limits around the kind of content that generative AI will be able to produce convincingly.

The Lovelace Objection, and the definition of *creativity*

Chapter 1 began with a vignette featuring Ada King, Countess of Lovelace, one of the greatest mathematical minds of the 19th century. She was the only child of the poet Lord Byron's marriage to Lady Anne Byron, and from an early age, she was fascinated by mathematics, scientific engineering, and—potentially because of her father's reputed "insanity"—the human brain. Although a consummate member of the aristocracy both through her parentage and through her marriage to William King, the Earl of Lovelace, she worked within these fields throughout her short life. She collaborated with Charles Babbage, the engineer who theorized the first digital computer, and in this capacity she was tasked with translating and annotating an 1842 article by Luigi Federico Menabrea, an Italian professor of mechanics who outlined Babbage's machine for the Royal Academy of Sciences at Brussels. While Menabrea's original explanation was slightly over 8,000 words, Lovelace's notes and annotations would top 20,000. Famously, she described how one might feed the machine certain presets for an iterative task, creating what is generally considered the first computer program.[1]

It is writing these very notes where we joined Ada Lovelace in Chapter 1. In the first of these notes ("Note A"), she described the future potential of the computer. She theorized that any task that can be represented digitally, that is, in the "abstract science of operations," can be translated into a computational function. Singling out music, she writes:

[If] the fundamental relations of pitched sounds in the science of harmony and of musical composition were susceptible of such expression and adaptations [i.e., encoded in computer-readable formats], the engine might compose elaborate and scientific pieces of music of any degree of complexity or extent.

Later in her notes, however, she dismisses the potential of such machinery to ever exhibit true intelligence, stating that the output of such algorithms would simply reorder the components put into them. In other words, computers can only ever process the content given to them, and anything they generate would be a reshuffling of their source content rather than anything creative or new.[2] In Note A, she claims a computer "weaves algebraic patterns" just as the "loom weaves flowers and leaves" into fabric using presets and human-made designs, while in Note G, she writes:

> The Analytical Engine has no pretensions whatever to originate any thing [sic]. It can do whatever we know how to order it to perform. It can follow analysis; but it has no power of anticipating any analytical relations or truths. Its province is to assist us in making available what we are already acquainted with.

In 2024, the Recording Industry Association of America filed a lawsuit against the music-generating AI companies Udio and Suno. This lawsuit follows many similar ones filed by authors, newspapers, visual artists, and graphic designers against a number of AI companies, and the list of such suits gets longer every day. These lawsuits allege precisely what Lovelace argued 181 years prior: Whenever a computer generates content, that content is not *new* and *original* but rather the reordering of the computer's source material. Following this logic, when 21st-century machine learning models train using the work of authors, musicians, or graphic designers, the resulting content is a reconstitution of the original dataset of text, music, or images.

In Lovelace's estimation—and in the allegations of these lawsuits—a computer cannot be *creative*. In Chapter 2, I relied on a basic definition of "creativity" with two essential criteria: that a creative act must 1) make new, novel content that 2) conforms to some series of norms rendering that content understandable and valuable to an audience. In that discussion, I worked under the assumption that a process that did not directly replicate its source material *verbatim* was generating something novel and was therefore "creative."

Lovelace, however, suggested a higher bar. To her, processing and reorganizing source material is just reshuffling, even with the complex processes we see used in contemporary neural networks.[3] To Lovelace, computers are not creative. Instead, she imagined some deeper transformative process at the root of true human creation, some spark that produces original content fundamentally distinct from any previous creation.

This argument makes a lot of sense, given how I've described AI's learning processes. In Chapter 2, I outlined how these systems identify patterns in some datasets, and in Chapter 4, we saw how these patterns are represented as mere strings of references within a computer's digital mind. Given that these patterns are regurgitated from the source content, they are not "creative" under Lovelace's logic. Instead, they are better understood as presets determined by the original dataset. This is the *Lovelace Objection* to artistic generative AI. Here, computational creativity will always be limited to reshuffling its source material, regardless of how complex its reorganizing process is. The Lovelace Objection also moves beyond the definition of creativity I adopted in Chapter 2. It assumes that true human creativity involves something more than reordering source data, some more holistic and synthetic method of creating content.[4]

Before complicating this objection and diving into various rebuttals, I want to outline the basics of a second historical objection to generative AI, that of the mid 20th-century neuroscientist, George Jefferson.

The Jefferson Objection, and the humanity of art

In 1949, George Jefferson, a professor of neurosurgery at the University of Manchester, published "The Mind of Mechanical Man" in the *British Medical Journal*. The article is a response to the new "calculating machines" ("computers" to us) that burst onto the scene in the handful of years since the end of World War II. Jefferson noted that computer engineering has many similarities to the human nervous system in the way that it sends, stores, and analyzes information through a bevy of interconnected electric pulses. These similarities made him wonder whether mechanical minds could have the capacity to mimic human cognitive processes. Jefferson summarized his conclusion:

> *Not until a machine can write a sonnet or compose a concerto because of thoughts and emotions felt, and not by the chance fall of symbols, could we agree that machine equals brain—that is, not only write it but know that it had written it. No mechanism could feel (and not merely artificially signal, an easy contrivance) pleasure at its successes, grief when its valves fuse, be warmed by flattery, be made miserable by its mistakes, be charmed by sex, be angry or depressed when it cannot get what it wants... I conclude, therefore, that although [an] electronic apparatus can probably parallel some of the simpler activities of [the] nerve and spinal cord... it still does not take us over the blank wall that confronts us when we come to explore thinking, the ultimate in mind. Nor do I believe that it will do so.*

To Jefferson, any computational system will be found lacking because it doesn't experience, interact, and feel the world around it. Importantly, he doesn't seem to care whether it *can* "write a sonnet or compose a concerto," but that it does so "because of thoughts and emotions." If Lovelace focuses on the mechanical processes underpinning the creation of new content, Jefferson worries about the *cause* behind the process. He believes any art or music that AI generates will be found hollow because it lacks the experience and motivations that define a flesh-and-blood human mind.

Again, this argument makes sense, given what we've seen in previous chapters. In particular, Chapter 4 showed the level of abstraction and removal that a tokenization process engages in. Not only are deep learning machines focused on the patterns within a dataset rather than the underlying meaning of those patterns, but the items of data in an AI's "mind" are mere computational placeholders for whatever original content may have existed in its dataset. Machine-learned models, then, are several layers removed from the actual feeling—the pleasure, grief, and misery Jefferson describes—that might have inspired the dataset.

The *Jefferson Objection*, then, posits that human experience forms the essential foundation for creative and artistic content. By definition, computational systems can never replicate this experience. Because expression relies on human experience, AI-made visual art, music, dance, and literature will be hollow. Regardless of how complex, detailed, and human-like a computational system might become, because it does not share our lived experiences, there will always be a chasm between human- and AI-produced content.

As with the Lovelace Objection, there are plenty of pros and cons surrounding the Jefferson Objection. To begin engaging with these issues, I'll outline two famous rebuttals to these arguments, beginning with one from a founder of modern computing, Alan Turing.

Turing's retort

In Alan Turing's 1950 paper, "Computing Machinery and Intelligence," he argued that computers will likely exhibit some form of intelligence at some point in the future. The paper is famous for proposing the *Imitation Game*, what later researchers would call a *Turing Test*. In its original form, the Turing Test involves a human having a conversation with another entity via text, typing on a computer, and seeing responses on the screen. The interlocutor is either a human or a text-generating chatbot, but its identity is unknown to the conversing human. If a chatbot fools the human into believing it's another human, it has won the Imitation Game. This paradigm has been extended and abstracted into several creative domains and is often used to judge whether some computer program produces content that's passable as a human creation. If a human audience believes that some prose, poetry, image, or music generated by an AI was actually created by a human, that AI has "passed the Turing Test."

Turing did not originally view his test as a method of AI quality control. Rather, he imagined his test as a way to determine whether a machine can exhibit some form of intelligence. In Turing's estimation, we only base our belief that other humans are "intelligent" according to the content of the various sorts of communication we exchange with one another. We do not peer into the neurons within our fellow humans' skulls to deduce whether they have a consciousness and intelligence similar to our own. No, we make this deduction by exchanging conversation, text, art, music, and so on. If someone produces intelligent content, they must be intelligent. They've passed a simple version of the human-to-human Turing Test.

Turing extended this logic to computer programs. If computers create content that *seems* to come from human-like intelligence, we can reasonably assume that the computer possesses such intelligence. By locating the definition of "thinking" in this way, Turing argued that a machine that reliably produces human-like content can "think." In this logic, the underlying programming or engineering is beside the point. It doesn't matter whether a program's inner workings mimic neurology or whether its consciousness is structured exactly like that of a human. After all, given that we never glance into other humans' consciousnesses or brains, those facts don't really matter to our day-to-day definition of consciousness anyhow.[5]

Turing therefore has no time for the Lovelace and Jefferson Objections.[6] It doesn't matter what sorts of experiences or processes lie behind an AI, only that it *acts like* it's intelligent. From this standpoint, an AI that reorders its source data so convincingly that its content seems "new" will counter the Lovelace Objection. An AI that creates content that seems like it's experienced deep human emotion similarly undercuts the Jefferson Objection. And from where Turing sat in the middle of the 20th century, he saw no reason that sophisticated future computers would not be able to accomplish both tasks with flying colors.

The Haugeland-Chalmers retort

Some theorists go even further. They suggest that AI doesn't just act like human consciousness, but that it can feature the same inner workings as a human's consciousness. To these thinkers, computers are theoretically capable of learning, remembering, thinking, feeling, and producing in much the same way as humans, and technologies like neural networks and LLMs go some distance in this direction.

In 1985, the cognitive philosopher John Haugeland coined the term *Good Old Fashioned Artificial Intelligence* (GOFAI) to describe the majority of 20th-century computer modeling. At the heart of GOFAI is the idea that an analyst can pinpoint specific ways objects or concepts are represented within a computer program. For instance, if you were to examine the computational framework of a GOFAI designed to generate images, you could precisely identify the individual parts of the program responsible for creating images of teddy bears and those responsible for skateboards. Similarly, in a music-generating GOFAI, it would be possible to specify exactly which parts of the program are responsible for creating specific musical elements such as scale degree 1, scale degree 5, half notes, quarter notes, downbeats, and phrase lengths.

Haugeland contends that the human brain and mind do not operate like GOFAI. It's notoriously challenging to identify the particular neurons associated with particular cognitive concepts or actions.[7] Unlike a library where each book has a specific place on a specific shelf, the human brain is not compartmentalized into discrete slots for each thought or idea. Instead, human cognition resembles ever-changing cloud formations, congealing into shapes only to dissolve and rearrange into new configurations. Brain regions interact dynamically, resonating with various networks of neurons to generate thoughts, memories, or emotions.

Haugeland argues that more recent and complex computational architectures like neural networks mirror the abstract and interconnected nature of the human brain. He refers to these systems as New Fangled AI (NFAI). Unlike traditional AI systems, the complex neural networks that form the basis of deep learning systems do not maintain straightforward one-to-one correspondences. For example, within the computational architecture of Google's chatbot Gemini, there is no single location where the concept of a "sonnet" resides. Nor can one pinpoint a specific node in the neural network of the image generator Dall-E where the shape of a teddy bear is stored. The same goes for trying to locate a distinct place in the Udio musical AI that represents scale degree 1. Instead, these concepts exist as part of a complex web of interlaced connections that extend deep within the network's layers.

To Haugeland, the amorphous and complex networks of connections within modern AI systems closely resemble the dynamics of human cognition. This logic suggests that contemporary deep learning models like LLMs, with their enormous computational architectures, are structured in ways that parallel human thought processes. This design allows them to approximate how the human mind operates, making them increasingly capable of mimicking human reasoning and learning.

The philosopher David Chalmers adds a further layer to this argument. Chalmers emphasizes a key aspect of human cognition: our minds integrate various senses and modes of expression in composing our thoughts. For instance, red and orange remind us of warm temperatures, and that association is an important part of how and where those colors are used in images. A picture of a cookie might remind us of a particular taste associated with a specific childhood memory, while a musical gesture might be informed by the types of dance moves it often accompanies. Such associations will contribute to how a painter or composer might use these ingredients. Colors, cookies, and musical gestures gain meaning by reaching across different senses, types of experience, and modes of expression.

Chalmers contrasts this with the domain specificity of current machine-learning models. Chatbots, for instance, operate primarily with linguistic data, image generating AIs handle visual inputs and their descriptions, and music-making LLMs focus on auditory elements. These systems are constrained within one or two mediums and therefore cannot make complex connections across different senses and modes of experiencing the world. An image-generating AI might know how to place a picture of a cookie in a larger tableau to evoke a sense of nostalgia, but it wouldn't know anything about the cookie's taste or its reference to times past.[8]

However, Chalmers argues that recent advancements in AI technology are gradually overcoming these limitations by integrating multiple types of knowledge. He introduces the concept of an *LLM+*, a more advanced model that learns connections between several domains. Such a system would enhance the AI's ability to generate more sophisticated and nuanced content. Imagine a music-making machine that understands the imagery of lyrics, an image-generating program that connects pictures of baked goods with actual tastes, or a chatbot that knows the warmth of a color. The operations of such models would better approximate human cognitive processes. They would learn and create in a manner much more similar to how humans undertake these tasks.

Chalmers envisions LLM+s incorporating sensory data from optical scanners, audio processors, or even tactile sensors to create a richer, more interconnected AI system. This integration would enable the AI to associate sensory experiences with data inputs, like linking the tactile sensation of heat with "warm" colors, or a specific taste with the image of a cookie. Theoretically, an LLM+ that harnesses datasets across a wide range of media and sensory inputs could parallel human consciousness by learning, thinking, and interacting with the world across different senses and domains, creating memories and associations like a human.

The Haugeland-Chalmers retort further undercuts the Lovelace and Jefferson Objections. Lovelace focused on the limitations of computational systems, suggesting they could only reshuffle existing inputs, while Jefferson emphasized the absence of emotions and experiences in machines. Contrary to these views, Haugeland and Chalmers propose that, through the advancement of abstract programming and the use of increasingly diverse and integrated datasets, computers might indeed mimic human cognitive processes and potentially share a similar inner life. They argue that these technological improvements could enable AI to perform tasks with a complexity and adaptiveness that resembles human thought, erasing the cognitive gap between machines and humans.

Intentional artistic creativity

But I don't buy it. I think these retorts are so mesmerized by AI's output and engineering that they forget the crucial role the audience plays in realizing artistic expression and how the audience relates to the creators of that expression. Do we value the origins of creative content? Do we consider the internal experiences and emotions of the creators? Is an artist's or composer's identity important to us when we engage with their work?

To my mind, the answer is a clear and resounding "yes." My reasoning focuses on three words: *Intention*, *Art*, and *Creativity*.

I find philosopher Daniel Dennett's concept of the *Intentional Stance* particularly useful in approaching the first part of my formulation. Dennett's theory focuses on the many different ways that humans interpret events in the world. For instance, when we think of a car starting, we make sense of that event in terms of the mechanical processes involved. The car is switched on as a result of the interaction of its ignition system with the rest of the internal combustion engine. As we ponder the car, we might also consider how useful it is as a mode of travel, or we might worry about the machine's contributions to air pollution. However, we do not consider the car's *intention*. Because it's a machine, we don't ask ourselves about the car's motivation for switching on.

In contrast, when we focus on a *person* starting a car, our interpretation shifts. When a human turns an ignition switch, it's not a strictly mechanical event. Rather, it is the result of some human motivation. Perhaps the driver needs to travel somewhere. Perhaps they need to pick up their child at school or get groceries. Or perhaps they're starting the car to run an engine diagnostic. Whatever it may be, they started the car *for a reason*. When we observe human actions, we attribute to them some series of motivations.

This is the Intentional Stance. It's a viewpoint that believes actions are undertaken for some reason and with thoughtful motivation. On the one hand, the Intentional Stance involves empathy. We know what motivates our own actions when we engage a car's ignition, and we project that motivation onto other humans. On the other hand, it depends on viewers' expectations of the sophistication of outside actors. We do not imagine an automobile having consciousness, but we do imagine another human driver having a thoughtful inner life.

We constantly navigate the Intentional Stance in the realms of art and creativity. Consider a subway map displayed on a train platform. We would likely interact with it like we would the mechanics of a car's engine. We engage with it pragmatically, and we use it to figure out which trains to take to our desired destination. If the map is particularly well designed, we might even admire its clarity, usefulness, and aesthetic appeal. However, our appreciation remains anchored to its functionality and efficiency in fulfilling its purpose.

But what if an artist created that same subway map and hung it in a museum? Staring at the map as an installation, our stance would be dramatically different from when we stood on the train platform. We would wonder what the artist meant to convey with their choice of a subway map. We'd consider what the creator was trying to express. Maybe we'd wonder why they chose a particular set of colors or why they used a particular layout. Maybe we'd even scoff at this piece of modern art, thinking how silly and gimmicky it is to hang a subway map in an art gallery. Maybe we'd shrug our shoulders, bewildered at the artist's objectives.

Whatever our reaction, we'd be taking an Intentional Stance toward the map. The platform map and the gallery map may be identical in terms of visual content, but because we know the gallery map was placed there by a human for some reason, we make sense of it very differently than the utilitarian map on the subway wall. We *interpret* the gallery map while we *use* the map on the subway wall.

These different paradigms begin addressing the second of my trio of words, "Art," and these differences can be usefully articulated in the age-old distinction between Artworks and Craftworks.[9] According to this traditional dichotomy, a Craftwork is characterized by its remarkable construction. It engages its audience through its complexity, sophistication, and the skill used to create it. It elicits pleasure, enjoyment, and occasionally awe. Typically, Craftworks serve some practical purpose or utility. Examples abound: a well-crafted table, a handmade pot, finely wrought jewelry, or an elegantly designed subway map. Each of these items not only performs its intended function effectively but also delights the senses through its craftsmanship.[10]

However, Artworks are, in the words of the philosopher Arthur Danto, "interpreted things."[11] An Artwork compels an audience to probe deeper into its meaning, to feel emotions, and to ponder some underlying message. It invites the audience to find meaning and expression in its contents. When a painting encourages introspection, a poem makes you cry, or a novel gives you chills, these things become Art. (From now on, I will use capital-A "Art" when referring to this concept, differentiating it from the more general visual "art.")

Just as in the Intentional Stance, Art depends on how humans engage with some given content. The content will change in the mind of the viewer depending on how they are encouraged or inspired to interpret it. In my formulation, the Intentional Stance and Art are intrinsically linked. A piece of content is elevated to the status of an Artwork when it compels its audience to ascribe meaningful interpretation and adopt the Intentional Stance to discern that underlying meaning and motivation.

This definition of Art and Intention can lead to a honed understanding of the last of my word triplet: "Creativity." In Chapter 2, I described creativity as a process that generates new, useful, and legible content. By integrating Art and Intention in this definition, we can carve out a special case for creative content that encourages an audience to interpret, analyze, empathize, and find meaning. I'll refer to this sort of content as *intentional artistic creativity*. Works of intentional artistic creativity are those that provoke thought, encourage interpretation, or foster emotional engagement with an audience. The audience believes that the content has some motivation or expressive intention behind it, and they are compelled to interpret it accordingly. Intentional artistic creativity is understandable and useful, but it is also *meaningful*.

By shifting the focus toward the entity that creates the content, the concept of intentional artistic creativity begins to undercut Turing's retort. In this paradigm, an audience isn't simply consuming a complex Artwork, shrugging their shoulders, and assuming the entity that created that Artwork must be correspondingly sophisticated. Instead, the audience probes and considers that Artwork, in part, by trying to figure out what sorts of motivations and inner life might be behind the content. Here, we care about who made the content and why it was made. Unlike the Turing Test, in which the identity of the creator is completely removed from an audience's interpretive calculus, the intentional artistic creativity paradigm requires that Art encourage an audience to probe the identity and intention of its creator to figure out the underlying meaning.

But surely a computer program can exhibit "motivations" and have an "inner life." After all, the Haugeland-Chalmers retort suggested that sufficiently complex computer engineering could exhibit human-like consciousness. Couldn't such a sophisticated model exhibit intention and artistry?

Once again, I assert that the answer is a resounding "no." My position is grounded in the essential role that lived human experience plays in intentional artistic creativity. But before I can effectively revisit and reframe the Lovelace and Jefferson Objections through the lens of intentional artistic creativity, we must first delineate the role that bodily, lived human experience plays in musical and other forms of artistic expression.

Associational versus experiential knowledge and the importance of the lived experience to Art

As I write this, my son is in a developmental stage in which he asks a lot of questions about words. Once, when we were talking about a car being parked "under a tree," he interrupted to ask what it means to be "under." I gave him a series of descriptions, explaining that when two things are stacked, one will be above and one will be below. "What's it mean to be 'stacked'?" he then asked, followed by, "What's it mean to be 'below'?" I found myself in an increasingly complex tangle of synonyms and self-referential definitions. Finally, I took two objects from his pile of toys and showed him the toys stacked on top of one another to illustrate what it means to be "below," "above," and "under." He then mimicked the activity, and as he stacked, unstacked, and restacked objects, he proudly narrated the different relative positions of his toys.

My son's questions highlight the difference between what I call *associational* knowledge and *experiential* knowledge. When I was listing off synonyms, I was giving my son associational knowledge. I was showing him which words are similar to one another and indicating situations in which each might be appropriate. I was listing off the contexts he could *associate* with the words "under," "above," and "below." This sort of knowledge is about meanings, definitions, and usage, and it hinges upon the web of connections between these meanings and how they are used.

In contrast, when my son was stacking toys on top of one another, he developed physical, relational, spatial, and bodily understandings of those words. This experiential learning grounds the definitions of words in the tangible world and our interactions with it. Here, words like "under," "above," and "below" derive their meaning from our lived experience with them.

Both approaches are important to learning and communication. I have, for instance, never been to Antarctica. However, I'm confident it's cold there because I've read and heard about the temperature in that part of the world, and the pictures I've seen of Antarctica are replete with snow and ice. I've *associated* the word "cold" with Antarctica. While I have never *experienced* Antarctic weather, I have experiential knowledge of "cold," "ice," and "snow." I've held ice in my hands, bundled myself against the cold, and felt snow against my skin. I can rely on associative knowledge to connect these words, images, and ideas with Antarctica, and ground those associations in my prior experiences.

Humans employ both systems when creating content. Consider an individual who composes a poem about romantic heartbreak despite never having personally endured such an experience. This person might research the topic, studying how other poets have expressed those feelings and analyzing accounts of what it feels like to be rejected by a loved one. Armed with this knowledge, they can craft a poem that encapsulates the essence of heartbreak. This creation is rooted in associational knowledge. The poet draws on information and emotional descriptions from others to construct narratives and turns of phrase that align with shared cultural understandings of heartbreak. However, if someone gets their heart broken and then expresses those emotions through poetry, they would be using experiential knowledge to write a poem. They choose words and phrases to reflect what they're feeling, and the poet pours their own emotions into the resulting lyrics. They are creating content to express a lived experience.

Experiential knowledge captures lived human meaning, while associational knowledge operates within the realm of how words and symbols convey that meaning. Again, this distinction has been explored by scholars from various disciplines. For instance, the early 20th-century philosopher Maurice Merleau-Ponty argued that all human perception is based in our bodily experiences. To Merleau-Ponty, words, concepts, and ideas all point back to some basic embodied experience, from the chill of low temperatures against one's skin to the neuro-chemical wrenching of heartbreak.[12]

Contemporary cognitive scientist Stevan Harnad arrives at a similar conclusion by examining how meanings are attributed to words, concepts, and images. Harnad's concept of "symbol grounding" occurs when words, images, or references ("symbols") are linked to real-world experiences. Without this grounding, words and images are merely referential, existing in a vacuum where symbols only relate to other symbols, like the piles of synonyms I shuffled in front of my frustrated son. However, when a symbol is connected to an experience—as when my son saw and felt the positions of his toys in front of him—that symbol becomes anchored to a concrete meaning.

Intentional artistic creativity relies on experiential knowledge. For a reader, viewer, or listener to take the Intentional Stance and ask themselves, "What does this content mean?" or "Why did an artist make this?," they need to be convinced that whoever made that content was motivated by some actual idea or experience. If an audience is to view something as an Artwork to be interpreted, they must believe there is something concrete to interpret—the grounded ideas of experiential knowledge—rather than empty self-referential symbols of pure associational knowledge. We don't simply want words, images, and melodies to *seem like* there's intention, understanding, and motivation behind them. We want there to *actually be* some intention, understanding, and motivation behind them. And for there to be meaning behind that intention, the meaning must be grounded in experience. In short, we need to see experiential knowledge inside intentional artistic creativity.

Of course, we don't hold all content to such a high bar. We certainly don't scrutinize every piece of media we consume for its intentional artistry or for some deep experiential meaning, and I will address these cases shortly. Not all content, in other words, is intentional artistic creativity. However, music strongly exemplifies the dynamics of intentional artistic creativity, and very often, it connects to the lived experience of both its creator and its listeners. Therefore, before returning to the larger idea of artistic expression and AI, I want to survey music's particular role in the dynamics of intention, expression, and human experience.

Music as a radically experiential and intentional Art: meaning, social functions, and expressions of authenticity

Music is a deeply emotional art form. As I noted in Chapter 1, when I was a teenager, closeted and struggling with depression, I would end tough days by putting on my headphones and blaring my favorite albums alone in my room. Music became a tool for me to process and cope with my emotions and helped me grapple with my position in a difficult world. A decade later, when my husband and I got married, music was central to some of the most meaningful and memorable parts of the service. The hymns, songs, and instrumentals were vectors in one of the happiest moments of my life. Then last year, when my dad entered hospice and we began planning his funeral, one of our first discussions was about the music we would include. Music would be a focal point for my family's sadness at my dad's passing.

While every art form evokes strong emotional connections, music's connections run particularly deep and are especially dependent on how an audience views a creator's intention and lived experience. This linked reliance on human experience and intention is evident in at least three aspects: the music's meaning, its social role, and the way we associate musical "authenticity" with the identities and biographies of its creators.

A staggering amount has been written about this first category— the ideas and concepts that music communicates to its audience, or in other words, what music *means*.[13] Despite the multitude of debates and disagreement on the topic, a perennial issue tends to pervade these arguments. Namely, music does not possess clear lexical meaning, at least not as clear as words or objects. You can't pinpoint the concrete *meaning* of a chord or melody as straightforwardly as you can look up the definition of a word in a dictionary or as obviously as you can describe the objective contents of a picture.

The word "cat" and a picture of a member of the species *Felis catus* both have very clear meanings. They both directly indicate a small, furry semi-domesticated creature, and if you or I were to look at that word or that image, we'd both have the same basic associations. The meaning of the musical climax of your favorite song, on the other hand, is far more amorphous. While it might evoke feelings and emotions, these effects are not specific, they're hard to describe, and you and I might experience very different emotions at that moment. We can't just look up the meaning of some musical gesture in a dictionary.

Despite its indeterminate nature, there is no doubt about music's ability to evoke feelings and meanings within listeners. Philosophers often note that musical gestures have recognizable emotional analogs, which Suzanne Langer describes as music's "general forms of feeling." Thinkers like Robert Hatten and Peter Kivy discuss this aspect in terms of metaphor and simile, showing how music can *act like* an emotion or idea. For example, if a melody repeatedly strives but fails to reach a particular note, it can elicit feelings of frustration, disappointment, or sadness, emotions that mirror the melody's failure to achieve its goal. This approach views music as a form of emotional onomatopoeia, where the sounds of music reflect the emotions they evoke. Theorists like Arnie Cox and Janna Saslaw further this notion by suggesting that such a melody gains meaning by triggering our preconscious mind to empathize with its struggle or failure. We imagine what we would be feeling if we were experiencing the same struggle as the melody.

Because musical meaning is amorphous and does not rely on concrete symbols, it directly appeals to our lived experience, becoming rooted in experiential knowledge. When writers like Arnie Cox suggest that we empathize with some musical gesture and imagine ourselves undertaking the same action as some musical phrase, they are suggesting that human experience bestows meaning into the music. When theorists such as Suzanne Langer and Robert Hatten argue that the melodies, harmonies, timbres, and phrases that hit our ears have some foundational similarity with the emotions we feel in our guts, they are also arguing that music gains meaning via human experience.

Despite having varied approaches, all such theories draw a direct connection between musical meaning and lived embodiment, underscoring how music's expressivity relies on the human condition and our collective experiences. These various theories of musical meaning suggest that music's ability to evoke emotion or empathy within us creates direct, immediate, visceral effects in its listeners. It is almost as if music cuts through any layers of associative knowledge altogether to elicit experiences in its audience. And of course, in order for music to express some kind of lived human experience, we need to imagine that experience coming from a musical creator—actively and intentionally—who shares or understands that experience. This is the first of music's deep connections to intentional artistic creativity: its meaning has a direct and raw connection to human experience.

The second crucial connection between music, experience, and intention is its social component. Music gains its potency from being a *social act*. Again, music is not alone among Art in this fact. The Russian philosopher Leo Tolstoy, for example, highlighted Art's ability to forge connections within a community as one of its primary benefits. This sentiment is supported by evolutionary biologists who suggest that artistic activities like sculpture, painting, and music may have supported social bonding in early human societies.[14]

However, many scholars argue social connections are especially essential to music. Theorists like Theodor Adorno and Cora Palfy consider music a container for communal values and meanings. Palfy describes music as a "virtual agent," a persona built from the collective parallels we make between music and human actions. Mariusz Kozak similarly argues that musical concepts like rhythm and meter gain meaning from communal experiences of movement and dance. Furthermore, thinkers like Walter Benjamin, John Molyneux, and Christopher Ariza contend that seeing, feeling, and hearing an actual human perform is a crucial component of musical meaning. Benjamin or Molyneux, for instance, point to the fundamental difference between experiencing live performances and listening to music via a device like a streaming service or radio. Ariza, on the other hand, argues that the embodied process of creating music together—jazz musicians improvising intertwined melodies or a vocalist collaborating with a pianist as they interpret a phrase—is inseparable from musical meaning. In each of these instances, music is tethered to how we experience the world in community with other intentional and expressive humans. This is the second of music's connections to intentional artistic creativity and experiential knowledge. It gains its value, meaning, and content from being shared between humans, and it is used by those humans to create social experiences and community.

Finally, notions of "authenticity" undergird many musical styles. These tend to rely on the identity and background of the human making the music. Scholars like Justin Williams, Keith Negus, and Pete Astor examine how genres like rock and hip-hop are often deemed more authentic when created by individuals from specific racial, socio-economic, or regional groups. For instance, hip-hop and rap are genres deeply rooted in the specific lived experiences of economically and racially oppressed communities. As a result, "authentic" expressions of these genres are often tied to those experiences. Creators from outside these communities may not have the lived experience necessary to access an authentic rap or hip-hop voice. (Consider, for instance, the dissonance some listeners feel between the artist Drake's affluent background and his hip-hop persona.[15])

This interest in a composer's biography can extend to how we interpret individual pieces of music as well. The public's decades-long obsession with connections between Taylor Swift's love life and her music provides a clear example. We attempt to identify the true ("authentic") meaning behind her songs by voyeuristically scrutinizing the twists and turns of her personal life.[16] We find meaning in trying to identify what aspects of Swift's lived experience she is intentionally embedding into her songs.

The third broad connection between music, experience, and intentional artistic creativity is, then, in the link between human biographies and the meaning and authenticity of the music. Our experience with music is bound to the identity and expression of the artist who made it. Once again, music is tethered to actual, lived human experiences and the intention of the artist.

Revisiting the Lovelace and Jefferson Objections in the face of music and AI

In the rooms of closeted teenagers, wedding celebrations, and parents' funerals, music bolsters the Lovelace and Jefferson Objections while deflating the retorts of Turing, Haugeland, and Chalmers. Meaningful and expressive music asks an audience to take an Intentional Stance. It asks its audience to find their own embodied, lived experience in the music. It invites listeners to empathize with the performer or creator, and it trades on notions of meaning and authenticity that are tied to the artist's lived experience. It acts as a tie to bind us together as a society while connecting to our own individual embodied human experiences.

These dynamics suggest that we won't find music—or any other Art for that matter—truly "creative" if we know it's made by AI. Lovelace argued that we care about the process by which content is created, and the same holds true for the plaintiffs in the many contemporary lawsuits alleging copyright infringement by AI companies. They assert that an algorithmic process is somehow fundamentally different from the way human intuition works. Algorithms merely reorder the source content fed to them, while humans can create something new. Turing attempted to undercut this objection by focusing on the content itself, suggesting that humans can be won over by sufficiently sophisticated computationally generated content and that these impressive machines can even be considered "intelligent."

But, intentional artistic creativity—and especially artistic music—requires an audience to connect and empathize with a creator in order for that Artwork to be understood as true creativity. I maintain that the transformative spark that Lovelace finds lacking in computer algorithms *can be located in the audience's knowledge that a human intentionally produced that content.*

When we want to engage with meaningful Art, we will search for content that we know was made by other fleshy, experienced humans. If we don't know whether a piece of content was made by a human, we will try to find out. And, if we can't be assured that it was, in fact, created by a human, we won't find it artistically creative. Even if an AI produces flawless music that passes Turing Tests with flying colors, we won't take the Intentional Stance toward it unless we see a human behind the creative process. Instead, as soon as we know the content was created by a computer, we'll treat the music more like a car's engine than the human starting the car.

To my mind, these dynamics vindicate the Lovelace Objection. By eliciting a connection to a composer, producer, or performer, the Lovelace Objection suggests that artistic and creative music cannot be generated by a computer, simply because we need to see an intentional human behind the creative process.

But *why* do we need a human behind that process? The answer lies in the dichotomy between associational and experiential knowledge. This is what corroborates the Jefferson Objection and deflates the Haugeland-Chalmers retort. Machine-learned models, even very complex LLMs, create content using only associational knowledge. As we saw in Chapters 2 and 4, these deep learning systems learn the patterns of some datasets by turning them into arbitrary referential symbols, the very epitome of associational knowledge. A neural network knows where to place a word, how to arrange objects in an image, or which note to place in a phrase, because it's learned the appropriate contexts and behaviors of those words, objects, and notes. But it has no access to the experience-based meanings behind these patterns and symbols.

At its core, an AI does not experience the world. "Solving" this problem by giving the models more data with more complexities—expanding AI's abstract connections using Haugeland's New Fangled AI or reaching across different domains as in Chalmers's LLM+ concept—merely kicks the can down the road. Adding more and more associational knowledge into these systems is not going to flip their understanding into the realm of experience. More associations will never add up to an experience. Just as the potential poet reading all he can about heartbreak won't *experience* that emotion until he's been faced with a devastating personal loss, complex associational systems can only ever *know about* ideas and emotions. They will never *experience* those concepts.

An excellent AI musical model will know where to write a downbeat and may even be able to list all the social, embodied, theoretical, and expressive reasons to write a downbeat. But because it has never jumped or danced or clapped its hands, it will never know what it's like to feel the bodily thud that accompanies a particularly satisfying arrival of a strong beat.

The Jefferson Objection posited that the experience of being human was crucial to Art, and because of the role that experiential knowledge plays in intentional artistic creativity, that rings true to me. When an audience takes an Intentional Stance and actively interprets Art, its members are looking for aspects of their own lived experience. This is particularly relevant in the case of music, where the basis of expression is abstract, embodied meaning and emotion. Here again, for something to become Art, we need to see a human creating it, and this is especially true for music.

These ideas aren't just theoretical. They're supported by observable human behavior. Researchers like Chiara Longoni, Luca Cian, Francisco Tigre Moura, and Charlotte Maw have shown that humans are uncomfortable with AI undertaking more subjective, taste-oriented tasks like recommending clothing or the best recipe for dinner. Further, these studies show that, when we spend our money, we would rather not spend it on something made by AI. Humans also like art less when they believe it's made by AI than when they believe it's by another human. The labs of Lucas Bellaiche, Linwan Wu, Taylor Jing Wen, Nils Köbis, and Daniel Shank have conducted behavioral studies showing over and over again that people like poems, images, and music less when they *believe* they were made by AI, even when they are indistinguishable from human-made content. Participants in these experiments report that the AI doesn't seem to be telling a story, isn't writing from experience, and isn't being truly creative. In other words, these experiments tell us that people view AI as not intentional and devoid of experiential knowledge.[17] On several levels, our guts seem to be telling us that AI-generated content cannot be intentional creative Art.

But what of the more speculative and futuristic side of Chalmers's argument? Wouldn't his idealized LLM+, trained on all sorts of media and integrated with sensory data from a digital body, *experience* the world? By connecting sensory and musical data, couldn't that sort of model *feel* the rising and falling of musical phrases? Couldn't it *experience* a downbeat by mapping the feeling of dancing onto musical beat patterns? Couldn't these complex interconnections lead to consciousness and even creative intention? Couldn't it even experience grief and write music about that feeling?

These are interesting if speculative eventualities, but I remain skeptical. Even if something like this superintelligent experiential consciousness came to pass, its intentions and experiences would be different from ours. It might be very smart and knowledgeable, and it might know a huge amount about the human world,[18] but it would be a silicon-based mind with an inner life very different from our own. It would not be *human*.

And humanity is important. It's hard to imagine a teary-eyed teenager running to their room, throwing on headphones, and listening to music generated by an algorithm, regardless of the quality of the music or the AI that created it. That computer might know a lot about sadness, and it might have more raw data associated with depression than any human could. But it won't be capable of feeling sad in the way that a human feels sad. A computer can't be bullied. It will never cry.

My dad died shortly after entering hospice. I wrote and arranged several pieces of music for his funeral. Of course, I could have used a musical AI to help with this music. The prospect, however, seemed bizarre, almost disgusting. The idea of using an AI in a religious service celebrating life and mourning death would be antithetical to the essence of such an event. Funeral music facilitates our collective experience of something deeply human, and my dad's family and friends were coming together in empathy and community for such an experience. A musical AI could have a mountain of data about funeral music, and about what sad and mournful music should sound like. Maybe it could put all the notes in the right places. But mourning families do not program funeral music just to hear the right notes played at the right times. Funeral music connects us on a human level as we express human emotions. During my father's funeral, it mattered that humans wrote, arranged, and performed the hymns, anthems, and solos. It mattered that there was a lived experience behind the notes we were hearing and singing.

These dynamics return us to the musical scene in *1984*. As the protagonist listens to the laundress inject her humanity into the shallow AI-generated tune, Orwell adds some further descriptions of the surrounding scene. He writes:

> *But the woman sang so tunefully... He could hear the woman singing and the scrape of her shoes on the flagstones, and the cries of children in the street, and somewhere in the far distance a faint roar of traffic, and yet the room seemed curiously silent.*

When the protagonist hears the woman transform the song into something artistic, the world becomes quiet, and his thoughts turn to the footsteps and voices around him. His attention is heightened as he connects the woman's singing to audible expressions of humanity. As the song becomes Art, it sonically magnifies the surrounding human world. When the music switches from plastic AI-generated content to embodied creative expression, the protagonist becomes more intertwined with the human, embodied, social, and visceral world around him.

This expressive, communal, and human experience is exactly what generative AI cannot provide. If musical AI begins to produce flawless content, we would—as the Lovelace Objection notes—find its combinatoric computational process deeply inhuman. We would not take the Intentional

Stance toward that computational algorithm, and we wouldn't find it creative. Even if a complex futuristic model replicates human expression, it will be the result of silicon-based processors rather than emanating from a fleshy, warm, fragile body. As the Jefferson Objection argues, this computational experience will be foundationally different from human experience. It won't know what it's like to cry. Its computational replication of tears would be some manufactured analogy. It won't know what it's like to lose a father. A computer was never born, and it cannot die, at least not in the human sense.

Even if we shovel new and diverse data into future AIs, the pile of information won't replicate a human's actual lived embodied experiences. Given that intentional artistic creativity—and musical creativity, specifically—relies on human experience and community, that distinction will remain important.

AI as wallpaper, Craftwork, and tool

Not every piece of content requires its consumers to plunge into the Intentional Stance and treat the item as an Artwork. Indeed, much of the content we consume in our day-to-day lives is useful, well-made, and enjoyable without being Art. To my mind, well-made AI music can fill these sorts of non-artistic roles.[19] I believe this type of musical content will function in one of three ways: as a background wash, a tool, or a Craftwork.

There's a lot of music in the world we're not meant to pay attention to. We don't consciously listen to music in elevators, bathrooms, hotel lobbies, or five-second commercials on social media. Sometimes we don't even pay much attention to film scores, our exercise playlists, or podcast intro music. So much background music doesn't need to be *good*; it just needs to be *there*. Such enjoyable background sound wash is one of the three ways that I see musical AI being used in the future. When the purpose of music is not to be meaningful but, rather, to fill silence, AI will be a useful tool. Because we don't usually understand this music as capturing or expressing the human experience—it's not meant to be intentional, artistic, or creative—we'll be happy to use AI to fill silence and color the background sonic landscape.

The second role I envision for musical AI is as an aid to human composers. Just as David Cope used his 1980s AI to pull him out of writers' block, musicians can use AI to generate nearly infinite amounts of melodic and harmonic ideas for musical inspiration. Let's give credit where it's due: AI excels at detecting and reconfiguring patterns with a speed and precision beyond human capability. Musicians can leverage this capacity to spark new ideas, accelerate their compositional process, and even solicit edits to refine their work. In this capacity, AI will function as an aid to human creativity, acting as a tool in service of the final musical product.

Finally, meticulously constructed AI music will be regarded more as impressive Craftworks than Artworks. Recall from our earlier discussions that audiences find Craftworks to be beautiful and impressive, but they don't inspire that audience to seek meaning, expression, or intention within them. In a Craftwork, our focus is less on expressive meaning and more on the pleasure and utility the work provides. We do not engage with a Craftwork through the Intentional Stance, nor do we necessarily find ourselves intrigued by the identity or biography of its creator. While the intricacies of a marble carving might prompt us to ponder a sculptor's expressive intent, we don't usually ask the same questions when admiring the beauty and design of an ornate piece of jewelry. Artworks invite interpretation and meaning. Craftworks are to be appreciated for their design.

Future musical AI will excel at Craftwork. Even now, when I listen to an exceptional piece of AI-generated music, I hear moments of well-made content. Some of the tunes are catchy, and I've even encountered turns of phrase that I find clever. I can find pleasure in the beauty of an AI's chord progressions and delight in the elegant construction of its melodies. Yet, I never find myself pondering the music's meaning, and I won't attempt to interpret an AI's song or use it as a lens for introspection. As long as audiences care about the humans behind musical Artworks, even the finest and most convincing pieces of AI-generated music will be devoid of true human expression. They will, therefore, remain outside the realm of Art. Compelling and impressive AI-generated music will instead be better understood as pieces of Craft.

Some thoughts on the future

I began this chapter by evoking a famously dystopian novel and referencing the bevy of lawsuits that creators are currently bringing against AI companies. I ended by outlining several situations in which AI-generated music will likely succeed in our society. These sentiments were sandwiched by a step-by-step argument about the specific circumstances in which AI will *not* succeed.

I'm a realist. AI will soon be *very good* at making content of all kinds. Will these advances eliminate jobs? Yes. Will humans try to pass off AI music as their own? Certainly. Will fewer kids be inspired to learn to read music and gain fluency on an instrument when they can create impressive content at the press of a button? Likely. Will the next decades be laden with lawsuits about musical ownership surrounding AI models, their outputs, and their training data? Probably. Will younger generations be more open to finding meaning and expression in musical AI? Maybe.[20] Do I wish I could limit or reverse these eventualities? Definitely.

We should engage in pro-music, pro-musician, and pro-creator advocacy. We should pressure regulators and the AI industry to clearly label machine-generated content. We should educate our students about the limits of AI. We should expose our audiences to the beauty of human-made music and live performances. And we should be smart and thoughtful consumers of AI-generated content.

However, AI music will never stamp out human-made Art. Streaming services, records, radio, the printing press—none of these extinguished our collective craving for live performances or newly composed, human-made music, and yet each elicited worry that they would do exactly that.[21] If Art is about expressing the human experience, generative AI will never be able to create it. It simply cannot capture the full depth of human emotion and the complexities of our experiences. AI lacks the ability to feel and to live through the unique circumstances that shape each composer's—each human's—voice. While AI can mimic patterns and styles of human-made content, it cannot experience a human life. And audiences will continue to care about this, because we care about the people who make the Art we love.

I also think that music will be at the frontline of the discomfort with, and even the resistance to, AI-generated content. For one, as we have seen, musical AI simply develops more slowly than other media. This will give us the opportunity to more thoughtfully reflect on its expansion and evolution. As my previous chapters argued, musical AI is allocated fewer resources for research and development than other areas of AI research, has smaller datasets available to it, is more difficult to represent to a computer, and contains structures and organizations that are difficult for machine learning to identify and learn. However, at some point, musical AI will be capable of truly excellent outputs. When this happens, I believe that music's foundational human components will be put into stark relief. We'll realize that machine-made music lacks a reliable human connection, and we won't like it.

AI will be a tool. It will produce background music. It will even produce beautiful Craftworks. But, as long as we place value on genuine emotional expression and the unique perspectives that only humans can provide, human composition will remain irreplaceable.

Summary

In this chapter, I have argued that audiences do not interpret music generated by AI the same way as they do human-made music. While generative AI may one day create technically perfect music, we will continue to value the lived experience behind musical expression, a lived experience that will remain inaccessible to AI.

I began by outlining two reasons that we might perceive AI-generated music as unsatisfying: 1) AI programs are not truly creative, and 2) AI does not experience the human world. I connected these arguments to two historical thinkers, Ada Lovelace and George Jefferson, and suggested that their skepticism still applies to contemporary generative AI. In the Lovelace Objection, computer-based intelligence is unable to generate truly novel ideas because it is limited to the information fed into it. The Jefferson Objection, then, argues that artistic expression is based on embodied human experience, and computers will never have access to that experience. I first contrasted these views with arguments from Alan Turing, who believed that, if AI can convincingly mimic human outputs, it should be considered intelligent. I also outlined the thinking of contemporary scholars John Haugeland and David Chalmers, who argue that sufficiently complex computer models might, indeed, have experiences and consciousnesses similar to those of humans.

My own thinking, however, is that human interaction and emotional input are essential for music to be fully appreciated as Artwork. Both aesthetic theory and behavioral data suggest that audiences care deeply about the identities of the artists creating content, and that music is a particularly potent example of this dynamic. Even as AI becomes increasingly human, the very fact that it is *not human* precludes it from creating content that a human audience will interpret as Art.

I ended by suggesting that generative AI will produce music to fulfill three musical roles: as a sonic background filler, a compositional tool to aid human musicians, and a producer of technically proficient but emotionally detached content. Each role leverages AI's strengths in pattern recognition and efficiency while acknowledging its limitations in providing genuine artistic and emotional depth. While AI can support and enhance the process of musical creation, it cannot replace the human elements essential for true artistic expression. The human experience, with its inherent emotions and contextual understandings, remains central to creating music that moves and connects with human audiences. As long as we place value on emotional expression, human experience will remain vital to music as an artform.

Some final thoughts

At the beginning of this book, I outlined five forces that affect musical AI's development. My first chapter explored these five key forces: 1) the *motivations* behind AI development, 2) the *examples* used to train these systems, 3) how music is *represented* to a computer program, 4) the *structures* a program needs to generate coherent music, and 5) how humans *interpret* and consume AI-generated music. The second chapter addressed the first force. Using some basic market analyses, I showed that musical AI research receives less investment and fewer resources compared to other forms of AI, and that this imbalance is at least partly due to its limited commercial applications.

AI needs vast datasets to learn how to successfully replicate a given medium, and Chapter 3 discussed the scarcity of usable musical datasets. I described the challenges in extracting reliable information from both audio files and musical scores, and I contrasted this with the relatively straightforward ways that information is extracted from text and images. Chapter 4 examined the complexity of music's overlapping elements, which make it difficult for researchers to provide their AIs with digestible musical chunks and cause AIs to stumble when creating new music.

Chapter 5 then analyzed the types of patterns and structures that AI excels at learning, particularly *nested determined proximities*, sequences of nearby, frequently occurring events that follow some overarching logic. I reviewed music generated by some current musical AIs and demonstrated how these systems favor nested determined proximities. I contrasted these characteristics with the more varied, dispersed, and unpredictable structures of human-made music.

Finally, the current chapter connected these engineering problems back to how we enjoy and value music. In the last several pages, I argued that even if AI produces flawless music, it won't resonate with people as much as human-made music. These issues then connect back to the broader problems that began this book. If the human element is a crucial reason that audiences value music, why should we expect users and financiers to invest in musical AI? The lack of motivation is compounded by the lack of value that listeners place on music created by AIs.

At the end of the classic 1939 movie *The Wizard of Oz*, the mechanical Tin Man famously receives a "heart" from the titular wizard. The Tin Man had been constructed with nothing in his chest, which he believed made him unable to feel or experience emotion. The wizard then presents the Tin Man with a plastic trinket in the shape of a heart with the words, "A heart is not judged by how much you love, but by how much you are loved by others."

This sentiment represents an issue underpinning this entire book, and especially this final chapter. We can worry about market forces, and how computers represent music. We can dive deeply into how machine learning models work, and scrutinize the datasets they require. We can wring our hands all day about whether an AI can truly be conscious, or if some computer is capable of feeling. We can theorize about different types of knowledge, and we can make analogies between neural networks and the brain all day long. But, if we do not value music made by a computer as much as human-made compositions—as I believe we do not and will not—there will be limited motivation to develop musical AI, compile large datasets, parse that data, and train it to learn sophisticated meaningful musical structures. We won't believe that musical AI has a "heart," and that belief will undercut all other forces that might otherwise support the technology's development.

If that turns out to be the case, I'll be very happy.

Notes

1 See Menabrea (1843); Stein (1984); Hollings, Martin and Rice (2018); and McCully (2019).

2 Lovelace's criticism was itself influenced by contemporary British Romantic aesthetic theory. English thinkers like John Keats (themselves influenced by continental philosophers like Immanuel Kant and Georg Hegel) argued that original creativity arises from the artist's connection to some set of ethereal larger truths, and the artist transforms their relationship with those truths into a new and unique work of art (Stein 1984; Bonds 2006). Because of her Romantic sensibilities, Lovelace would doubtlessly argue that a computer could not generate poetry of the quality created by a human. More important to my logic, her criticism is also about the authorial process. To Lovelace, a true artwork does not involve cutting and pasting from past artworks, but from an artist's personal relationship to the creative process.

3 Notably, this distinction is nowhere near new and has many precedents in theories of creativity in general. To Plato, the lowest form of Art involved copying while the highest was some representation of a larger ideal. Several millennia later, Samuel Coleridge Taylor would make a distinction between "Fancy," which takes items in the memory and reorders them, and "Imagination" which dissolves these associations and creates something truly new. Immanuel Kant considered someone a "genius" when they could synthesize something truly new from their intuition (Bonds 2006).

4 Other theorists have made similar arguments. In 1980, the philosopher John Searle criticized supporters of AI through his "Chinese Room" analogy. Imagine a man in a locked room with a library of Chinese phrases organized by some coding system. Intermittently, the man receives a letter with a sequence of codes on it, and he walks through the library withdrawing the corresponding Chinese phrases. He meticulously copies the phrases onto a paper, stuffs the result into an envelope, and returns the letter. In the parable, the man can *produce* Chinese, but he does not *know* Chinese. Searle suggests that this is the way AI works. When computers learn to generate an appropriate series of symbols in an appropriate context, they don't actually know about the content they're generating any more than the man in the room knows Chinese.

5 This sort of approach to AI would come to be known as "Strong AI." In Strong AI, we "don't need to know how the brain works to know how the mind works" (Searle 1980). Rather, we just need to analyze the behavior of humans and AIs to understand their intelligence. This contrasts with a "Weak AI" stance that argues that computational systems should be evaluated based on their outputs and utility. To a theorist of Weak AI—and I must admit that I

count myself a member of this club—an AI can act *like* a human and can even *model* a human thought process, but it cannot actually *be the same as* human intelligence.

6 By calling these the "Lovelace Objection" and "Jefferson Objection," I'm giving homage to Turing's original paper, in which he describes "Lady Lovelace's Objection" and directly cites Jefferson's argument.

7 See Satel and Lilienfeld (2013).

8 Proust (1913).

9 It's likely that debates over the definition of Art began as soon as the paint dried on the earliest cave drawings. The contours of the debate about "What is Art," how that conversation has changed over time, and the different notions of art between cultures fill piles of books. In *The Transfiguration of the Commonplace* (1981), for example, Arthur Danto suggests that part of what makes something an artwork is that it offers the possibility—if not the necessity—of interpretation. Importantly, Markowitz (1994) argues that the distinction between what is art and what is not is based on the race and class of both the viewer and the creator. I must admit that I hold a particularly Romantic/modernist default in my own thinking, insomuch as I center expressive meaning and authorial intention in my discussions and definitions of Art.

10 See Markowitz (1994), Danto (1981), and Dissanayake (2015).

11 Danto (1981), 135.

12 While I've singled out Merleau-Ponty, ideas of embodied cognition weave their way through many academic discourses. Indeed, much intersectional feminism and Black feminism locates issues of identity and politics in how bodies exist in the power structures of the world around them (Richardson 2013, Allen 2011, Davis 2001, Laqueur 1990), and many theories of the mind rely on bodily metaphors (Saslaw 1996). In the past several decades, music studies in particular have seen increased focus on the role that the body plays in musical experience (Kozak 2019, De Souza 2017, Le Guin 2005, Palfy 2022, Cox 2016). Additionally, several AI researchers have explicitly focused on why physical neurons are different from the silicon-based processing chips of computers (Block 1995, 2009).

13 For a few reviews of these discussions, see Agawu (1991), Cook (2001), and Palfy (2022).

14 See Piilonen (2024) and Tomlinson (2015) for sophisticated and subtle descriptions of music's role in theories of evolution.

15 See Pope (2016) and Isai (2022).

16 See, for instance, Spanos (2016) or Greene (2022). This sort of "authenticity" extends to classical music as well. Studies have shown that people like classical music more when they know that it was written by someone respected and famous (Fischinger *et al.* 2018, White *et al.* 2022), that it was made by people whose biography is similar to their own (Greenberg *et al.* 2021), and that it is relatable to their own experience (Pelowski *et al.* 2017). For a review of a how the framing around a piece of music influences our assessment, see Leder and Pelowshi (2022).

17 Bigman and Gray (2018).

18 My argument here interacts a bit with the concept of AI superintelligence. A model would be "superintelligent" if it can undertake some reasoning or investigation faster and with more sophistication than could a human, and even could identify some solution using logic that humans can't comprehend (Bostrom, 2014). For instance, a superintelligent AI might be able to make pharmaceutical breakthroughs by understanding interactions between organic and bodily chemistry that extend far beyond the capacity of human

researchers. This type of superintelligence would be impressive, useful, and even scary—but, its knowledge would still be associational. My hypothetical pharmaceutical breakthrough would come from the superintelligent AI reading and studying inhuman amounts of biological, and chemical research about the human body, not because the AI *has* a body.

19 To use a term from Chapter 5, this music would achieve the status of an "adult" model.

20 Indeed, Deirdre Loughridge's historical analysis of how humans relate to "human-like" mechanized sounds shows that the relationship between humans and machines has changed over time. It's a definite possibility that future generations will have very different understandings of mechanized expression and creativity than those I am describing here.

21 See Blair (2003) and Fischer (2010).

References and Further Reading, Chapter 6

Agawu, K. V. 1991. *Playing with Signs: A Semiotic Interpretation of Classic Music*. Princeton: Princeton University Press.

Ariza, C. 2009. "The Interrogator as Critic: The Turing Test and the Evaluation of Generative Music Systems." *Computer Music Journal* 33(2): 48–70.

Allen, J. S. 2011. *¡Venceremos?: The Erotics of Black Self-Making in Cuba*. Durham: Duke University Press.

Bellaiche, L., R. Shahi, M. H. Turpin, et al. 2023. "Humans Versus AI: Whether and Why We Prefer Human-Created Compared to AI-Created Artwork." *Cognitive Research: Principles and Implications* 8(1): 42. https://doi.org/10.1186/s41235-023-00499-6.

Benjamin, W. 1935 (1968). "The Work of Art in the Age of Mechanical Reproduction." In *Illuminations: Essays and Reflections*, edited by Hannah Arendt, translated by Harry Zohn, 217–251. New York: Schocken Books.

Bigman, Y., and K. Gray. 2018. "People Are Averse to Machines Making Moral Decisions." *Cognition* 181. https://doi.org/10.1016/j.cognition.2018.08.003.

Blair, A. 2003. "Reading Strategies for Coping with Information Overload ca. 1550–1700." *Journal of the History of Ideas* 64(1): 11–28. https://doi.org/10.2307/3654293.

Block, N. 1995. "The Mind as the Software of the Brain." In *Thinking: An Invitation to Cognitive Science*, edited by Edward E. Smith and Daniel N. Osherson, vol. 3, 377–425, 2nd ed. Cambridge, MA: MIT Press.

Block, N. 2009. The mind as the software of the brain. In S. Schneider (Ed.), *Science fiction and philosophy: From time travel to superintelligence*: 170–185. Wiley-Blackwell.

Bonds, M. E. 2006. *Music as Thought: Listening to the Symphony in the Age of Beethoven*. Princeton: Princeton University Press.

Bostrom, N. 2014. *Superintelligence: Paths, Dangers, Strategies*. Oxford: Oxford University Press.

Braguinski, N. 2022. *Mathematical Music: From Antiquity to Music AI*. New York: Routledge.

Chalmers, D. J. 2022. *Reality+: Virtual Worlds and the Problems of Philosophy*. New York: W. W. Norton.

Chalmers, D. J. 2022. "Could a Large Language Model be Conscious?" Talk Given at NeurIPS. https://philpapers.org/archive/CHACAL-3.pdf.

Cook, N. 2001. "Theorizing Musical Meaning." *Music Theory Spectrum* 23(2): 170–195.

Cox, A. 2016. *Music and Embodied Cognition: Listening, Moving, Feeling, and Thinking.* Bloomington: Indiana University Press.

Danto, A. 1981. *The Transfiguration of the Commonplace: A Philosophy of Art.* Cambridge, MA: Harvard University Press.

Davis, A. 2001. "Black Women and Music: A Historical Legacy of Struggle." In *Black Feminist Cultural Criticism*, edited by Jacqueline Bobo, 217–232. Malden, MA: Blackwell Publishing.

Dennett, D. C. 1971. "Intentional Systems." *The Journal of Philosophy* 68(4): 87–106.

Dennett, D. C. 1981. "True Believers: The Intentional Strategy and Why It Works." In *Scientific Explanation*, edited by A. F. Heath. Oxford: Oxford University Press, 150–167.

Dennett, D. C. 1987. *The Intentional Stance.* Cambridge, MA: MIT Press.

De Souza, J. 2017. *Music at Hand: Instruments, Bodies, and Cognition.* New York: Oxford University Press.

Dissanayake, E. 2015. *What Is Art For?* Seattle: University of Washington Press.

Fischer, S. 2010. "A History of Media Technology Scares, from the Printing Press to Facebook." *Slate*, February 15, 2010. https://slate.com/technology/2010/02/a-history-of-media-technology-scares-from-the-printing-press-to-facebook.html.

Fischinger, T., M. Kaufmann, and W. Schlotz. 2018. "If It's Mozart, It Must Be Good? The Influence of Textual Information and Age on Musical Appreciation." *Psychology of Music* 48(4): 579–597. https://doi.org/10.1177/0305735618812216.

Gray, H. M., K. Gray, and D. M. Wegner. 2007. "Dimensions of Mind Perception." *Science* 315(5812): 619. https://doi.org/10.1126/science.1134475.

Greenberg, D. M., Kosinski, M., Stillwell, D. J., Monteiro, B. L., Levitin, D. J., & Rentfrow, P. J. 2021. The song is you: Preferences for musical attribute dimensions reflect personality. *Social Psychological and Personality Science*, 12(3), 300–308.

Greene, J. 2022. "Taylor Swift's Dating History: How Her Past Boyfriends Wind Up in Songs." *Today.com.* October 10, 2022, updated April 18, 2024, posted at https://www.today.com/popculture/music/taylor-swift-boyfriends-dating-history-rcna50748.

Harnad, S. 1990. "The Symbol Grounding Problem." *Physica D* 42: 335–346.

Haugeland, J. 1996. "What Is Mind Design?" In *Mind Design: Philosophy, Psychology, and Artificial Intelligence*, edited by John Haugeland, 1–16. Cambridge, MA: MIT Press.

Hollings, C., U. Martin, and A. Rice. 2018. *Ada Lovelace: The Making of a Computer Scientist.* Oxford: Bodleian Libraries.

Hong, Joo-Wha, Katrin Fischer, Yul Ha, and Yilei Zeng. 2022. "Human, I Wrote a Song for You: An Experiment Testing the Influence of Machines' Attributes on the AI-Composed Music Evaluation." *Computers in Human Behavior* 131: 107239. https://doi.org/10.1016/j.chb.2022.107239.

Huang, C. A., C. Hawthorne, A. Roberts, M. Dinculescu, J. Wexler, L. Hong, and J. Howcroft. 2019. "The Bach Doodle: Approachable Music Composition with Machine Learning at Scale." In Proceedings of the 20th International Society for Music Information Retrieval Conference, 100–107. Delft, The Netherlands: ISMIR. https://arxiv.org/abs/1907.06637

Isai, V. 2022. "When Drake Is on Your Course Syllabus." *New York Times.* www.nytimes.com/2022/01/22/world/canada/drake-course-toronto-ryerson-university.html.

Jefferson, G. 1949. "The Mind of Mechanical Man." *British Medical Journal* 1(4616): 1105–1110. https://doi.org/10.1136/bmj.1.4616.1105. PMID: 18153422; PMCID: PMC2050428.

Kivy, P. 1980. *The Corded Shell: Reflections on Musical Expression*. Princeton: Princeton University Press.

Köbis, N., and L. D. Mossink. 2021. "Artificial Intelligence Versus Maya Angelou: Experimental Evidence That People Cannot Differentiate AI-Generated from Human-Written Poetry." *Computers in Human Behavior* 114. https://doi.org /10.1016/j.chb.2020.106553. (https://www.sciencedirect.com/science/article/ pii/S0747563220303034)

Kozak, M. 2019. *Enacting Musical Time: The Bodily Experience of New Music*. New York: Oxford University Press.

Kozak, M. 2021. "Feeling Meter: Kinesthetic Knowledge and the Case of Recent Progressive Metal." *Journal of Music Theory* 65(2): 185–237. https://doi.org /10.1215/00222909-9143190.

Kramer, L. 2002. Musical Meaning: Toward a Critical History. Berkeley: University of California Press, 2002.

Langer, S. 1942. *Philosophy in a New Key*. Cambridge: Harvard University Press.

Laqueur, T. 1990. *Making Sex: Body and Gender from the Greeks to Freud*. Cambridge, MA: Harvard University Press.

Leder, H., and M. Pelowski, 2022. "Empirical Aesthetics: Context, Extra Information, and Framing." In *The Oxford Handbook of Empirical Aesthetics*, edited by Marcos Nadal, and Oshin Vartanian. Oxford: Oxford University Press. Online edition: https://doi.org/10.1093/oxfordhb/9780198824350.013 .43.

Le Guin, E. 2005. *Boccherini's Body: An Essay in Carnal Musicology*. Berkeley: University of California Press.

Long, R. 2022. "Key Questions about Artificial Sentience: An Opinionated Guide." *Experience Machines* (Substack). https://experiencemachines .substack.com/p/key-questions-about-artificial-sentience.

Longoni, C., and L. Cian. 2020. "Artificial Intelligence in Utilitarian vs. Hedonic Contexts: The 'Word-of-Machine' Effect." *Journal of Marketing* 86(1): 91– 108. https://doi.org/10.1177/0022242920957347.

Lonsdale, A. J., and A. C. North. 2009. "Musical Taste and Ingroup Favouritism." *Group Processes & Intergroup Relations* 12(3): 319–327. https://doi.org/10 .1177/1368430209102842.

Loughridge, D. 2023. *Sounding Human: An Expansive Analysis of the Relationship between Human and Machine in Music*. Chicago: University of Chicago Press.

Markowitz, S. J. 1994. "The Distinction between Art and Craft." *Journal of Aesthetic Education* 28(1): 55–70. https://doi.org/10.2307/3333159.

McCully, E. A. 2019. *Dreaming in Code: Ada Byron Lovelace, Computer Pioneer*. Somerville, MA: Candlewick.

Menabrea, L. F. 1843. "Sketch of the Analytical Engine Invented by Charles Babbage, Esq." In *Scientific Memoirs, Selections from the Transactions of Foreign Academies and Learned Societies and from Foreign Journals*, edited by Richard Taylor, F.S.A., vol. 3, article 29, 666–731. London: Richard and John E. Taylor. Originally published in *Bibliothèque Universelle de Genève*, no. 82, October 1842.

Merleau-Ponty, M. 1945. *Phénoménologie de la perception*. Paris: Gallimard.

Molyneux, J. 2020. *The Dialectics of Art*. London: Haymarket.

Orwell, G. 1949. *1984*. London: Secker and Warburg.

Ostermann, F., I. Vatolkin, and G. Rudolph. 2021. "Evaluating Creativity in Automatic Reactive Accompaniment of Jazz Improvisation." *Transactions of the International Society for Music Information Retrieval* 4(1): 210–222. https://doi.org/10.5334/tismir.90.

Palfy, C. S. 2022. *Musical Agency and the Social Listener.* New York: Routledge.

Pelowski, M., P. S. Markey, M. Forster, G. Gerger, and H. Leder. 2017. "Move Me, Astonish Me… Delight My Eyes and Brain: The Vienna Integrated Model of Top-Down and Bottom-Up Processes in Art Perception (VIMAP) and Corresponding Affective, Evaluative, and Neurophysiological Correlates." *Physics of Life Reviews* 21: 80–125. https://doi.org/10.1016/j.plrev.2017.02.003.

Piilonen, M. 2024. *Theorizing Music Evolution: Darwin, Spencer, and the Limits of the Human.* Oxford: Oxford University Press.

Pope, A. 2016. "Musical Artists Capitalizing on Hybrid Identities: A Case Study of Drake the 'Authentic' 'Black' 'Canadian' 'Rapper.'" *Stream* 9: 3–22.

Proust, M. 1913 (1992). *In Search of Lost Time.* Translated by C. K. Scott Moncrieff and Terence Kilmartin. Revised by D. J. Enright. 6 vols. New York: Modern Library.

Richardson, M. 2013. *The Queer Limit of Black Memory: Black Lesbian Literature and Irresolution.* Columbus: Ohio University Press.

Sarmento, P., L. Jackson and B. Mathieu. (2024). Between the AI and Me: Analysing Listeners' Perspectives on AI- and Human-Composed Progressive Metal Music. 10.48550/arXiv.2407.21615.

Saslaw, J. 1996. "Forces, Containers, and Paths: The Role of Body-Derived Image Schemes in the Conceptualization of Music." *Journal of Music Theory* 40(2): 217–243.

Satel, S., and S. O. Lilienfeld. 2013. *Brainwashed: The Seductive Appeal of Mindless Neuroscience.* New York: Basic Books.

Searle, J. 1980. *Minds, Brains, and Programs.* Cambridge: Cambridge University Press.

Shank, D. B., C. Stefanik, C. Stuhlsatz, K. Kacirek, and A. M. Belfi. 2023. "AI Composer Bias: Listeners Like Music Less When They Think It Was Composed by an AI." *Journal of Experimental Psychology: Applied* 29(3): 676–692. https://doi.org/10.1037/xap0000447.

Spanos, B. 2016. "Ex-Factor: Taylor Swift's Best Songs About Former Boyfriends." *Rolling Stone.* https://www.rollingstone.com/music/music-lists/ex-factor-taylor-swifts-best-songs-about-former-boyfriends-19644/.

Stein, D. K. 1984. "Lady Lovelace's Notes: Technical Text and Cultural Context." *Victorian Studies* 28(1): 33–67.

Tigre Moura, F., and C. Maw. 2021. "Artificial Intelligence Became Beethoven: How Do Listeners and Music Professionals Perceive Artificially Composed Music?" *Journal of Consumer Marketing* 38(2): 137–146. https://doi.org/10.1108/JCM-02-2020-3671.

Tolstoy, L. 1897 (1995). *What Is Art?* Translated by Richard Pevear and Larissa Volokhonsky. London: Penguin.

Tomlinson, G. 2015. *A Million Years of Music: The Emergence of Human Modernity.* New York: Zone.

White, C. Wm., M. O'Harra, K. Coker, I. Fuentes, S. Franciosa. 2022. "Exploring Implicit and Explicit Bias in Music." Paper Presented at the *Society for Music Perception and Cognition,* Portland, Oregon.

Williams, J. A. 2011. "Historicizing the Breakbeat: Hip-Hop's Origins and Authenticity." *Lied Und Populäre Kultur* 56: 133–167.

Wu, L., and T. J. Wen. 2021. "Understanding AI Advertising from the Consumer Perspective." *Journal of Advertising Research* 61(2): 133–146. https://doi.org/10.2501/JAR-2021-004.

Wu, Y., Y. Mou, Z. Li, and K. Xu. 2020. "Investigating American and Chinese Subjects' Explicit and Implicit Perceptions of AI-Generated Artistic Work." *Computers in Human Behavior* 104: Article 106186. https://doi.org/10.1016/j.chb.2019.106186.

INDEX

Note: Page numbers in **Bold** indicate Tables. Page numbers in *Italics* indicate Figures.

For Product Safety Concerns and Information please contact our EU
representative GPSR@taylorandfrancis.com
Taylor & Francis Verlag GmbH, Kaufingerstraße 24, 80331 München, Germany

www.ingramcontent.com/pod-product-compliance
Lightning Source LLC
Chambersburg PA
CBHW070946050326
40689CB00014B/3365

* 9 7 8 1 0 3 2 9 5 9 7 5 7 *